D1431974

LAND OF AEOLIA

Ilias Venezis, thought to have been
photographed in the United States in 1949
during his visit there.

LAND OF AEOLIA

BY

ILIAS VENEZIS

Translated by

THERESE SELLERS

PROLOGUE

BRUCE CLARK

DENISE HARVEY (PUBLISHER) · LIMNI, EVIA, GREECE

First published in 2020 by
Denise Harvey (Publisher), 340 05 Limni, Evia, Greece
www.deniseharveypublisher.gr

This book was first published in Greek
by Hestia Publishers and Booksellers, Athens, in 1943,
with the title *Αἰολικὴ Γῆ*
and has since been reprinted sixty-nine times

Land of Aeolia
is the twenty-sixth publication in
THE ROMIOSYNI SERIES

ISBN 978-960-7120-43-4

TO THE MEMORY OF MY FRIEND
MICHALIS ACHILA
LIEUTENANT COLONEL – POET
WHO DIED IN GREECE
FROM GERMAN BULLETS
1942

Contents

PART THREE

MAN

TRANSLATOR'S NOTE

IN NOVEMBER OF 1987, several months after I first moved to Athens, a Greek friend who belonged to Venezis' generation gave me a copy of *Αἰολικὴ Γῆ*. It was one of the first books I read in demotic Greek. My friend told me it was his favourite book, and since the time I began translating it and telling Greek acquaintances about my project, I have heard this reaction again and again. The edition he gave me had a plain, manila-coloured cover and the kind of folded pages you have to cut with a letter-opener before reading. When I read the opening passage, I thought I had misunderstood the Greek. First, the waves of the Aegean seemed to be talking to each other. Then the mountains of the Anatolian mainland seemed to be leaning over to observe an island. My sense of reality and of how novels most usually begin were stronger than my confidence in my Greek reading comprehension.

Such was my introduction to *Land of Aeolia* and the lost world that Ilias Venezis recreates in its magical pages. It is a world where the lives of men and the natural world are so inextricably linked that they feel and express each other's deepest being. Waves and mountains speak, so do rivers, trees, birds, bears, salamanders, eels, worms, drops of blood, drops of dew and Night herself. As the story of the principal characters unfolds, so do the parallel stories in the world of nature. It reminded me of Greek tragedy, where the chorus amplifies the actions of the main characters and projects them onto the plane of myth. Also, like Greek tragedy, Venezis' text fuses lyricism with human drama. At the same time, his simple and delicate prose seemed like something I could render in my own words. And so I began translating.

When I found out that the book had already been translated into English,[1] I secretly hoped the translation would seem antiquated, so as to justify a new translation. What I discovered was more troubling.

---

[1] *Aeolia,* translated by E. D. Scott-Kilvert, William Campion, London, 1949; US edition, with the title *Beyond the Aegean,* The Vanguard Press, New York, 1956.

This first English edition had deleted nearly every part that personified nature. The opening passage was gone, so was the conversation between the two drops of blood, the thoughts of the salamander as it is carried skyward by a hawk, and the story of the two walnut trees who suffer homesickness after they leave their homeland in the Caucasus mountains. Every passage where, in the height of human drama, Venezis pulls back from the world of men to evoke the animate world of nature was gone. In some places a few sentences were deleted, in other places whole paragraphs and pages. The edition also omitted the two chapters which tell the fairytale-like story of the beautiful Scottish protagonist Doris and of her Greek origins, and how she came from Scotland to Anatolia.

It seems whoever decided to eliminate these passages from the first translation did not, or could not, believe that readers of English would tolerate such nonsense. The very passages that made the book unique, that made it resonate so deeply for me, were excised. From the perspective of the person who insisted on these deletions, it must have been considered within the scope of an editor to remove content that was perceived as outside of an English reader's ken. And yet isn't the very purpose of translation to convey something that is by definition something other? I was inspired by the task of giving Venezis' complete text to English readers for the first time.

When it came time to publish my translation, I had the good fortune of finding an editor who believed that English readers deserved — and could handle — a complete and faithful rendering of what Venezis committed to print for his Greek readers. This included not only the personifications of nature throughout the book, but certain stylistic choices that I, as a writer in English, initially felt compelled to correct. One example is Venezis' slipping into the present tense to heighten the drama of a moment, only to switch back into the past tense in the next sentence. This device may be unfamiliar to English readers, but it is not a mistake that needs correcting. My publisher encouraged me to present Venezis to English readers with all his idiosyncrasies and his full range of expression throughout, and I hope as a result that my readers will feel some of the same jolts of disbelief and delight that I felt when this masterpiece fell into my hands for the first time.

* * *

Saint John the Russian of Prokopi was the patron saint of this book project, and the present edition would not have come into being without his intercessions.

I also wish to acknowledge some earthly helpers. Thanks first to Erasmia Sidiropoulou, who cared for my infant daughter while I was in the library translating. Thanks to Susie Irving for going through the whole translation, word-for-word, checking it against the Greek. Thanks to my first readers: Panayiotis Roilos, Donald Carne-Ross, and Georgia Stathoupoulou, who made me believe I had something new to offer as a translator of Venezis. Thank you Lia Papadaki, Krystalli Glyniadaki, and Cecile Margellos for practical help and encouragement on the path to publication. Thanks to Joanne Crerand for reading the final proofs, and to Ayse Gucer Kayali for help with Turkish words. Special thanks to my sister, Lucy Bell Wait Jarka-Sellers, for creating the cover art with speed and grace. Thanks to my husband, Geoffrey Gordon, for being by my side every step of the way. And thanks to Denise Harvey for being the best editor and publisher I could ever have dreamed of working with.

I dedicate my translation of Αἰολικὴ Γῆ to the memory of Anna Cosmetatos, the author's daughter, who longed to see this book come out, but died before it went to print.

Therese Sellers
Gloucester, Massachusetts
October 6, 2020

EDITORIAL NOTE

Exegetical remarks on places, events, individuals, etc., are given in the Endnotes and are indicated in the text by an asterisk. Words in italics in the text refer the reader to the Glossary.

It was decided to include the Prologue to the second Greek edition (1944), by the major Greek lyric poet Angelos Sikelianos, and the Preface to the first English edition (1949), by the British writer Lawrence Durrell, in the end matter as being of particular literary interest.

Prologue

AS AN ABSORBING NARRATIVE OF A LOST CHILDHOOD WORLD, stirring deep emotions but never sliding into maudlin sentimentality, *Land of Aeolia* marks a literary milestone. Its publication was a huge event in the letters of modern Greece, and in world literature too. That is why a fresh English translation, one that follows the author in all his caprices and refuses to ignore his lapses into a methodical kind of madness, is immensely welcome.

Land of Aeolia is the best-known work of Ilias Venezis (real name, Elias Mellos) who lived from 1904 to 1973. It reflects his childhood summers on a family farm in the hinterland of Aivali, or in Turkish Ayvalik. Ethnic Greeks were expelled from that region in 1914, only to return around 1919 and then face a second, definitive expulsion in 1922 after the Greek army's defeat and withdrawal from Anatolia. The situation described in the novel is that of Greek communities prior to 1914, when to a child at least it would have seemed that life was secure and carefree.

As conjured up by the author, the patch of ground between the mountains and the sea was abundantly blessed with rivers, birds, animals and flowers, as well as colourful but mostly benign human characters. To the book's child-narrator, Petros, it seemed obvious that all these elements and creatures were in easy communication with one another. And this was an endless, playful conversation in which he and his four sisters could eagerly and effortlessly join.

Because the child's voice is so authentic, all manner of unlikely details and sub-plots, some rather fuzzy at the edges, can be introduced without jarring. Stories heard in childhood are remembered as vividly as the events of real life. Take, for example, the sweet white-headed camel whose master regrets having sold him and goes crazy as he searches the world for the beloved beast. Or the meandering saga of a simple-minded saddle-maker who is maddened by desire for a grand local lady. For a child whose world is fundamentally secure, all kinds of human oddity, real and imaginary, can safely be observed and enjoyed.

The narrative slides seamlessly from early childhood to adolescence, with the appearance of mysterious objects of desire such as Doris, a young lady of Scottish origin. Only in the final pages do the dark shadows descend. It is the boy's grandparents who take centre-stage, as they sail away from their adored homeland, pathetically clutching a handful of soil.

This book has a timeless attraction as a celebration of the child's instinctive empathy with all manner of creatures and things. With its talking seas, mountains and lizards, it anticipates the magical realism of Latin American fiction. There are shades at times of William Golding's Lord of Flies, and of the boy naturalist, obsessed with frogs and dragonflies, described in Seamus Heaney's most famous poem. Venezis matches C. S. Lewis in his ability to describe the intimacy of young siblings whose secrets and adventures are lived out on many levels. It is no surprise that the book has been enjoyed in places far from the eastern Aegean, translated for example into Estonian and Afrikaans.

The novel also had a specific place in the annals of Greek literature, and of modern Greece generally. Of all unlikely times, it was published in December 1943, when Greece was in the depths of Nazi occupation. Shortly beforehand, Venezis had endured a spell as a prisoner of the German authorities, who released him in response to protests from prominent Athenians including the nation's spiritual leader, Archbishop Damaskinos.

In the book, Venezis brought a flash of Aegean warmth and light to a country in the throes of tyranny and deprivation. It forms a pair with his earlier, much darker autobiographical work: *Number 31328*, which describes his experiences as a captive of the victorious Turkish forces after 1922. (Of the 3,000 men from his home town who were subjected to compulsory labour, only twenty-three returned alive.) The first novel evoked the most painful recollections of the Asia Minor refugees, albeit in a way that avoids anti-Turkish chauvinism; the second celebrates much happier memories from an earlier era.

It is sometimes said that *Land of Aeolia* finally 'broke the silence' of the newcomers from Anatolia and Thrace who had cascaded into

Greece, in varying degrees of destitution and misery, two decades earlier. Numbering at least 1.2 million, they had transformed the country's economy and demography and now constituted between a quarter and a fifth of the total population.

The claim of broken silence demands some explanation. As of the 1930s, writers originating from the eastern Aegean (if one includes island of Mytilene as well as the adjacent mainland) were already becoming the most powerful voice in Greek letters. At a humbler level, the bustling refugee quarters of Athens and other Greek towns where newcomers were forging new lives could hardly be described as silent places.

Yet during the early years of their life in Greece, the refugees faced spiritual and psychological struggles that were masked, only in part, by the daily battle for physical and economic survival. They felt compelled not to differentiate themselves sharply from the rest of Greek society. If they had a distinctive form of speech (be it Turkish or an idiosyncratic Greek dialect) they were under pressure to forget it and use nothing but standard modern Greek.

Generally they felt obliged to play down their collective memories, whether happy or dark, and integrate seamlessly into a national mainstream which was circumscribed by the borders of the Greek state. Especially after 1930, when Eleftherios Venizelos and Kemal Ataturk ushered in warm political relations between Greece and Turkey, the refugees were under pressure not to rock the boat by speaking of lost homelands in ways that could be interpreted as revanchism.

Although the effect was probably not immediate, the publication of *Land of Aeolia* helped to break that taboo. Venezis had given the refugees permission to celebrate and to mourn everything that was peculiar to their own collective memories, including the lands which they had lost. At least in the realm of the mind, the shackles imposed by the narrowly-defined nation state had been cast off. (A similar liberation took place in Turkish fiction in the 1980s, as Iraklis Millas has shown.)

More than seventy years on, in a world where tens of millions of people are on the move because of war, anarchy and economic inequality, those national shackles seem even slacker. Whatever other pressures they may face, migrants arriving in Europe or America are not expected to forget their homelands or the loved ones they left behind. Technology makes it vastly easier for them to remain in contact, and to keep social and economic networks intact across vast distances.

Yet none of that diminishes the human appeal of *Land of Aeolia*. In truth, all adults are in mourning for a lost world. That is the case even if the social and geographical environment where we grew up stays roughly intact, and even if we never leave it. Reality shifts around us as older generations pass on, and above all as our own relationship with that home patch loses its innocence. To that extent, even the most stubborn stay-at-home will know the feeling of inhabiting a strange land.

In a sense, the trauma of a child such as Petros, finally uprooted by war, revolution or disaster from a once-secure environment, is only an extreme example of a universal human experience. If we are fortunate, we spend the first few years of our lives among adults who offer unlimited security, demonstrate consistent love, and expose us to the delights of the natural world. Inevitably, even in places of peace and prosperity, bad things happen that undermine the child's security and bring home the hard reality that grown-ups cannot offer unlimited shelter. Nor, even if nothing terrible happens, can the toddler's pure delight in the world last for ever. In a lucky childhood, the transition is a gentle one and the shocks are manageable.

My own interviews with people whose early years were affected by the Greek and Turkish upheavals of the 1920s brought home the truth that psychological security is more important than the physical sort. Terrible danger and hardship could be endured without lasting damage as long as the child continued to feel protected by at least one significant adult, ideally several. (The reverse, of course, applies: if a sense of consistent love is absent, no amount of material comfort will make that child into a healthy adult.)

The voice of Petros is that of a child whose primordial environment was warm, secure and offered huge enjoyment of the human and physical worlds. He could bear the loss of his beloved Aeolian land precisely because it was all so good to begin with, and it therefore stayed with him forever.

That, in turn, helps explain why the story is universal, and has equivalents in so many other places and times. To take one example,

Serge Schmemann, an American journalist, was raised in New York amidst family stories about idyllic lands he never expected to see. He recalls being told by his White Russian grandfather about a village called Sergiyevskoye where his forebears had been landowners, a 'place where the river flows east and both banks are high, and therefore especially lovely.' In a letter, the old man explained to his progeny that for him, the village was as much a spiritual reality as a physical one: 'I believe everyone in a hidden corner of his soul has his Sergiyevskoye ... here the soul first opened to receive God's universe and its marvels ... [It] is that lost worldly paradise for which we all yearn, believing that if only we could return, we would be happy.'

Ilias Venezis, whether writing as Petros or speaking for himself, clearly knew all that too. The Aeolian lands had claimed a place in his soul, and the memory was powerful enough to sustain him through Nazi prisons as well as Turkish ones. Better still, he had the literary gifts to share that memory.

Bruce Clark
Maghera, County Derry
December 2019

PART ONE

THE WORLD

∌ Chapter One ∍

When the waves of the Aegean parted, and the mountains of Lesbos* began to emerge from the depths, damp, shining and serene, the waves were astonished to see the island, their new friend. They were used to travelling from the regions around the sea of Crete and breaking on the shores of Anatolia. All they knew of dry land were hard mountains, gigantic cliffs, and yellow, rocky land. But this, this new island, was something different; how very different it was! And that's why the waves said:

'Let's take the news to the nearest land, to the land of Aeolia.* Let's tell it about the island, the new land that married light with serenity.'

The waves came and brought the sea's news to the Aeolian shore. Other waves came, and still others — all the waves. They told of the play of the island's lines, the play of harmony and silence.

The first day that the hard mountains of Anatolia heard the waves, they remained aloof. They heard them the next day and still did not react. But then, when it became too much, when every second they heard nothing but the roar of the sea telling them about the miracle, the mountains gave up their indifference. Curious, they leaned over, above the waves, to see the Aegean island. They were envious of its harmony and said:

'Let us, too, make a place of serenity in the land of Aeolia that will be just like the island.'

Then the mountains moved aside and drew back, further inland. The place they left became the place of Serenity.

Those mountains of Anatolia are called the Kimindenia.

My ancestors worked hard on the land that lies below the Kimindenia. By the time I was born, a large part of the region belonged to our family. In the winter we lived in the town, but as soon as the snows left the Kimindenia mountains and the earth began to turn green, our mother took all of us, my sisters Anthippe, Agapi, Artemis and Lena, and me, and we went to spend the summer on the estate with our grandfather and grandmother.

The sea was far away from there, and at first this was a great sorrow for me, since I was born near the sea. In the silence of the land, I remembered the waves, the shells, the jellyfish, the smell of rotting seaweed and the travelling sails. I was still very young and didn't know how to express this. But one day my mother found her boy flung face down on the ground, as though he were kissing the earth. He wasn't moving at all, and when his frightened mother came near and lifted him up, she saw that his face was flooded with tears. Alarmed, she asked him what was the matter. He didn't know how to answer, and said nothing.

But a mother is the most feeling creature in the world, and my mother understood. After that she took me with her many times to a place high up into the Kimindenia mountains where I could see the sea. While I lost myself in the distant magic of the water, she said nothing so I could feel as though we were alone, the sea and I. A lot of time passed in this way; my eyes grew tired of looking, my eyelids drooped and I sank down onto the ground. Then the trees that surrounded me became ships with tall masts; the leaves that rustled became sails; the wind stirred up the earth and lifted it into high waves. The crickets and the birds became goldfish sailing along, and I was travelling with them.

When I woke up, I saw my mother's eyes above me, waiting.

'Was it beautiful, my boy?' she asked, smiling sweetly.

'Oh, Mother, it's always beautiful with the sea!'

ON ONE OF THOSE SUMMER DAYS, returning with my mother from the 'trip-to-the-sea-in-the-Kimindenia,' we stopped by the bed of a small river. The riverbed was full of clean sand, but there was also a little water flowing.

'How can there be water,' I asked, 'since it's summer, and no water is coming down from the Kimindenia?'

'Come!' said my mother. She had spent all her childhood in the Kimindenia and knew the area well. 'Come and see!'

We walked in the riverbed, following it deep into the valley. Then, in a small hollow, we found the spring where the water was welling up. It was very cool there, even though there was no moss and no plane trees, as there should have been in such a damp place.

'Try the water,' said my mother. 'See how fresh it is!'

I took some water in my cupped hands and brought it to my lips. But as soon as I touched it, I let it spill and wiped my tongue.

'That's seawater!' I said, astonished.

My mother laughed with delight. She took me in her arms and said: 'You see? The sea is everywhere!'

Then, as we started home, she became serious and explained to me how the whole region at the foot of the Kimindenia had once been bad land because very deep within it lived the sea. The sea went through it. It had taken the unending labour of my humble ancestors, generation after generation, to get rid of that salt water and for the trees and grapevines to grow.

BY MY GRANDFATHER'S TIME, the time of my mother's father, the land was ready and the farming estate came into being. I learned from my mother how the first hut was built; I learned about when my grandmother planted the plane tree in the courtyard with her own hands, and when they planted the vines.

You entered the compound through a large door made of carved wood. The courtyard was in the middle, and all around it were the buildings, one next to the other. The storerooms and stables were on the ground floor; on the upper storey were our grandparents' residence, then the guest rooms, and next to them the living quarters for the women and ploughmen who worked on our property year-round. A wooden staircase from the courtyard led up to my grandfather's rooms, and from there, a wooden balcony extended along all the buildings, joining them in a circle. The windows all looked onto the courtyard. Only grandfather's rooms had one iron-barred window that looked out at the world outside the great door. In this way, for fear of brigands, the farmstead resembled a monastery or a fortress, built completely out of strong Sarmousak stone.* But it had nothing of the ascetic austerity of monasteries or the fierceness of fortresses. It was painted sky blue.

The weapons were stored like precious objects in a special room. There were rifles from Europe and swords: enough to arm all the ploughmen in an emergency, if brigands should attack us. We called this room the Yellow Room because it was painted bright yellow. Our own room, the children's room, was next door to the weapons, and their proximity to us made us think about them a great deal. Since the Yellow Room was always locked, and no one had permission to open it except for grandfather, our imagination gave it extraordinary dimensions. We conceived it as the secret refuge of mythical creatures.

At night, after it grew quiet outside, after the jackals stopped howling and all you heard was the leaves rustling, every slightest sound that reached us seemed to come from the forbidden room. Then one child would wake another.

'Did you hear that?' little Artemis would say, nudging me.

I'd wake up frightened and ask:

'What is it?'

'Listen, something is happening next door! In the Yellow Room . . .'

I would concentrate all my attention and listen. The earth was resting and fertilizing the seeds. From that secret activity comes a very faint sound that only a child can hear. The roots of the trees stir in the darkness, looking for water to drink; the bark of their trunks moves so that the sap can flow into their branches and leaves. The sightless worms pursue their little struggle alone. A roe deer passes and disappears. Another, hunted by a larger animal, is not able to cross the forest, not able to escape. Its rending cry is heard in the distance, the voice of death. After that everything settles, and the Great Silence arrives.

'Listen!' says Artemis again when it is still.

'It must have been a jackal. It's gone now,' I say.

'No! Not the jackal! There! Now, now! In there! Listen!'

I strain my ears and open my eyes as wide as I can. My heart beats in anguish, because I feel an urgency to hear whatever she can hear. Finally I cry out in despair:

'I can't hear anything, only the leaves . . .'

'Pathetic! The leaves! Why are you talking about leaves?' says her voice in the darkness, and I know that her eyes are shining with contempt. 'Are you such a baby?'

I was six years old, and she had already turned eight. That didn't bother me so much. But I wanted to cry with frustration because it wasn't fair: Artemis was a girl, and a girl should not know more than a boy. Yet that's how it was. There was great injustice in the world.

'You're talking nonsense!' I say at last, angrily. 'You hear the leaves on the trees and you think it's in the Yellow Room. Ha!'

'You poor thing! I'm talking nonsense, am I?' Artemis retorted. 'Don't you remember how you heard the swords walking around in the Yellow Room the other day and talking to the pistols? And now you say I'm talking nonsense!'

Artemis was right. The other night there had been a lot of wind after midnight, and the whole farmstead had seemed to be moving. From high up in the Kimindenia mountains came the lament of the trees wrestling with the wind. Neither the jackals nor the deer had dared come out of their hideouts that night, and not a voice was heard. Then we heard the mysterious sound coming from the Yellow Room and agreed, Artemis and I, that the swords were talking. So why should I not believe it now?

'All you do is sleep, that's what it is!' Artemis concludes, to explain my inadequacy. 'I stay awake, and I've trained my ears to catch everything.'

'All right, all right!' I cry. 'You know everything! So, stay up then, stay awake in the darkness . . .'

I turn over in my small bed and pull the sheet up over my head. But at exactly that moment a distinct, a perfectly distinct sound, a *tik-tik*, comes through the night from the direction of the Yellow Room.

'Did you finally hear it?' whispers Artemis' voice in the darkness, and I think she's trembling. 'Did you hear?'

'Ah! I heard it!' I murmur anxiously. 'What do you think it is?'

'The swords are waking up . . . ,' she says.

But then Anthippe wakes up. She is our oldest sister. She is twelve years old and like a second mother. We always tell her our secrets.

'What's the matter, you two?' she asks quietly.

'Anthippe, listen!' says Artemis, and her voice sounds like she's asking for help. 'The swords have woken up in the Yellow Room . . . !'

Anthippe listens and then says, unperturbed:

'It's mice, don't make such a fuss. Go to sleep.'

We hear her turn to the other side and go to sleep as though nothing had happened. I cover myself too, up to the top of my head, but my eyes don't close. The sounds of the forest, the earth, and the deer become one; they become the strange music that tells of fairy tales and dreams and the journeys of children who ride goldfish in search of Rose Slipper, with her white dress and silver hair, and the Great Dragon who keeps watch at her door.*

The swords and pistols in the Yellow Room are no longer savage creatures; they only woke up because they were jealous, because they wanted to ride goldfish too, not be locked up and all alone. They quietly open the door of their prison, they stretch out their hands, and they know that even if there isn't a goldfish, a good little dolphin will wait to take them. As the goldfish start their journey, sailing through the air, they hear the voice of the swords behind them, riding on a dolphin and pleading:

'Wait for us! Wait for us to come with you to Rose Slipper's house!'

'Come on!' says the little boy very kindly from astride his goldfish. 'Come on, we're waiting for you!'

The next morning Anthippe asks me:

'Who were you waiting for last night?'

'Was I waiting for someone?'

'Yes! You were calling out in your sleep for someone to come.'

I don't remember anything and tell her it must have been a dream.

➤ Chapter Two ➤

THE EVENTS OF A FLOOD
AND A FEARSOME BRIGAND NAMED LAZOS-*EFE*

G randfather was a large-boned man, bursting with health despite his seventy years. He was a noble soul. He had spent all his life in the Kimindenia, a harsh life until he had established the farmstead. But the only trace that difficult life had left was the deep lines on his face, nothing more. In his blue eyes a childlike goodness reigned, and when he laughed, the kindness of the world shone on his lips. Since he had entrusted the management of his farm to a loyal overseer, he could spend all day dressed in his expensive felt clothes, with the traditional breeches sewn in the austere Aivali* fashion. He was incredibly meticulous in how he dressed, and I don't remember ever seeing him unkempt in all the summers we spent at the farmstead. He did not know how to read or write, so his faithful companion, my grandmother, helped him with the bookkeeping. It seems that all grandmothers are tender creatures, but mine was the sweetest and gentlest of all the grandmothers in the world. She shared all the sorrows and difficulties of life with grandfather. By his side, year after year, she saw to the upbringing of the children, the grandchildren, the trees, and the vines. A great part of all this was her work. And yet, even in old age, her relationship with our grandfather was rooted in the formality of their younger years.

'We owe all this to your grandfather,' she would say, pointing around her with a gesture that encompassed the land, the trees, and us.

And whenever grandfather came in, she was always the first to stand up to receive him, always standing. It was not only to teach us to respect him, but because she, too, felt it was her obligation.

Then, as soon as grandmother stood up, we children, my sisters and I, would all get up and run to kiss grandfather's hands or stroke his legs up to his knees, whatever we could reach. Laughing, he would make his way through us with difficulty, as though he were wading through waves. He went to where grandmother stood waiting for him at the back of the room.

'Sit down, Despina,' he would say, and stroke her back, while from his face radiated the joy of a person who has been useful, whose life has not passed from this earth without bearing fruit.

On summer days, when evening was beginning to fall, they would always go to sit, just the two of them, under the oak tree outside the large door at the entrance to the farmstead. There was a small bench there, just big enough for two people. There they would sit. They spoke at rare intervals with long pauses, and their memories kept them company. Their eyes rarely looked down, but remained fixed, needing nothing. Free from the agitation of youth, they rested peacefully on the clouds, the trees, the Kimindenia mountains. Then, approaching slowly and distinctly, the memories would come from the past.

He would say:

'Do you remember when our first child came? It was the year the river flooded.'

'Do I remember, Yannako? How could I forget?'

They remain silent for a long while. Then the light breeze turns into a strong north wind, and the travelling white clouds become gigantic black mountains that cover the land below the Kimindenia. It is night, and the storm rages. It rains and rains without stopping. In a small room, lit only by the fireplace, a very young woman moans softly with stifled cries, bringing a child into the world. Around her stand two or three of the women who work on the estate, while outside the door, her strong and rigid husband paces with large, nervous steps. Suddenly the night thickens, and the storm becomes more savage.

At that moment, a terrified servant boy with clouded eyes arrives, drenched from the downpour.

'The river is flooding!' he cries. 'It's going to drown us!'

The woman's young husband starts to run. He calls for all hands to come and save the land — so much labour — but at the last minute he hesitates. How can he go and leave his wife alone when she is in danger, giving birth to his son? His son!

'You go!' he says at last, in a decisive voice, and instructs his men how to combat the flooding. 'I'll stay here.'

But his companion understands what's happening. She clenches her pain in her teeth, makes a tremendous effort to appear calm, and sends someone to call in her husband.

'Yannako,' she says, 'it will be a while more. My time hasn't come yet. What's happening outside?'

'Nothing,' he says. 'Just a little flooding.'

'Go, Yannako,' she says, calmly and convincingly. 'If there is something you should do, go. I will be a while yet.'

But when he still hesitates she cries out:

'In the name of God! The land! Our land!'

Her husband was persuaded. He went and worked hard all night with his men. They dug trenches and diverted the water. Returning at dawn, no sooner had he arrived at his wife's room than he noticed a strange silence inside. He opened the door abruptly. All the peasants who stood around gasped and looked down, afraid of what was going to happen. The young woman, motionless on her bed, looked at him once, with a kind of wonderment, then turned her face, stamped with pain, towards the tiny child, all bundled up and resting beside her.

'Forgive me,' she whispers humbly, 'it's a girl.'

Then the man understands. He runs near, bends over his young wife, and caresses her face. His eyelashes flutter with emotion.

He says only:

'May I see?' as though asking permission.

The new mother uncovers the child who has just come into the world. Her husband leans over the shapeless, dark thing, stays that way for a little while and then leaps up.

'Well, go tell them to slaughter the white calf!' he shouts thunderously to the women. 'Give food and drink to all the ploughmen and any travellers who pass through! Tell them that my daughter has been born!'

And while the new mother, looking for his hands to kiss, began to weep silently in gratitude to this man who could be so kind, he gave to the child — my mother — her first tenderness. He covered her carefully, just as he would care for her all his life.

'And the land?' murmured his wife through her sobs.

'Everything went well. Now rest.'

'You see, Despina, how our life has passed by?' says grandfather softly, returning from the depths of the years, while his hand lightly touches grandmother's hand.

'Yes, Yannako, my life was good by your side,' she whispers. 'You were my crown and my joy . . .'

'Come, come, enough of that,' he says, and smiles at her happily. 'You were the one who helped me. I am indebted to you.'

After a little while he says:

'How good that God gave us only girls at the beginning! That way you were never lonely and without help in this remote place.'

Then after a little while he says:

'What happened the year our second child was born, Ourania?' He is trying to remember which event on the farm was linked to that child, because that was the only way that the sequence of the years made sense to him: bound to the history of the land.

'You really don't remember?' grandmother asks, amazed. 'It was the year the trees burned, the year Lazos came.'

'Oh, yes! When Lazos came! How could I forget?'

He seems to suddenly think of something.

'Come on, tell me now, you were really scared then, weren't you?' he asks, smiling.

'But don't you remember? By the time I knew about it, it was all over. And besides, I was never afraid for myself, only for you . . .'

Lazos was a fearsome Turkish brigand, the terror in those years of the whole region, from Pergamum and even further, from Kirkagats to the Gulf of Andramittium. He was reputed to be an unthinkably cruel and bloodthirsty man, without a scruple towards his own race or towards Christians. Everyone called him *kafir* — infidel — since they knew that no faith in God could have found a home in such a wild beast.

One day at noon, while the ploughmen were resting under the olive trees, and grandfather — a young man — was resting with them, they saw in the distance a shepherd from the neighbouring mountains running towards them, shouting:

'Where is Yannako-Bibelas? Where is Yannako-Bibelas?'

They motioned for him to come closer and saw a man pale with fear and dripping in sweat from running.

'Master!' he said to grandfather. 'Master! Lazos!'

'Speak, man! What is it?' said grandfather, trying to appear unmoved by the unexpected news in front of his men.

Then the shepherd told him in a rush how, while he was sitting on a summit in the Kimindenia watching his sheep, some fifteen tall men with beards and wild eyes had suddenly jumped out in front of him. They had cartridge belts crossed on their chests and rifles in their hands. After they had interrogated him about how many men were on Bibelas' farm, whether they had weapons, how much livestock and other property there was, whether any government troopers had been seen in the vicinity, and other such questions, the brigand who seemed to be the chief said to him:

'Take this and give it to Yannako-Bibelas! Tell him that it's from Lazos and that Lazos will be putting up at his lodgings tonight. Tell him to have five hundred gold pounds ready. Have him send one of his men back with you to get me. We will be waiting here.'

And he gave the shepherd his token, which was a terrifying warning to grandfather. It was a red handkerchief in which he had rolled and knotted a bullet, after first biting it hard.

This was what the shepherd said.

The distress that his words produced among the ploughmen cannot be described. Some wanted to flee immediately, to try to make it to the coast and hide there. Others said they should arm themselves and resist the brigand and his band after first sending someone to Dikeli for help. Everyone had something different to say.

'We have women at the farm. What will happen to them?' one man suddenly remembered.

'And with the master's wife in her condition!' said another, recalling that just one day before their mistress had given birth to her second little daughter, Ourania, and was not doing well.

Then grandfather, who had kept quiet all the while — partly to have time to think and decide on the right thing to do, partly to avoid betraying any fear before his men — raised his eyes, looked around at all the ploughmen one by one and then, turning to the shepherd, he said decisively:

'You will go back with one of my men. Tell Lazos that at Yannako-Bibelas' house, everyone who passes through finds food to eat and a place to sleep. If he wants, he is welcome to come. As for the five hundred gold pounds, I don't have the amount he's asking for. I can send him only one hundred. I am sending them with one of my men. I don't have any more.'

That's what happened. The shepherd left with the overseer of the estate. The sun was already setting. The ploughmen, the women, everyone returned from their work. Grandfather gave strict orders that the news should not reach the ears of his wife, the young mother. Everyone spoke in lowered voices. They stood about the courtyard in small groups talking about it. The men were uneasy and scared. They privately debated their master's decision not to resist. Some said, 'What was he supposed to do? Abandon his wife in her current state?' They concluded that he had made his decision for her sake. The women labourers, especially the young girls, hearing all this, ran to and fro, from one group of men to another. Their cheeks were flushed, and in their eyes, the tumult of the male adventure blazed.

'What will happen? What is going to happen? Maybe there will be killing! Maybe they will take us!'

From time to time, one would rush to the great door of the farmstead and look out. She would shade her eyes with her hand and look high up towards the Kimindenia mountains, while the others waited inside in anguish.

'Nothing yet.'

'Nothing!'

They sighed, but no one could say what weighed on them more heavily: their fear, or the anguish of waiting.

Finally, one woman could stand it no longer. She began to cry and blurted out:

'Just let them come! Whatever is going to happen, let it happen! Let them come so we can get it over with!'

Evening fell. Night was descending on trees and men, and the darkness was a new weight on their troubled hearts. Many men went and lay down in their rooms exhausted, smoking one cigarette after another, while the women sat outside keeping vigil, their eyes wide open under the stars, every pore of their bodies open.

The stillness was vast. High up, where the austere divinity of the land loomed, in the Kimindenia mountains, a large tree was thirsty. It moved its roots slowly, to the right and to the left; it stretched them out, looking for water.

The worms wake up from their slumber. 'What is it?' says one. 'Nothing,' answers another. 'The tree was thirsty.' They turn over and go back to sleep. But then the earth wakes up. 'What's going on?' it asks. But as soon as it sees the roots in their desperate struggle, it understands and smiles tenderly. 'I'll bring you water,' it says to the tree. The earth moves a little, it brings forth water from the secret hiding place where it is stored for times of need, and the tree drinks. At the same moment, on the surface, a large rock stirred by the earth's moving, loses its balance and rolls a little.

Those things were happening up high, and the mountains were listening, unperturbed. Unperturbed, they were also listening to what was happening down below, under their shelter, among the men.

'Nothing yet?' the ploughmen were asking from inside their rooms. Their eyes were clouded and red.

'Still nothing!' the women answered from outside.

'Still nothing!' they said, and the tone of voice showed that they had reached their limit, that they couldn't stand waiting any more.

At that moment, one voice, trembling with emotion, rang out:

'Listen! Listen now!'

Muffled, but very distinct, came the strange sound.

'Is it horses?'

'Yes! It's horses! It's them! They're coming! They're coming!'

They all jumped up and came out of their rooms. The confusion grew inside the stronghold that was waiting to be taken. They notified grandfather discreetly as he sat by his wife's side, and asked him to come out.

'What is it?' she asked.

He smiled at her kindly:

'Soon we'll have a new calf. The white cow is giving birth.'

He stepped outside and his expression changed at once. He became stern and rigid. He ordered two men to light resin torches and wait at the great door. Then he gave orders to all the ploughmen and the women who were wandering around in the courtyard:

'All of you, go inside and lock yourselves in your rooms! No one come out unless I order him to!'

It wasn't long before the brigands finally arrived. They dismounted outside the great door. Half of them stayed there to keep watch, and Lazos, with five of his companions, approached the men with the torches.

'Where is your master?' he asked savagely.

Trembling, they told him Yannako was waiting for him, and rushing ahead, they opened the gate and lit the way to the wooden staircase. The women and the ploughmen, hidden behind their grillwork windows, saw in the torchlight a tall young man walking ahead of the others. He had a small blond mustache and a sunburned face. A red scarf was tied around his head, and a double cartridge belt crossed his chest. In his belt were a pistol, a knife and a silver dagger; a rifle hung from his shoulder. He walked behind the torches fearlessly, with large steps. His men followed behind him.

Grandfather was waiting for him at the staircase.

'Welcome to my household, Lazos-*Efe*!'

'Are you Yannako-Bibelas? I am glad to meet you!' responded the brigand.

Grandfather led them to the room where the food was ready on a low, round table.

The chief brigand sat down first on the wooden bench that was built into the wall. His men sat down beside him on either side. He looked around, examining his surroundings, then fixed his eyes on grandfather.

'Where are your men?' he asked.

'They are all in their rooms.'

'Where are your weapons?'

'There are no weapons in here,' answered grandfather calmly, avoiding a direct answer.

Lazos glanced at the bare walls, then ordered his men:

'Search him!'

They searched, but there was nothing on him. He was completely unarmed.

'All right!' says Lazos.

Then, after a pause:

'Have you heard of me, sir?' he asks grandfather.

'I have. All the country around here has heard of you.'

'Then you know that what I say, I say only once. I told you I wanted five hundred gold pounds from you. Why didn't you send them?'

Suddenly his expression became hard. His eyes fixed piercingly on grandfather. How could that almost boyish face possess such eyes?

'And my word is good too,' answered grandfather, calmly. 'I don't have the sum you asked for. My land is not good land, and what I sent you was earned through hard labour. It's all I have.'

The eyes blazed again.

'We'll see!' said Lazos, and a strange smile, burning with sarcasm, appeared on his lips. 'But know one thing, Yannako-Bibelas: not many men have spoken to me that way.'

'Whatever you see fit to do, do it,' he said, maintaining his frozen composure. 'I have men who could have guarded my gate and kept you out. But I didn't do that. Because . . .'

He was going to speak of his wife's condition, but considered it dishonourable. His lip trembled slightly.

'Why?' asked the brigand.

'Nothing. Nothing.'

And then, after a little, he added:

'No man who came to my house looking for bread was ever turned away.'

He softened his voice.

'Let's eat now,' he said to Lazos.

And he stood up with the air of a person who must attend to his guests.

'Welcome,' he said again and was the first to bring bread to his mouth.

On the table, there was a roast lamb, eggs, cheese, wine and honey. Grandfather barely touched the food and drink. It was for his guests. But those men, half-starving as they were, soon forgot completely that he was there too. They ate and drank like beasts and talked among themselves, laughing and shouting. One of them glanced over at grandfather for a moment as though he'd only then remembered his existence.

'If you only knew what was waiting for you, *ulan*!' he said, laughing. And all his companions laughed. 'If only you knew Lazos-*Efe*!'

More time passed. It was clear now that all the brigands were drunk. Then the blond brigand, Lazos-*Efe*, began a song:

From far away, from the depths of Asia, down from the high, bare mountains, comes the pack of wolves. They go towards the lowlands, towards the plain, towards the land near the sea to find food. They go from place to place, laying them to waste, but they cannot satisfy their hunger. The trees and the wild animals all tell them: 'Go further down! Go down to the sea!' And the wolves keep on running. They pass the Salt Desert, but not a soul is there. They find only a stray bird, and they ask him: 'Where is the sea?' 'Go further down! Go further down!' says the frightened bird, and vanishes. The sea! What can it be, this country of water that everyone is desperate to reach, all beasts and birds and men who are hungry in the bare mountains? The wolves cross the Salt Desert and enter the great forest. There, in the hollow of a tree, they find an old stag, who has withdrawn there to die. They say: 'Tell us, you who ran so far in your life, tell us about the sea. Will it be much longer before it is in sight?' And the stag, who has lived a long time in the forest, has lived only in the forest and seen all the deer of his race give birth and die under the great trees, answers them: 'You will never reach the sea. You will never reach it.' Then, with a wild moan, the wolves sink to the ground and begin to cry, bemoaning their fate, bemoaning their devastation, since now they know for sure that they will never reach the sea, that the sea is not for wolves.

That song about the wolves was a strange, distressing song about exile and loneliness, overflowing with anguish and unsatisfied passion. A bitter veil covered the brigands' eyes as the song was unfolding, and their hearts beat hard until it ceased. Then the sorrow came and settled over them. The hard lines disappeared from their faces, their hands with swollen veins relaxed. Then very slowly the hour of truth drew close and was present among them.

Just then, at that crucial moment, a sound was heard from inside: insistent and unbroken came the plaintive cry. A baby was crying with its high, piercing voice: helpless, utterly helpless. Into the atmosphere of the wolves, among the ammunition belts and the weapons, into the male odour of dirty bodies came the incredible new voice, to say it existed and to implore.

The blond brigand, Lazos-*Efe*, found his voice first. He blinked his eyes several times, as though he wanted to make sure he had heard right. Then he looked at his comrades as though he were trying to find out from them. Finally, he looked at grandfather.

'What is that?' he asks at last in astonishment.

Grandfather looks him in the eye gravely.

'It was born yesterday,' he answers. 'It's my daughter. Her mother is seriously ill.'

The high, helpless cry, as it passed through the walls, became increasingly insistent and pleading. For one moment, a deathly silence took hold of the brigands. Then finally Lazos jumped up, rushed at grandfather, and grabbing him by his jacket, he shook him violently.

'Why didn't you tell me that, *ulan*? Why didn't you tell me?' he screamed.

As though suddenly something terrible had happened to him, he stamped his feet on the ground and beat his chest with his hands. The bullets in the cartridge belts rattled.

'Why didn't you tell me that, *ulan*?' he kept bellowing, as though they had forced him to do an awful, cowardly thing.

Some time passed before he calmed down. He sank onto the bench and said nothing for a little while. His men stood over him in silence, to avoid upsetting him.

Finally he stood up. He was calm now, and his resolve showed on his dry face.

'Call a servant girl,' he ordered grandfather.

The old woman who was taking care of the sick young mother came in.

Lazos took a small black pouch from his belt, the purse with the hundred gold pounds that grandfather had sent him.

'Give this to your mistress,' he said, giving her the purse. 'Tell her that it's from Lazos for her daughter's dowry.'

He went out first and the other brigands followed. The Pleiades trembled in the west. It was cold.

When they reached the large outer gate where their horses waited, they stopped.

'*Allaha ısmarladık,*[1] Yannako-Bibela!' said the brigand.

'*Uğur ola,*[2] Lazo-Efe!'

He mounted, his companions mounted, and they disappeared into the night.

Such were the stories that our grandfather and grandmother would remember and tell in the evening hours, alone and apart on the wooden bench under the oak tree.

'How far away all those things are ... ,' murmured grandmother.

'See how the years have passed, Despina,' he would say.

As the stars came out, and the birds grew silent, and the cool of night descended and covered everything, grandmother would stand up first.

'Shall we go in, Yannako?'

'Let's go, Despina.'

And since she had grown heavy, and her legs didn't help her much,

---

[1] Allah be with you.   [2] Farewell.

she leaned on her husband, and they walked together, making their way slowly. At the large outer door of the farmstead, they would stop and make the sign of the cross. Then grandfather drew the crossbar.

Those were the two things in the ritual of our life below the Kimindenia mountains that never changed: in the evenings, only our grandfather and grandmother could sit on the bench under the oak tree. And only grandfather could open the great door in the morning or close it at night; because grandfather had to pray for all of us: for the men, for the trees, for the flocks and for the livestock at the beginning and the end of every day.

That is how I learned in time to love that land, where peace had dropped anchor.

⋙ Chapter Three ⋘

THE HUNGRY JACKALS

There were nights when nothing was heard, when nothing was happening outside in the Kimindenia. Those were the lifeless nights. In silent waves, the dew came down from the clouds and mountains and settled in drops on the leaves. Their journey was uneventful. They encountered no evil in the clean atmosphere where they floated, with the stars as their only guide and companion. Yet they needed neither guide nor companion. From the time the drops of dew were born, way up high, earth was the magical land where they were destined to go. They knew that place was their destiny, so the earth tugged at them to fall and disappear. The attraction of their end drew them on.

The children, my sisters and I, were gathered in our grandparents' room, worried by so much quiet. We leaned out of the window in the hope of hearing some sound.

Nothing. Not a living voice. But the magic of the night, a deep and unexplored world, spoke to our hearts.

'Grandfather, what's happening outside?' we asked.

'What's happening? Nothing.'

'Nothing? But listen!'

He listened carefully, then verified his first answer:

'I told you. I don't hear a thing.'

Then we turned to our grandmother.

'Do you hear anything, Grandmother?'

She was a woman, she was a grandmother, and she understood.

'Of course I hear,' she said gently, blessing us all with her eyes.

'What is it? What is it, then?' we asked, impatient to learn.

'The Night has woken up, children,' she answered calmly and conclusively.

So that was it. The Night had woken up . . .

'But what happened to the jackals? What happened to the foxes? Why aren't they howling?'

'Don't you know? The Great Dragon took all the deer into his cave. He fed them and put them to bed.'

'So that's why . . .'

The Great Dragon was our grandmother's favourite creature. From the people-eating hero of fairy tales, he gradually became, in grandmother's telling, a beneficent divinity of the forest. He was the one who closed children's eyes for them to sleep. If they did something bad, like disobeying their mother, or forgetting to say their prayers, he punished them with a switch so light and thin it was like a caress. He showed lost strangers the path through the valley; he set the table and invited the poor jackals in to eat when they were howling the most.

When we heard those things about the Great Dragon, we imagined him like God, who was painted in the domes of churches. We imagined him with a great white beard, wearing a hood and a gold crown on his head. He moved silently, striding over the trees on his long legs. In front of him went forty small dragons, and behind him another forty. The heavy bells that hung from their necks echoed through the forest, *glanka, glounka*, so that everyone would know the Great Dragon was passing by.

All this happened on quiet summer nights under the Kimindenia mountains. But it wasn't always quiet. There were other nights, and these were more common, when the Great Dragon, tired of feeding the jackals and putting them to bed, let them loose over the plain, over the ploughed land, to eat and satisfy their appetites. In the spring, before the fruit had ripened, their forays were harmless, and no one on the farm bothered about it. We would hear their wild howling far off in the distance, faint at first, and wait for them in suspense and fear.

'Do you think they'll come *here*?'

'Why, are you afraid?' grandfather would say. 'Let them come!'

'Let them come!' I would say too, as the boy of the house, to show courage to my sisters. 'What are you afraid of?'

Little Artemis, Agapi and Lena were literally trembling. Seeing me act all brave made them mad.

'You pathetic little boy!' they cried with unbearable scorn. 'Look who's pretending not to be afraid. You, who are afraid of lizards!'

I am afraid of lizards, true. So what? Lizards run between your feet and slither like eels. Isn't it natural to be afraid of them? But in here, the walls protect you from the jackals.

'Ah, of course, you're only a daring man inside the walls.'

The girls hadn't finished their laughter when the howling of the jackals, which had now got very close, cut their voices short and stopped the blood in their veins.

'My God! They're coming!'

It came through the silence of the earth, heart-rending and sacred: the voice of hunger. Never did the anguish of man or the pain of death resound so wildly. Nothing we had ever heard could compare with this. The leaves shuddered on the trees and fell silent. The drops of dew, struck suddenly by the wind, stopped falling to earth. The roots in the ground did not move, the stars stopped travelling, and the subterranean veins of water froze, because that harsh and merciless divinity, Hunger, had come to the Kimindenia.

We were young children then. The good earth gave us grain, the trees gave us fruit; we did not yet know what hunger was. But our pure hearts were a good guide, and all the mysteries of the world could find a receptive place inside us. We could feel those mysteries and understand them. In the safety of the high walls that protected us, in the shelter of our grandfather, who shaded us like a great tree, we were not like grown-up people, pitiless and indifferent when they themselves do not suffer. We experienced the drama of the night as powerfully as was possible.

'I can't stand it!' Agapi would always cry out first, since she was the weakest and most sensitive of us all. She started to cry and sob as though her heart would break. Once we saw her, we let ourselves go too, Artemis, Lena and I. We began crying and shouting:

'Why do the jackals have to be hungry? Why do the jackals have to be hungry?'

Then there was great pandemonium: outside the wild animals were howling, and inside we were wailing. At first grandfather laughed at these outpourings of children's hearts, while our mother and grandmother ran to hug us and calm us down.

'Yannako!' said grandmother sternly. 'Stop that! Don't you see them?' she said, indicating our distress.

Very rarely did she speak to him in that tone of voice, as though she were scolding him. And he immediately became serious, like a person who has been in the wrong, and stopped laughing.

'Come on now, calm down,' grandmother said soothingly. 'God will find food for the jackals. He is good, and He will find food. Now go to sleep.'

It was very late when the voices of the jackals died out. Then there wasn't a sound. We said our bedtime prayers and, as always, asked God to protect grandfather, grandmother, our father, our mother, the trees and all mankind. We lay down, but did not sleep. Sleep weighed on our eyelashes, but we used all our strength to keep it away until we could make sure that the jackals had gone. And then, when we were certain they were gone, we whispered our prayers again to ourselves, and along with mankind and with the trees, we also prayed for the hungry jackals of the world.

HOWEVER, THE SEASON WOULD COME when the fruit was ripening, and the half-ripe clusters of grapes hung from the vines. For the jackals to overrun us then was not without danger, as it had been in the spring. If such a big pack of hungry animals went through the property even one night, there would be no fruit left the next morning.

For this reason, people looked for a way to fight this evil and to withstand it. Everyone who worked on the estate, men and women, divided into three shifts. The first shift kept watch until ten o'clock, the next until the middle of the night, and the third until the morning hours. They would wait, and as soon as the jackals came near, they would all rush to the outer boundaries of the estate, shouting wildly and striking tin pans or drums. If the night was dark, many of them held flaming resin torches of split pine in their hands.

The frightened beasts would retreat, howling furiously, and run to other neighbouring estates. In a short while, shouts came from the people on the other properties as they, in turn, tried to defend themselves, turning the pack of hunger somewhere else. Some time would pass and again the cries were heard, now from deeper in the distance, from another estate. It was like a terrible wave, which rolled, possessed, striking here and there until it could find a place to break. It didn't find one, and the circle began again. Again it hit us, and again our men drove it away. There were nights when the chase of fear and of hunger lasted until morning.

Our first encounter with this cruel game brought real distress to us children. One evening there was a curious commotion in the courtyard of the farmstead. The women, especially the young female labourers, and the men were in small groups talking, laughing, and preparing resin torches, tin pans and drums. We had all gone to our room early, little Lena, Agapi and I, and were busy making toy boats out of pinewood. We didn't notice what was going on outside. Only Artemis was missing. She was probably looking around downstairs. No one thought anything of it.

Artemis was the most restless of us all. She had an extraordinary curiosity for her age, a curiosity that amounted to a mania. It was as though she sensed already that she was going to leave us early and was in a hurry to learn everything about this world before her time came and it was too late. While the most off-hand answers that the grown-ups gave to our questions sufficed the other children, Artemis, ever distrustful, always sensed another truth hidden behind the veils that enveloped the world. She would ask, she would probe, she would insist that they tell her and insist on learning. Because of this, the grown-ups found it difficult to answer when she asked them about things she wasn't supposed to know yet. They told her something off the top of their head, and the world's veils grew darker. Artemis sensed it and stamped her feet crossly.

'No! That's not it! That's not it!' she would shout, ready to cry.

But she didn't cry, very rarely did she cry. A premature sense of seriousness held her back, a dignity entirely unnatural for a child.

So while we were playing that evening with little pine boats, the door opened suddenly and Artemis rushed in. Her face was bright, and her pale cheeks were flushed. Sparks flew from her big dark eyes.

'Have you heard? Have you heard?'

We jumped up, abandoning our boats, and hung eagerly on her every word.

'What is it, Artemis? What is it?'

As though she wanted to torture us, she cast a contemptuous glance at our feet, at the toy lateens and caiques that lay abandoned.

'You are playing with boats, when tonight . . .'

'Oh, Artemis, tell us what it is! Tell us!' we begged her.

Suddenly she became serious. She looked at us once and then:

'Didn't you see the torches and drums they're getting ready?'

'They're getting torches and drums ready? What for? Why?'

'*War!*' says Artemis, looking us straight in the eyes.

War? What did that mean? None of us knew. We had never heard of such a creature: bird, beast or tree.

'Tonight, war on the jackals begins,' Artemis said. 'Alexis told me.'

We jumped with joy at the thought that something new was going to enter our lives. Surely it would be some game, this 'war'.

'Really? It's going to happen? What did you call it? There will be . . . war?' We shouted and jumped up and down.

But Artemis didn't jump or laugh with us. Her lips were tightly closed, and she shuffled her feet nervously. It was as though she guessed something, foresaw something.

Agapi, a girl of ten at the time, was the first to notice the serious expression on our younger sister's face, so inconsistent with our delight.

'What's the matter, Artemis?'

And immediately connecting the doubt that suddenly rose up inside her with the expression on Artemis' face, she asked fearfully:

'And what is this game, Artemis? What is war?'

Yes, really. What is it?

Our jumping and shouting stopped at once, and our eyes fixed on Artemis again.

'What is it, Artemis? What is war?'

But Artemis didn't know; she had not been able to understand. Alexis, our best friend among the ploughmen, had reported the news to her. But he was in a hurry and short-tempered, and Artemis hadn't asked anyone else, impatient as she was to be the first to bring us the news. But the mystery of the word, the fact that she couldn't find out its meaning, together with her own forebodings, disturbed her deeply.

'I don't know!' she said. 'How should I know? Why are you asking me?' She stood for a second wavering, and then said:

'I have to find out! I have to find out! I am going to grandfather!'

She rushed to the door, and we ran behind her. Since we were all upset over the news, we expected to find our grandfather agitated too. Not in the least. He was sitting calmly, as he did on other evenings, as though nothing was happening and nothing was about to happen.

'Grandfather, is there going to be war tonight?' said Artemis, and fell at his feet out of breath.

He turned around and looked at her in surprise; he looked at all of us and our questioning eyes.

'Is *what* going to happen?' he asked.

'War, Grandfather! Won't there be war tonight?'

Staring and quivering with hunger for the unknown, our very eyes trembled.

'War?' whispered grandfather. 'Who told you that word? Who told you there would be war?'

'Come, Grandfather, don't hide it from us,' cried Artemis. 'I learned for sure that we're going to make war on the jackals!'

Then grandfather began to laugh that happy, childlike laugh of his. He laughed and looked at all of us.

'Oh, is that what you're talking about? Is that it?'

He wiped his eyes and patted Artemis.

'It's nothing, children, it's nothing.'

'What do you mean it's nothing, Grandfather! What do you mean it's nothing?' said Artemis, and we cried out with her. 'Then why are they getting torches and drums ready?'

'But really it's nothing at all! The hungry jackals can do us harm now, so we'll beat them off. That's all.'

'Ah! We're going to beat off the hungry jackals!'

'Of course. We'll beat them off.'

Nameless feelings took hold of us that night. What had happened to our grandmother's kind God, the one who we secretly asked in our prayers to find food for the hungry jackals? Why had the Great Dragon disappeared, the divinity of the forest who was so friendly and benevolent, who fed all the jackals and put them to bed when they were very hungry and howled? And since God and the Great Dragon had gone up in smoke, and the jackals were hungry, how could the men beat them off so harshly?

It was impossible for us to understand. The jackals, after being creatures of the forest that had the right to eat, now had to become the enemy. Until then, we had only known that we were afraid of them because they were foreign to us, because all we knew was their voice, and their voice was wild. Now we had to get used to fighting them, we had to make our first steps towards that inexhaustible resource of men: hatred.

We were lying awake in our beds that night waiting, when we heard the howling of the jackals coming closer. We held our breath. Suddenly, at a signal given, who knows how, a wild uproar echoed through the night; the men were rushing out. They were yelling, hitting the drums and tin pans, and shaking the flaming torches. From time to time a shot was heard. The wild animals, struck suddenly in this way, let out heart-rending cries and pulled back at once. Again, they ran forward, raging. Again, the shouting of the men rang out in the night as though it were striking copper. Again, the howling resounded. The air was thick and heavy with heartbreak and suffering. The stars were hidden for a while by the smoke. Then a big cloud came and covered them. We were silent and listened. Not even tears would come to bless our tired eyes. Trembling, we came to understand the hard law of the world.

⋟ Chapter Four ⋞

Gradually, as the days below the Kimindenia mountains dawned and set, I began to understand the different meanings of many things there, close to the land and to nature: the earth, the trees, the clouds. In the town, there were also trees and earth and clouds. There too, the leaves fell from the branches in winter, and later, spring would come, and leaves and flowers would burst out of the naked sticks again. The clouds there cast down rain, or travelled along, all white, or painted the sky with fantastic colours when the sun was about to set. All those things were beautiful in the town. But they were only beautiful. It was the decorative magic of the world, which surely existed only for the amusement of children, like little ships made of pine, and wooden elephants with blue hides, and yellow rubber rabbits.

It was outside of the town, close to the earth, that I began to learn about the secret life of trees. It was there that I began to learn about the profound bond between man and the sun, the earth, and water.

Uncle Joseph was the Nestor* of the estate, its spirit, as everyone said. His hair was completely white, and the skin on his face and hands was furrowed with wrinkles and burned by the sun. As a very young man, he had set out from his poor island, Lemnos,* to find sustenance in the rich land of Anatolia. He never returned; the Kimindenia mountains kept him.

In the time of his distant youth, there was a girl on Lemnos with very bright eyes. Joseph was a beardless young man, a fisherman who worked on trawlers. One night he went out and found the girl looking at the stars. He asked:

'Maria, what are you thinking about?'

She was startled and turned round frightened, because her conversation with the sky was solitary and sacred; she was afraid of betraying it.

'What are you thinking about?' he asked again.

'Nothing,' she answered, trying to seem off-hand. 'I was looking at the Pleiades.'

'Really? You were looking at the Pleiades? And where did you learn about the Pleiades and the stars?'

She told him that an old captain who passed by the island once had taught her how to read the stars.

'Really? He taught you how to read the stars?'

No, he didn't teach her how! He had only showed her the way people study them. But there were so many stars, and she was so simple and so young. How could she work it all out? The old captain had studied the stars all his life. How long had she been alive? Perhaps that was why they were all obscure, mixed up, and she had to struggle to figure out their secret meaning.

Joseph, a spirited lad, put his arms around her and kissed her on the lips and told her: 'Forget the stars, Maria, I came to talk to you.'

They sat on the ground, below the night sky. Only the night, serene and mysterious, heard them.

'Do you see those mountains beyond the sea?' he asked, and pointed to the east.

'I see them.'

'Today a boat came from there. I was at the harbour and saw the travellers. They spoke of a rich land with tall trees and fertile earth. You throw one seed into it and it gives you back five hundred seeds, a thousand seeds. The mountains there are filled with countless herds of animals, not to mention the deer, bears, and wild boars that live in the untrodden places. It is the most blessed land in world. Are you listening?'

'I'm listening, my love.'

'Here, our land is poor and bare. It doesn't have trees, it doesn't have flocks of sheep, it doesn't have wild boars and deer. And our sea, no matter how hard you work it, gives nothing. No matter how I calculate it, I will never be a captain. I will never have my own trawler. Where am I going to find the wealth to own a trawler in this place? And yet, you should not go hungry. I should give you all the good things in the world. Are you listening?'

'I'm listening, my love.'

'Well, I'm going to leave for that land beyond the sea. I'll work for a short while, but I'll work hard. As soon as I've gathered some resources, I'll come back for you. Then we'll have the best trawler on the island. Her name will be Vangelistra. We'll paint her with red and yellow paint, not plain yellow, canary yellow. And you will be the captain's wife.'

Maria is silent. Very silent. Then she begins to cry softly, steadily, without caring, as though she were alone. She makes no attempt to stop him. She knows it would be in vain: the stars were so confused tonight, so dark . . . And even if she didn't know how to read them very well, she had guessed their secret meaning.

'I knew it,' is all she says. 'I knew,' she repeats, as though talking to herself, 'that my time had come.'

That's what happened that night on Lemnos. Joseph left his quiet island, crossed the sea and came to the land opposite. He came to the Kimindenia. But he never got his own flock, or any other wealth. After the first year had passed, he looked at what he'd saved from his work and said:

'It is very little. I can't buy a trawler with this money and marry Maria. Maybe I can manage it next year.'

The next year came, and still he did not have enough. The next year came, and the next.

'This will be my fate,' he thought.

But he did not give up. He wrote to the island: 'Wait for me. Soon I'll have the money for us to buy a trawler. Then I'll come for you, Maria.' More years passed. When Joseph finally knew for sure that it isn't easy for a fisherman to make a fortune working the land, even if that land is in Anatolia, he gathered all the savings from the years of his youth that he had wasted in the foreign land and set out to return to his island. On the road, before he reached the sea, he was fallen upon by brigands, who stripped him of everything. He went back to the Kimindenia. He began to work again, not wanting to return to his island poorer than he had been when he left. He started over again. But by now his faith had deserted him. He would say over and over to himself:

'Maybe it was for the best that I met with brigands. Maybe better years will come. I'll make money and I'll buy the trawler.'

But deep inside he didn't believe it anymore. He was only fooling himself. After that, years came when there were floods, and the crops were destroyed. Many misfortunes befell the Kimindenia, and Joseph was sick for many summers. Then, finally, he accepted once and for all that this was his fate: he would never have a trawler of his own; trawlers were not for Joseph.

Beyond the sea, Maria waited for him for many years. Then one day an American came to their island, a compatriot who had become a foreigner. He had gold coins and gold teeth; he was mean and withdrawn, and his face was yellow from the diseases of the great world. It was to this man that Maria's parents gave their daughter in marriage, and in her green eyes, the story of the stars ended. Maria submitted, like all the women of her land and her position. And from that time, not even once was she able to read the stars again. The secret bond between them, the privilege of her youth, was lost forever. She cried the first night she saw the stars close their mouths and not tell her anything. But later she got used to it; she didn't even remember there were stars in the sky.

Time passed in this way, and Joseph grew old in the Kimindenia. His hair became completely white, and the skin on his hands and face became furrowed with wrinkles and burned by the sun. Of all the jobs on the land, there was only one at which he truly succeeded and became a master: it was the grafting of trees. His hands had brought about the metamorphosis of thousands of wild olive trees, pears and other kinds of trees. He knew every one of them. At first, he even gave them names. He called them *Maria*, he called them *Vangelistra*, he called them *Nikolas* and *Petrakis* — the names of the girl who knew the stars, the boat he would never own, and the children he did not have. But when there were too many Marias and Vangelistras and Petrakises, he began to confuse them, so he gave up on names. And when the trees he gave new life to became nameless, he learned to share their life more deeply, not only as desires that had never been satisfied.

He became their true friend. He knew them individually; he remembered the year he had grafted each one, their circumstances. And as he studied them in this way, following their resurrection in the world, as he shared their life in this way, his own life gradually found a purpose. He distanced himself from men; he became one with the trees. He became one of them, a great old tree that blessed and protected his small friends. He didn't care about anything else in the world. He didn't know what had become of the world beyond the Kimindenia and no longer cared to find out.

Sometimes, very faintly, distant memories would come to him at night: they spoke of a dry island in the Aegean, of an azure sea, of seashells, and ships with mermaids on their prows. The ships sail along, the masts and the rigging make them into a forest. Then the mermaid on the first ship cries out triumphantly to the others: 'Make way! Make way, she's coming!' All the mermaids are astir. Their eyes brighten and they put on their good clothes. The masts shake, and the ships part. They make a passageway between them like a river. The wind stops blowing, and through the stillness of the sea river, striking the water slowly with her oars, comes the *Vangelistra*, all freshly painted. 'Welcome to our sea!' cry the mermaids on the prows. 'I am glad to be here!' answers the trawler.

'I am glad to be here . . . ,' murmur the lips of the old man.

He opens his eyes wider, as wide as he can, to hold onto the vision. But it's slipping away, forever slipping away. Only a misty azure veil remains. It moves like waves. Ah, yes, the waves have come back. Shadows come slowly from inside them, trembling. From deep inside them come the masts. They flutter to make way, but they cannot. They just become more clearly defined and gradually take on a stable form. They become trunks and leaves, trees that are growing among the waves.

THE SEASON FOR GRAFTING TREES was approaching. All the rest of the time, Uncle Joseph spent his days peacefully on the farmstead, since they didn't let him do any work. But now he displayed a curious agitation. He could not stay still. He kept walking around on the thick layer of sand where he kept the cuttings for grafting.

Finally, one day, grandfather called him:

'What do you say, old Joseph? Has the time come?'

'It has come, Master.'

'Good. Start tomorrow morning.'

Later he sent for us children.

'You will go with Uncle Joseph tomorrow morning to see where he will graft the trees.'

Turning to the old man he said: 'Let each child choose a tree, and graft it in its name.'

The next day we set out very early. The sun had just come up. Uncle Joseph went first with slow steps, looking down at the earth, and we followed happily behind. We debated about which tree each one of us would choose, and made a great fuss. At last we agreed. Artemis chose a wild olive. She could not say why, but she loved the calm of the olive grove, the silver foliage and the tortured trunks. I chose a pear.

We arrived, and Uncle Joseph put down the bundle of cuttings he was carrying with him, the grafts. He did not see well anymore, so he felt the wild tree, fingering its branches, searching for the right place. His expression gradually became more severe. His eyes did not look to either side, not even at us. They slowly lost their luster, as though they were going out. His whole being shut down, so that only the intense life of his touch might remain. When he finally found the place he wanted, he lifted his eyes to the sun. He crossed himself three times, and his lips moved slightly as he whispered his secret prayer. He remained silent for a while and then brought his gaze down from the sun. Now he was calm and confident. With a steady hand, he cut with his knife and removed the scion from the cutting: a piece of bark in the shape of a ring. With the same knife, he carved the wild tree, and in the place where the bark had been cut away, he placed the piece of bark from the cutting. After that, he tightly bound the foreign body to the body of the tree.

He was finished.

The old man's face turned very pale. Again he looked towards the sun and again, trembling, he prayed:

'I give thanks to You that I was worthy this year to graft trees . . .'

Then, turning to me, he said calmly:

'That is all, my son. I entrust this tree to you. Love it as a thing of God.'

There was great sanctity in that moment and in his expression, which unwittingly entranced us children. But we did not understand why. What had happened? A bit of bark from a cutting had been attached to a wild tree. Nothing else had happened.

We looked at the old man in confusion. And as though he guessed what was going on inside us, he turned to me and said:

'Put your ear to the tree.'

I brought my head close and put my ear to the tree as he had told me to. He also drew his face near, laid it against the tree and listened. Our faces were so close, it was as though they were touching. I saw that his eyes were clouded. Slowly they grew heavy and began closing, as though he were sinking into ecstasy. Then they closed completely.

'Do you hear anything?' whispered his voice from the depths of that magic. Nothing. No. I couldn't hear anything.

'But I hear . . . ,' he murmured. His soft voice vibrated with joy. 'But I hear it,' he repeated.

Then he explained to me that he was listening to the blood of the tree from which he had taken the piece of bark, the graft, running slowly into the blood of the wild trunk, mingling with it, beginning in this way to bring about the miracle: its metamorphosis.

'If you love trees very much, then you will hear it too,' he told me. 'Will you love them, my child?'

I promised him I would:

'I will love them, Uncle Joseph.'

'Will you love them, Artemis?'

'I will love them, Uncle Joseph.'

THAT IS HOW I LEARNED TO LOVE TREES. And when its time came, on the night of a spring storm, and the great walnut tree at the entrance to the farmstead died, I had become its friend and wept at its leaving.

'Why did that happen? Why did the walnut tree leave us? Why?' I asked through my tears.

'That's the way it is, my child, don't be sad,' said my mother, comforting me. Despite her simplicity, she had had the wise instinct to protect me until that time, for as long as was possible, from the knowledge of death.

'But why is it like that? Why?'

'Because that is what happens, my boy. That's what happens to both trees and to people.'

'Did the walnut tree at least leave happy? It wasn't sad, was it?'

Oh, it wasn't sad at all! Its ancestors had come in the distant past from the region of the Caucasus. In those places, there is nothing but untrodden mountains inhabited by clouds. That is why the walnut trees there rarely see the sun. The world around them is dim and dark. One day a small wild bird passed by the mountains of the Caucasus. It was coming from the west, from distant realms, and it gave the walnut trees this report:

'Down there in the west is a land that is always bright. They call it the land of the Aegean. The Kimindenia mountains are there.'

Hearing this, two great walnut trees became very sad.

'How much time do we have left?' they asked. 'It's a shame for us to die without ever seeing that bright land.'

The great river of Anatolia heard and felt sorry for them.

'I have many sons and daughters,' said the river to the walnut trees. 'Where my own waters end, the waters of my children and of my children's children begin. The smallest one reaches as far as the bright land and lives there. I can give you passage.'

So that's how it happened: the great river took the two walnut trees in its water and carried them down. Then it passed them on to the other rivers, to its children and its children's children. And the smallest one, the *Tsakal-Dere*, the Jackal River, which is below the Kimindenia, brought them to our land.

At first the two walnut trees were enchanted, but later homesickness began to torment them. They would remember their homeland, the untrodden mountains of the Caucasus and the clouds that were always there. It took a long time for them to get used to the land of the sea.

They brought a new child into the world: our walnut tree. Since it was born in the Kimindenia and only heard them tell about the distant land of its ancestors as if it were a fairy tale, it never tasted the bitter longing of life in a foreign land, never suffered from homesickness. It lived for many years. It saw and heard all the storms that come down from the Kimindenia mountains. It sheltered our grandmother under its shade when she was a young girl, then it sheltered her children when they came, my mother, and then all of us. It gave us all its fruit. And now that it had grown old, it was going to sleep . . .

With wide-open eyes, I learned for the first time the story of the walnut tree. So that's it! Now it's going to sleep . . .

'But really, do walnut trees sleep?'

'Of course they sleep, when they finish what they have to do on this earth,' my mother assured me.

And since the woodcutter was going to cut the fallen tree into logs that same afternoon, my mother said, to prepare me:

'Look at the leaves. Look how they are beginning to wither . . .'

Yellow and shriveled, the leaves were slowly dying, ready to fall at the first touch. I pulled one off, rubbed it between my hands and smelled it. It didn't have that characteristic smell that I had breathed in so many times, rubbing together the leaves of the walnut tree to feel my eyelids grow heavy and to feel afterwards the sweet desire for sleep. No, the dead leaves didn't give off that fragrance anymore.

'The soul of the tree is no longer inside them,' my mother explained.

'That's why we can cut up the trunk and branches, knowing that we are not hurting its soul. And when winter comes, we will make fires with that wood which will warm us. That way, up until its very last hour, the walnut tree will keep us company and will help us with its red flames. But look, my boy! There. Look at the roots.'

Tortured by their hidden struggle of so many years, one entwined with another, like very tired hands, they lay there in the deep pit that the tree had opened when it fell.

'I'm not talking about the big roots,' said my mother, following my gaze. 'Those other ones, the little ones that stayed in the earth, look at those ones.'

While I looked, she explained to me that those tiny roots and the earth around them were the cradle for the new walnut tree that was to come. Tomorrow or the day after tomorrow, we would put two walnuts into that pit — fruit of the tree that had left us — and we would cover them with that earth. The tiny roots would gently embrace the two walnuts and protect them until they sprouted and came out through the surface of the earth into the sun. That is how a new walnut tree would come to us in the place of the one that was gone. But no, it would not be another walnut tree. It would be the same one, which would return to the world, fresh as a young girl, to make leaves and shade to shelter us again, and our children and the children who would come after us.

Hearing mother say these things, I understood that the soul of the tree that had left us was there in the tiny roots that remained in the ground. This greatly lightened my sadness.

LATE IN THE AFTERNOON, I went with Artemis to the open pit where the walnut tree had been. The tree was no longer there; they had cut it up and put the wood in the shed. I tried to explain everything to Artemis, who didn't know the story of the tree. I told her everything I had learned from my mother that morning, but when I got to the part about 'soul', I didn't know what that meant and couldn't make Artemis understand. It seems it must have been something like our small heart, whose beating we hear when we place our hand on our chest.

'Wait!' said Artemis. 'That must be it!'

She got into the pit, and bending down, she pressed her ear against the earth and the tiny roots that were left from the walnut tree. Her expression became serious, and I waited in suspense.

'Do you hear anything?' I asked her.

Her voice whispered: 'Nothing.'

After a little while I asked again:

'Nothing, Artemis?'

'Ach! Still nothing. You come too!'

I jumped into the pit, next to the little girl, and put my ear to the ground.

'Do you hear . . . ? ' she murmured.

'Nothing . . . Nothing . . .'

Our whole small existence, all the pores of our bodies and the blood in our flesh were throbbing only for that: for Artemis to hear, for me to hear. By that time both her heart and mine had begun to beat quite hard inside our chests, pressed against the ground.

Then the miracle happened.

'I hear!' I whispered, trembling with emotion. 'I think I hear something!'

'I hear it too,' says the voice of the little girl from deep within. 'I hear the tree's heart.'

That is how we were blessed that evening by hearing the heartbeat of a tree, when all we had heard was our own hearts: their beating, which the earth returned to us.

Night was coming down from the Kimindenia mountains with great strides. At night, all living things want refuge and shelter. So Artemis and I gathered earth in our hands and lightly covered the roots in the pit so that the walnut tree's soul would have a good night, so it wouldn't be lonely and afraid.

That same night Artemis, without meaning to, overheard this strange conversation. Grandfather was saying to Uncle Joseph:

'Joseph, the walnut tree is gone. I don't want that spot to be without a walnut tree. What do you think?'

'I agree,' he said.

'Well, do you want to plant another walnut tree there? Only if you want to, I'm not forcing you.'

Uncle Joseph didn't hesitate at all. He answered immediately:

'I want to.'

A moment passed. Then grandfather said:

'Honestly, you're not afraid, Joseph?'

'I'm not afraid, Master, you know that. I'm not afraid to plant a walnut tree. I'm not afraid of trees.'

After that he added that he didn't have much longer to live. By the time the walnut tree he planted bore fruit, he would have travelled on.

Grandfather clapped him kindly on the shoulder.

'Not yet, not yet, old Joseph! We still have many days ahead of us!'

Then he said:

'Very well, plant the walnut tree.'

After a little while Artemis went and found Uncle Joseph alone. She entreated him:

'Tell me, why are they having you plant the walnut tree? Are the others afraid?'

'Stuff and nonsense, little girl,' the old man assured her. 'Yes, they're afraid. Imagine being afraid to plant a walnut tree!'

'Oh, they're only afraid of walnut trees? But why?'

'Listen. They say that if you plant a walnut tree, you'll die as soon as the tree bears fruit. That's what they say. But on my island, we don't know that. We say that the walnut tree helps people to love each other.'

After a while Artemis asked:

'What time are you going to plant the walnut tree, Uncle Joseph?'

'Oh, tomorrow morning.'

'Good night.'

'Good night, my little girl.'

The next day, very early, Artemis is at the pit where the walnut tree will be planted. Uncle Joseph comes and is startled to find her.

'What are you doing here so early in the morning?'

'Nothing, Uncle Joseph. I came to watch.'

The old man puts fresh soil in the pit. He gets it ready and then takes the walnuts out of his pocket. He leans down towards the earth. At the same instant, Artemis darts forward like a deer and grabs the walnuts out of his hands. And before the old man has a chance to understand what's happening, Artemis has thrust them into the earth.

'What have you done?' cries Uncle Joseph in alarm.

She nervously brushes the soil from her little skirt. Her cheeks are red with emotion and she's breathing hard.

'I planted the walnut tree. Me! Now it's done.'

Uncle Joseph is not afraid to plant a walnut tree himself. He is not afraid for himself. But for this beloved little girl? Who knows what is true and what is not in the secret world of miracles? And if what they say in these parts about those who plant walnut trees is a little bit, only a little bit true . . .

Over the heads of the old man and the child circles a wild feeling of doubt and mystery.

'But why did you do it, my little girl? Why?' asks the old man, becoming increasingly upset and overwhelmed with fear.

Artemis no longer knows what to say, why she did it. Now she will wait for the tree to sprout, for it to come up out of the earth. Later she will wait for the first time it bears fruit. Then she will learn one more of the mysteries of the world that she was in such a hurry to learn: whether she will pay with death.

≫ Chapter Five ≪

In the Kimindenia mountains, close to the earth, I learned to read in men's eyes the daily, unremitting anxiety over weather, rain, and the wind. It was especially prevalent in the spring, at harvest time, and in the autumn. Every night my grandfather would consult the stars and the clouds that travelled beyond the Kimindenia. He leaned out of the window and gazed severely and insistently at the sky in deep concentration, while behind him everyone was silent and waited. The humble, solid and sacred experience of men of the earth, of his guileless ancestors, distilled in the blood in his veins, awoke. It calculated the movement of the clouds, the light in the stars, and the stir of the wind in the atmosphere. It was as though there was some secret voice in the wind, the clouds, and the stars. But none of us heard it, none of us had that gift, only he did.

When his conversation with the night ended, he would draw his head inside and turn to us. Then my grandmother's eyes and mother's eyes widened, and anguish throbbed in their moist light.

He would state simply:

'We will have rain by tomorrow night.'

Or, with the same simplicity:

'Dry weather. We will not have rain!'

Then, depending on the season, depending on whether rain was helpful or catastrophic for the crops, tranquillity or voiceless grief would pour into the women's eyes. The wisest of them, grandmother, had learned over time that she should not add her own distress to her husband's worries in times of sorrow. She should say nothing, but bite back her sadness. When the news from the sky was bad for the earth, she mustered all her strength to contain herself and whispered humbly, while crossing her arms stoically:

'Blessed be His name . . .'

Then immediately she would turn to us, the children, who were watching the rite with curiosity, and find her means of escape.

'You have to go to bed now,' she'd say.

Then she would always come with us. She signalled to our mother to go out, to leave grandfather alone with his thoughts. And while she led us to bed she said:

'Put this in your prayers tonight. Pray for God to send us rain.'

What else could grandmother do to help her companion? When she was young and alone, she had prayed secretly by herself. Maybe the miracle will happen, she would say, and the clouds that are always so slow in coming will hurry to the Kimindenia. When her children came, she taught them to pray — a child's voice is always better received. And when we came, her children's children, she taught us to intercede.

'Pray that we will have rain in the coming days,' she'd say.

And her voice trembled, as though she were begging us not to let her down.

We never denied her wish. Sometimes, according to her instructions, we prayed for rain to come, other times for it not to. It was like a game. However, there were times when we got mixed up and made a mess of it. One night, when she had told us to pray for rain, we prayed for the clouds to go away. And that time it happened that the clouds did go away. Early the next morning, as soon as we saw the blue sky, we ran to grandmother. And before we had time to notice how sad she was:

'Did you see, Grandmother? Our prayer worked! The clouds went away!'

Alarmed, she turned and stared at us. Her ingenuous eyes blinked rapidly.

'In the name of God! What are you saying? What did you make your prayer for last night?'

'For the clouds to go away, Grandmother. Isn't that what you told us?'

'Oh, my little children! Why did you do that? Why?' She was very upset. 'That's not what I told you. You didn't listen carefully. We want rain now!'

Afterwards, as though speaking to herself:

'How can it rain now?' she whispered. 'What can God do, since the children begged him not to send rain?'

We were sorry for what had happened. And another time, when

we got mixed up again and couldn't agree among ourselves what we were supposed to pray for, we sent Agapi in to ask:

'Grandmother, what do we want tonight? For it to rain or not to rain?'

IT RAINED. IT RAINED A LOT. The clouds appeared around ten in the morning and released their first drops, which later grew stronger. The rain lasted until evening. The earth was very thirsty, and everyone had been waiting for the rain as a blessing for the seeds. It was March. In the farmstead, the joy was evident in every face. The ploughmen, in the shelter of their rooms, made a great fuss. They told stories, played cards, and sang softly. They had nothing personally to gain from the rain bringing a rich harvest, but they worked the land and felt for the earth as for a living thing that could suffer. Their joy was as clean and powerful as physical joy.

In more than anyone else, the joy was apparent in the faces of our grandmother and mother. Only in grandfather's face could we detect nothing remarkable. He sat as he always did, calm and contented, as though nothing new or special had happened. He looked out of the window at the rain, the clouds, and the earth that was quenching its thirst.

At that time, we children did not know very well, did not yet understand the full meaning of the rain's blessing when the land needed it so much. However, we had our joy, too: the ditches and hollows would fill with water. Of course, it did not surge like the sea, but what did that matter? If you hit the water in a puddle with your hands, there are waves. If you throw green leaves in, they turn blue. They turn into blue waves, the beloved magic of our country; they become the Aegean. And the pine boats sail and travel. They are carrying gifts of gold, blue beads, and red marbles. They are carrying these gifts to Red Riding Hood, who got lost in the Kimindenia and never came back.

'Tell us about Little Red Riding Hood. Tell us, Grandfather,' begged Agapi and Artemis, as it rained outside.

'Come on, Grandfather, tell us!' I begged too and tugged at his hands.

Little Red Riding Hood was one of our latest acquaintances, and we adored her.

'But didn't your grandmother tell you the story yesterday?' he asked.

'She told it to us, Grandfather, but ...'

'Well, what is it?'

We didn't know how to answer, how to make clear what we wanted. Finally I thought I had it:

'She told it to us, Grandfather, but it was ... different.'

Then grandfather laughed heartily, and turning to grandmother, who was smiling too, he said:

'It looks like you didn't do too well, Grandmother.'

But I broke in again, protesting energetically:

'No, Grandfather! Grandmother's Little Red Riding Hood was good too. It's only that ..., only that it was ... different.'

I did not understand then that in my simple way, though still a small child, I was a sound critic. I evaluated the Little Red Riding Hood of my grandmother and the Little Red Riding Hood of my grandfather, not by the events of the story, which were the same, but by their personality, which was their style.

Grandmother gave a gentle and simple tone to the fairy tale. Her wolf, like her, was good; the unlucky creature went astray without meaning to. That was how he came to eat the grandmother and to later want to eat the little girl herself. But not out of evil: an evil hour befell him. This can happen to any creature in the world, and then they do evil deeds.

Grandfather's wolf, on the other hand, was a real wolf. He wandered in the Kimindenia, and when night fell he was very hungry. He came out of the forest, went beyond the riverbed and arrived in the valley. That was where the good old lady's hut was, the hut of Little Red Riding Hood's grandmother. The wolf stopped and thought:

'Should I eat the grandmother, or should I wait for Little Red Riding Hood, who has sweeter flesh?'

He had good taste and preferred to wait. But a long time passed, and Little Red Riding Hood did not show up. The wolf couldn't stand it any longer. He sat down and ate the old lady. Then he lay down in her bed, covered himself up to his neck and waited for the little girl. He said:

'She will come, she will see me in bed and think I'm her grandmother. Then I'll grab her and eat her.'

But Little Red Riding Hood did not show up in those parts that afternoon and was never seen again. A little oak tree that grew outside her family's hut saved her. The tree and Little Red Riding Hood were good friends. Every day they talked and told each other their secrets. The little tree told the little girl each day about its ancient ancestors, about the Great Forest of oak trees that was beyond the Kimindenia. It told her about the dense silence that reigned under their branches and the deep bed of leaves that had piled up on the ground over the years — thousands of years — until the leaves became water and earth and passed into the roots again and turned into branches again and green leaves. No human soul ever entered the kingdom of the oak trees. Every time men reached its borders, the trees that guarded the entrance wailed heart-rendingly and sent out a danger signal to their companions, the other oak trees of the forest. Then they all came running, frightful and ruthless; they drew up their trunks in formation and blocked the road.

When she heard all this, Little Red Riding Hood longed to travel to the kingdom of the Great Forest. She told her little friend, the oak tree. The tree answered her:

'When you grow up just a little more, I will take you. Only you, Little Red Riding Hood.'

This happened every day, and the sun rose and set many times before at last the tree decided that Little Red Riding Hood had grown up enough. She had turned five, and it was time for her to make the journey. The tree carried her astride its branches. They set the sails, and travelling through the air above the Kimindenia Mountains, they entered the land of the oak trees. Not a single tree blocked their entrance; they all knew and were waiting for her. That's why the guards at the border asked the breeze to blow through their branches when they saw the travellers. The breeze brought the message to the whole forest. All the leaves breathed it out:

'Little Red Riding Hood is coming! Little Red Riding Hood is coming at last!'

The little girl came down from the tree, straightened her dress and looked around, dazzled. The hard, unbending branches of the oak trees moved like arms above her and beseeched her. The leaves put on their best clothes and fell like golden rain. The springs rose from their hiding places underground and began to whisper songs of the forest. They were all begging her:

'Stay with us, Little Red Riding Hood. In the world down there, there are wolves and people that will eat you. Stay with us!'

Little Red Riding Hood could resist no longer. The Kimindenia mountains put a spell on her, and she turned into a deer, the only deer in the forest, and she lived for many happy years in the land of the oak trees.

IT RAINED AGAIN. But now it was summer. The fruit hung from the trees, and the vines and ears of wheat were ripe. All eyes turned again to the sky, but this time they were full of worry. And what they feared happened: the sun came out. A powerful wave of heat rolled down from the Kimindenia and spread out over the whole valley and plain. The blossoms of many trees burned. There was great devastation. People sat in distress without speaking. Silence reigned at the farmstead. Not even footsteps were heard; it was as though people were afraid to disturb the grief.

Only grandfather remained calm and gazed at the earth, the Kimindenia mountains, and the clouds. He had reached the threshold of that nobility and serenity that give meaning to all worldly things, viewing them only as events in a Great Law that was not in man's fate to learn. The anguish for the earth throughout his long life, the pain over so many rains that never came, the joy over so many others that came at the right time and made the seeds fruitful, had settled now into the calm philosophy of the world, into obedience:

'If *Yarabis* wishes it, it will rain.'

'If *Yarabis* does not wish it, then it will not rain. Blessed be His name.'

As for the fruit that was lost — so be it. The earth has given so much in years gone by. It will give again in years to come.

⇒ Chapter Six ⇐

THE STORY OF A MAN WHO WAS TRYING TO FIND THE CAMEL WITH THE WHITE HEAD, AND THE STORY OF ANOTHER MAN WHO WAS TRYING TO FIND PERPETUAL MOTION

I used to spend hours out in the fields with the ploughmen. I suppose they liked me. To amuse me, they recalled old stories about corsairs and the brigands of the mountains, stories about ghosts and the miracles of the saints.

Men came to work our land from many different places: there were islanders from the Aegean and mainlanders from distant places in Anatolia. The islanders told sailing adventures about mermaids and pirates, and their stories were filled with winds as light as air. There was one journey to lands of fantasy so convincing that a child could continue the story by himself, in his dreams.

The mainlanders were severe. They told of dark and silent smugglers carrying contraband tobacco with their camel caravans. They recounted the life and exploits of Tsakitzis, a mythical hero of Asia Minor in the last years of the nineteenth century.* But above all, they told about the lives and miracles of the saints.

Those saints were creatures outside the joy of the world: naked, emaciated, sunburned and vengeful. They blessed good deeds, but never forgave bad ones. They went out at night and lay in wait for sinners outside their huts and in their fields and called on the ghosts and the souls of the dead to punish them. In the end, it seems it was a great calamity to fall into the clutches of those saints.

However, I learned the true story of the world from the travellers who passed through. The main road that joined the shores of Aeolia to Pergamum, and from there to the interior of Anatolia, passed our property. There were almost always travellers on this great road. There were Jews, Armenians, Turks, and Christians, poor people, noblemen, peddlers and the sick. They carried their fates along with them: their passions and their misfortunes, ventures in their own interest and follies. On that long road, travelling under the strong sun, they raked up their anxieties; they lived them and relived them, until at last they were imprinted in the furrows of their faces and in their eyes. When evening found them in our vicinity, they came to the farmstead to seek refuge for the night: food and protection from the wild animals. Up until the very moment that night closed in, the great door of the farmstead was open for the travellers. A boy led them to the large room that was set up expressly for guests. He showed them where to sleep and gave them some of the small loaves of bread we made at the farmstead for passing travellers; he showed them where they would eat. The travellers would wash, and rest if they wanted. Then they went and sat with the ploughmen, smoking countless cigarettes and telling about their suffering and their joy.

Artemis, with her anxious curiosity, was always the first to learn about every new arrival. She would look him over, question him, examine the clothes he was wearing, and finally gaze at his face searchingly, looking him straight in the eyes. Then, once she had summed him up, she came running to us, the other children, shouting:

'Rainfall!'

From that we understood that a traveller of the right kind had come: one with stories, with bizarre clothes, with strange ideas or exotic merchandise, spurs to our imagination and our curiosity, like an unread book containing the destiny of the world. Then we ran, all the children, to find the stranger. We attended to him, we gave him milk or eggs, and once we had won him over, we sat down around him and waited.

Then, very slowly, the pages of the book began to turn. They turned so that a child might learn how, beyond external similarities, beyond joy and sorrow, another element as powerful as fire joined all men, made their fates all resemble one another: it was the pursuit of passion, the compulsion for self-torture.

The pages of the book turned:

THE FIRST TRAVELLER

'*Merhaba!*'

'*Merhaba!*'

He was a man of about forty-five years old, short and shabbily dressed in the baggy trousers of the Tsitmis camel drivers. The hair and beard that covered his head and face were thick and grizzled, but there was light in that face: it poured out and shone gently from his brown eyes. His name was Ali. His homeland was the gorge behind the Kimindenia mountains, three days away by foot. The Tsitmises live there, simple and good men who have never bothered anyone. They are a Muslim race and believe in Mohammed, but they also believe in the Christian saints, especially Saint George, the horseman. They say: 'Man is powerless down here on earth; the Christian saints live on high where the Prophet is; surely they must have a lot of power too. It's good for a poor Tsitmis to be on good terms with everyone who dwells in heaven.'

Most Tsitmises live by leading camel caravans, their own and other people's. They carry crops down from the Kozakia mountains to the coast riding astride their donkeys: behind them follow the male camels and female camels. Each camel has its own bell, and each bell has its own sound. The Tsitmis camel drivers travel the road slowly; they don't look back, they always look down, at the ground that shoots sparks from the sun and at the donkey's ears, which move now and then. Everything is the same, exactly the same. The animal under their legs gives a dull motion to their bodies, to their heads, which never look forward, never back.

The mind and body grow accustomed to this motion, which in time becomes as necessary as air and light; it numbs the man, he no longer desires anything; he covets nothing: this is life. Behind him play the different modes: six, seven, eight voices — these are all the voices of the world. The first mode, from the first camel — from the bell that hangs from her saddle — has a high, youthful sound that always says:

> *Evlendirelim . . . Evlendirelim . . .*
> *Evlendirelim . . . Evlendirelim . . .*

The second mode, from the second camel, speaks more deeply:

> *Narden boulaloum . . . Narden boulaloum . . .*
> *Narden boulaloum . . . Narden boulaloum . . .*

And the third, austere and slow, connects the first two and responds to them with assurance:

> *Sourndahn . . . bourndahn . . .*
> *Sourndahn . . . bourndahn . . .*

Nothing can disturb the strict discipline of these sounds. They affirm nature's harmony, the symphony of the world.

The Tsitmis hears them going along behind him and knows that all is well on earth. It can happen for one second — a single second — that one sound is missing. The harmony is affected at once and the Tsitmis understands that something has broken the world's order. Only then does his face take on a worried expression, and he turns his head back to see. He stops, gets down from his donkey, goes and refastens to the caravan the camel that had broken its rope. Then the symphony begins again.

GATHERED AROUND HIM, the ploughmen from the estate watch Ali silently roll one cigarette after another.

'Ali, where is your caravan?'

'I don't have a caravan, I came with only one camel.'

'With only one camel? Don't you work with caravans?'

'No, I don't work with caravans anymore.'

'Then where are you going?'

The light in Ali's eyes flickered uncertainly, revealing the doubt of a child.

'I am looking for the camel with the white head.' And before the ploughmen could say anything, he added, 'Have any of you seen it in some caravan? Have you seen it anywhere?' Ali's voice trembled with emotion. 'It's a small camel, about one year old. The hair on its forehead and its head is white.'

'Who ever heard of a camel with a white head?' The ploughmen broke into loud laughter and looked at Ali mockingly:

'Oh really? The camel with the white head? The camel with the white head! You will travel a lot more in Anatolia before you find her, Ali. You have got a lot of travelling ahead of you!'

Ali used all his strength to control the distress in his heart, to contain its beating, and he drew into himself in his seat like a wounded animal.

'Don't make fun of me,' he said very humbly, in a warm and trembling voice. 'I once had a camel with a white head. I lost it, I let it slip from my hands, but now I cannot live without it. I am looking, hoping to find it. Don't make fun of me . . .'

Very slowly the men grew calm under the thick layer of sorrow that flowed from Ali's face. The laughter died out, and all eyes converged on the same spot, trying to see through the smoke that filled the air, trying to come close to the passion that pursues a camel with a white head, the camel with the white head, along the roads of Anatolia.

Ever since he was a small child, Ali had worked with the caravans. When he began to understand life, the sounds of the bells that came from his ancestors, distilled in his own blood, awoke inside him.

'Take me along with the camels, Father!'

'Come along. Starting tomorrow you will go with the camels.'

And from the next day, mounted on the rear of the donkey, little Ali began to travel the roads of Anatolia. The camels were not their own. His father had never had his own camels. He worked for another master, and when he died, he left his son nothing but his bond to the sound of the bells.

Ali did not do much better than his father. When he grew up, he, too, began working with other people's camels. But when the time came when men marry, he managed to find a wife of his own.

The day after they married, when Ali was setting out with his caravan, his wife came out of their hut to see him off and said:

'In nine months we will have a child. Try to get your own camels, since we will have one more mouth to feed.'

Hearing this, Ali became serious and began to save money. As he travelled the roads of Anatolia, he ate only bread and didn't spend any late nights at the caravan inns. That way he was able to set a few piastres aside.

But when the nine months were up, no child came.

'Fine,' said his wife. 'We will have one next year. Keep on saving money.'

It went on like that for many years. Ali saved his money and his wife didn't give him any children, because she was barren. When they finally were certain they would never have children, his wife said:

'Count the money you've saved so far, Ali. Can we buy a camel of our own for our old age?'

Ali stayed up that night, and when the sun came up he had counted all his savings. No, it wasn't enough to buy a camel. They only had enough to buy half a camel.

Then Ali and his wife sat down together and stayed up another night trying to work out a way to buy half a camel. When the sun came up again, they had found a solution and agreed on what to do.

There was a fellow countryman of theirs, another Ali, who worked with other people's caravans in the Kaz-Dak region, far from their home. This other Ali came very rarely to the gorge where the Tsitmises live, only when his work brought him through those parts. At that time, he was there in the village.

The first Ali went to find him.

'Ali, for many years you also have been working with other people's caravans and do not have even one camel of your own. Wouldn't you like to have one?'

The second Ali answered:

'I would like to very much, but I don't have the money to buy a camel of my own.'

Then the first Ali asked:

'Do you know how much you have?'

'Yes, I know.'

'What does it come to?'

'To the cost of half a camel.'

'I also have enough money for half a camel. Why don't we put our savings together and buy a camel in partnership?'

They talked for a long time and reached an agreement. They bought a camel and put her to work in Ali's caravan. The second Ali later left for Kaz-Dak. Every time he came back, they would figure out how much money the camel's work had brought in and divide the profits.

Ali then hung a new bell on their camel's neck, tied her in the first row behind his donkey, and set out on the great road with his caravan. He was very proud and very confident about the future of the world; every so often he would turn around to make sure that the camel was following him, make sure that she existed.

A year passed in this way, and then something momentous happened. The shared camel gave birth to a baby camel. Ali had often seen other people's camels give birth, but now, seeing his own, he was deeply moved.

'Come look!' he cried to his wife. 'Now we have a child . . .'

They looked. And what they saw stirred their hearts like a strong wind. There was something unbelievable and singular about the little baby camel: the hide and hair on its head were not coffee-coloured, as on other camels. They were white. It was a baby camel with a white head:

the only baby camel with a white head ever born in all of Anatolia.

The news spread throughout the Tsitmises' village to the neighbouring villages that were in the gorge, and to everyone who travelled the great road that leads to the coast. They all hurried to see the wonderful white camel, and everyone considered Ali very fortunate.

Ali lived then in true happiness. He loved the young animal as he had never loved anything else on earth. He brought it up with affection and tenderness. He gave it names borrowed from the sky and nature — the names of trees and fruit — and he fed it not only the fodder that other camels eat; he gave it grapes and sugar and much more.

At last he bought a new bell, decorated it with red and sky-blue beads, and slipped it onto the neck of the small animal. After he had done that, he took it with him on its first trip to the coast. The little animal always went along next to its mother, and Ali kept turning back to look at it. But turning around exhausted him, since he was not used to it. The great sun burned above him, and Ali closed his eyes. The road was deserted, there was no sound and so, in the pure expanse, the new symphony rose up clearly, like a prayer. Mixed into the old, well-known sounds, the sounds that had followed Ali all the years of his life until today, was the new sound. It disturbed the old harmony; it erased the other notes and only the new ones remained. How good it was! How good it is to go down the great road of Anatolia and have it not be desolate behind you, to hear not only the voices of other people's camels, but to hear one that is your own, to have all the years that you toiled and suffered transformed into a melody on the neck of a small camel with a white head.

Ali was happy and at peace. At last life had meaning.

But the news reached the distant region of Kaz-Dak where the second Ali worked. He sets out and goes to the Tsitmises' village.

'Good day, my partner!' he says to Ali. 'What news?'

'We have good news, partner. Our camel gave birth, and now we have another little camel.'

'Let's see it!'

He looked at it but acted as though he didn't notice the white head. The Ali from Kaz-Dak said:

'All right, partner, now that we have two animals, I want to break up our partnership. You take one and I'll take the other. Choose which one you want.'

That Ali, who had travelled to distant places, had become clever and cunning. He thought to himself: 'My partner will keep the big camel. There's no doubt. He'll go from owning half the camel to owning the whole thing. But that way I'll get the camel with the white head. I'll take it to Kaz-Dak and sell it on the road to the bear trainers who have monkeys and bears and make money showing them to people. That way I'll get more than what one grown camel is worth.'

The first Ali sat up all that night with his wife trying to figure out what they should do.

His wife said:

'It's obvious, Ali! You should keep the big camel. When are we going to find such luck again to have a full-grown camel of our own?'

Ali was in distress. He could not imagine parting with the camel with the white head.

'But won't it grow up too?' he said. 'Why don't we keep it and bring it up?'

'How can you say we should keep it!' shouted his wife. 'And in the meantime, what can it bring in for us? What if it dies in the meantime?'

In the end, the practical mind of his wife proved more powerful than Ali's tenderness and weak will.

The next morning, his eyes clouded with sleeplessness and grief, Ali said goodbye to the camel with the white head. He stood upright and watched the vision, which left with the swift, bounding gait of a deer until it was out of sight. Then Ali understood that something had been torn from his heart. Everything around him was desolate since he would no longer have a companion on the great road, since the tenderness he had found so late no longer had a means of expression.

He became serious and silent. He had no appetite for food and grew thinner every day. Behind him, while he was leading his caravan, the sounds always followed him. Among the sounds was his camel, which was now completely his. But for Ali the voices had become silent, the melodies no longer spoke; because now, another, more powerful voice had taken their place, the one that comes to every man once and never again, and afterwards he chases it like a shadow that is forever slipping away.

AND ALI LEFT HIS WIFE in the gorge of the Tsitmises. He gave up working with other people's camels, because he had become a bad camel driver and they fired him. He took his own camel and set out for the region of Kaz-Dak.

He found his old partner and said to him:

'Take my camel. Take my donkey. Take my house in the gorge. Take everything I have, but give me back the camel with the white head.'

'I don't have it anymore,' Ali, his partner answered. 'I sold it on the road.'

Since then Ali wanders. As soon as day breaks, he goes out on the great road and sleeps wherever evening finds him. His little donkey walks patiently, and tied behind him, calm and alone, his camel follows him, the sound of her bell disturbing the warm silence of the earth. People mock and tease him. The more sympathetic ones tell him it's crazy, that there's no point in searching. They advise him to go back to the gorge and his caravan. But Ali doesn't hear them. Because he does not believe, because he cannot believe, that the camel with the white head is lost, that it will never be in his life again.

THE SECOND TRAVELLER

We knew Stephanos from the town. He was a bachelor who made saddles for a living. His shop was at the town's entrance, near the church of Saint Anthony, where the steep road that led to the hill of windmills began. Further on was the great caravan road to Anatolia. Wildflowers grew around the small church, and it smelled of rosemary. There was one cypress tree. Beyond the cypress was a row of wells with the best water in the area.

When it began to get dark, the young women fixed their braids, put water jugs on their shoulders and went with their friends to fetch water. They didn't go for the water. They went to see and be seen. When they reached Saint Anthony, they stopped to rest. They hung votive offerings — coloured ribbons and rags — on the old olive tree outside the small church. They hoped that after so much care the saint would visit them at night and tell them in their sleep of some good fortune. The breeze, coming from the sea, blew through the leaves and the coloured rags; the old olive tree looked like a boat getting ready to weigh anchor.

Stephanos had the best spot near Saint Anthony's church. He sat by the window of his shop, sewed his saddles, tied coloured beads to them, and watched the girls. In the summer, he left off work as the sun set and watered the small rise of land next to his shop. He brought out a kilim, spread it on the ground, and put flowerpots of basil all around. Then he sat, surrounded by the plants, and drew contentedly on his *nargileh*. He looked at the old olive tree with its coloured votive offerings fluttering in the wind. He rested his eyes there for a long time and admired the tree. How beautiful life is! How beautiful it is that the world ends in a tree adorned with coloured rags, a ship that is always ready to sail but never leaves.

'A man should stay firmly rooted where he is. All else is folly.'

Stephanos had worked hard to safeguard inside himself his love of the peaceful life. He had needed to work hard because he lived with temptation. He was surrounded by the craziest men in the world, in a nation of madmen. Most of his compatriots were either *yemitzides*, sailors, or *kontrabatzides*, smugglers. The *yemitzides* risked their lives on far away waters, on the Black Sea where the Danube flows into it. Many of them never returned. All that came back were reports of how they had been shipwrecked and lost in such and such a sea.

'It serves them right!' Stephanos would say. 'Don't we have a sea in our own country? A peaceful sea, sheltered by the Devil's Table, God's delight. Do you like the sea, man? Get a fishing boat and catch eels and sardines in the bay. But these sailors from Aivali will not settle for that. It serves them right!'

As for the other countrymen, the smugglers, hopeless cases! Every day the land buzzed with news of their feats, their unbelievable bravery, the blood they had senselessly spilled for fun and for honour, and their battles with the authorities.

Every now and then news would come:

'They killed so-and-so! So-and-so was killed!'

'It serves them right,' said Stephanos the saddle-maker to himself. 'Good-for-nothings! Why don't they stay out of trouble?'

Beyond the tree with the brightly coloured rags, at the end of the steep road, stood the windmills. There, every Sunday morning, the introduction to the symphony was played out: the smugglers' sons played stone wars. Played! They were preparing themselves for the other big game, the game they would play when the time came for them to take their fathers' places and become smugglers themselves.

For as long as the game was going on, the children's mothers stood at the foot of the hill, dressed in black and pale with anguish, watching and waiting. They waited until the sun had set and the game ended. Two rival teams of boys came down on separate paths. The strongest boys went in front, carrying in their arms their companions that had been killed. There were always one or two dead.

The procession descended slowly. It came closer and closer. Then the mothers could stand it no longer. They bit their lips until they bled and rushed towards the procession to find out. Those whose lot it was, the mothers of the boys who had been killed, fell hysterically on their dead sons and kissed them on the mouth. They tore out their hair and lacerated their cheeks with their fingernails. Then the procession began to advance again. The bravest boys always went in front with their dead companions, then the mothers of the dead. After them came the other mothers, and a wild joy shone in their eyes since their lot had not been drawn, not yet. The crowd followed behind. Not a voice was heard, only the mothers wailing their grief, cursing the hour when women were born.

Stephanos saw the procession pass in front of him and was very sad. But he said:

'Whose fault is it? The little hooligans! Why don't they stay at home? It serves them right!'

Because of all this, surrounded by raving lunatics, living in that town of passion, Stephanos avoided temptation and never went far from his saddles. Not even when the hill of windmills was deserted, not even then did he go up to look at the vast sea and the road that went on and on, never ending, the road to the great East.

'An evil place,' he thought to himself of the hill. 'Lunatic roads,' he thought to himself of the great sea and the caravan road. 'This world is made well, and it ends well in a tree with coloured rags, which is at the same time ship, sea and ocean: the whole world.'

Time passed, and the old olive tree with the votive offerings was always getting ready for a journey but never weighing anchor. Sometimes during lonely hours, the hours of their secret conversations, Stephanos would ask the olive tree:

'What do you say, comrade, will I leave some day?'

'You will leave,' it answered enigmatically.

And Stephanos, from the simple way that the olive tree answered him, thought he knew what the end of his journey would be. Because for the Stephanoses of the world, the end of the journey is fixed: someday he would like a girl, the daughter of a housewife whose husband was not a smuggler and whose son did not play in the symphony of the windmills. Then fresh air would blow through Stephanos' saddles, which were lined up in rows around him with their blue beads, waiting. After that, children would come. Nothing else.

'Should I go to the windmills?' his son would ask him.

Stephanos would answer him sharply:

'No! Your father didn't go to the windmills. No!'

But men's fates are not written that way, with straight lines. They are not always written that way, even if the men are named Stephanos. Squalls blow on the Aegean, the *meltemi* blows, and all the other winds. They blow without any rhyme or reason. Just when the sea is perfectly flat, waves suddenly come up; when there are waves, it becomes calm. The winds play, the clouds play, and God plays with men.

He also played with Stephanos, a law-abiding citizen who made saddles.

STEPHANOS COULD READ A LITTLE. He had a subscription to the *Amaltheia*, the newspaper of the big city, Smyrna. Everyone in Aivali who wasn't a sailor or a smuggler read the *Amaltheia*. That way, in the face of those rebels, they had a weapon that set them apart. The rebels, who heard them reading aloud the archaic language of the main article, didn't understand a word of those mysteries; they viewed their compatriots who read the *Amaltheia* with awe. From those mysteries came information about what was going on in the great wide world: in Russia, in Japan, and on the high seas. And there were even more astonishing things: information about what the weather would be, if the wind would pick up or bring rain and the like. The smugglers, who never shrank before any danger, would sit gathered round and listen like frightened children, their eyes filled with amazement.

Stephanos began with the *Amaltheia*. From the main article, he passed on to the serials. Norman dukes and counts duelled three times in twenty-four hours; the stranger with a mask ran his sword through the wicked and saved the weak. Florins and sovereigns flowed like a river. Later, Stephanos carried two armloads of old yellowed books he had bought from the bazaar to his saddle shop. They were synaxaria, lives of the saints, who, whether they were thrown into the mouths of lions, put among lepers or tied to burning logs, always came out unharmed. There were other books too: they told of magicians locked up all their lives in dark cells, trying to discover the laws governing life or how to defeat death by mixing secret liquid substances.

Stephanos threw himself into his treasure trove with passion. He read them all. Then his circumscribed, repressed and deprived life, the life he had so carefully planned to not be off by even a centimetre, took revenge on him.

He was forty years old. His hair was turning gray. Stephanos dyed it black and put on pomade. His clothes were covered with bits of string and horsehair from his saddle making. He put on new felt breeches, and when the sun set, he went out.

'Where are you going?' asked the olive tree with the coloured votive gifts, the rags. 'It's the first time I've seen you like that. It's the first time I've seen you leave.'

'I do as I please!' answered Stephanos.

He explained that he couldn't just look at saddles, water jars, and rags anymore. He was going for a stroll by the seashore, down by Saint Dimitris' church. This neighbourhood was the most amazing aberration in that town of smugglers. Real gentry lived there: people of extreme wealth, who were educated in Europe, had travelled widely and were deeply learned. There were girls who played Chopin, spoke foreign languages and were pale and thin like holy personages; Stephanos was afraid to look at them. The ambassadors lived there too, with members of the consular guard, who had feathers on their heads and wore clothes with gold buttons.

'I'm going there!' said Stephanos. 'Now I am their equal.'

He went. He was looking for a girl with white skin, golden hair and sparkling teeth who had slipped from the pages of his old books, who had escaped the clutches of the dukes of Normandy and come to the Aegean for him. He looked for her and he found her. She was a dream beyond anything he had ever dreamed. Her name was Gute, Miss Gute.

Stephanos keeps going back to the seaside mansion where Miss Gute is staying. Each morning, he waits impatiently for evening to fall, and then he goes there. He walks back and forth below the mansion. The waves break. The Devil's Table, the mythical mountain of the region, is stained with colour. And from inside the house comes the strange music. It is nothing like the smugglers' drums and bagpipes. It is an unknown voice, a soft voice that tells of travels and ships, of vast countries, forests and snow. Stephanos watches the Devil's Table and discovers that the strange music speaks of the shadows that advance across its deserted rocks. He looks at the sea and finds that the music tells of the sea. The stars start to come out, and Stephanos gazes at them. As the music tells of the stars, he whispers, overcome with agitation and emotion:

'Lord, what is happening?'

Afterwards he tells himself:

'It must be because she is playing.' And he sighs.

He sighs and sighs until his sighs reach the ears of Miss Gute.

She was engaged to the Ambassador of the Russian Empire. One evening, when they had company at the house, they talked about Stephanos, the saddle-maker who was in love with her. They had all heard about it.

'Why don't you bring him here some time?' everyone asked. 'We'll have some fun!'

'I'll bring him to you,' said the girl.

And she brought him.

Stephanos dusted off his felt breeches. He put pomade in his hair, and he went. There were a lot of guests. The evening air that came in from the balconies smelled of the sea. The women smelled of powerful perfumes. The lights shone. Stephanos entered the large hall with a supercilious air. But as soon as all eyes were turned upon him, and a curious whispering passed from mouth to mouth then turned into hushed laughter, he lost his bearings and was scared. As he looked around like a hunted deer, the girl went over to him to encourage him. She was leaning on the arm of the young Russian ambassador, who shone in white clothes and spoke to his fiancée in French.

Miss Gute said:

'The ambassador is glad that you came. He asks whether you desire anything, if he can be of use to you in any way.'

Stephanos made a deep, humble bow, bringing his right hand to his forehead in the manner of Turks. His dyed hair shone frightfully.

'We thank His Excellency,' he said. 'We do not desire anything.'

Miss Gute translated, smiling slightly. Then she said:

'The ambassador asks if you wish him to assist you in your work. What work do you do?'

It was a critical moment for his worthy saddles. If he denied them now, he would deny them forever. Because when you deny saddles once in your life, there is no going back. In that critical moment, the white uniform of the ambassador of the tsar of all of Russia shone. The girl shone like a flower from another world. Everything shone.

Stephanos' heart beat hard under the blinding light.

He denied them.

'We don't do anything anymore,' he said. 'We are engaged with books and promenades.'

They seem to have liked his answer a lot, because they said something in the foreign language, and then they laughed.

'And what about me?' says Miss Gute, and her eyes are sweet. 'What can I do this evening to give you pleasure?'

Stephanos says:

'Turn on that instrument I hear every evening below the window of your ladyship.' He imagined it was some kind of street organ or phonograph.

'But I play it myself!' says Miss Gute with a smile. 'I'll play for you.'

She looks at him strangely, and a wave of agitation passes over his whole body.

'I'll play just for you,' she says, '*only* for you.'

She sits at the piano and plays. Gradually everyone leaves Stephanos and goes to stand in a circle around the girl at the piano.

It is very quiet. He stays in his corner alone, Stephanos who denied the saddles. He stays there alone and listens to the sounds as they rise and speak. They speak softly at first, and Stephanos tries to remember the shadows on the Devil's Table, the sea, all the things that the strange sounds said to him when he listened to them under the window. Now that he is here beside the sounds, now that he sees her move the enchanted keys with her fingers, and the mysterious voice flows out like a river growing stronger, ever stronger, Stephanos doesn't see the shadows of the Devil's mountain anymore, doesn't see waves. Through a forest of tall pine trees, the wind moves softly. Inside a tower, a young girl sits and listens to the voice of the wind speaking through the pines. She is wearing a gold dress and red slippers. Suddenly it becomes still, not a voice is heard. It is as though the pine trees have been bewitched. The girl in the tower understands that finally her time has come, that the Great Duke is coming to take her away. She leans out of the window, looks down, and her heart beats hard. No, she was not mistaken, the pine trees did not deceive her. Astride his steed that froths at the mouth and strikes the ground with its hooves, the Great Duke, as young as an angel in his shining armour, draws his sword and lets it drop below her window as a sign of his submission.

'Will you come?' he asks her humbly.

'I am coming,' she replies. 'I have waited for you for years . . .'

And while the girl in the tower comes down for the journey for which she has waited so long, the wind in the spruces starts to speak again. The duke dismounts to take the girl in his arms. His weapons strike against his iron breastplate and shine like the sun.

'My love . . . ,' the Great Duke whispers humbly.

'My love . . . ,' whispers Stephanos deep inside, and the sweat drips from his dyed hair, the pomades and the oils drip.

The music has ended. Miss Gute stands up. Everyone applauds her. Her fiancé kisses her hand in adoration. She is very happy.

Stephanos stays alone in his corner, abandoned. Everyone has forgotten about him, including Miss Gute. A servant is serving lemonade. There is a straw in each drink. Stephanos sees the others put the straw in their mouth. Mechanically, he puts it in his mouth too and blows into the glass of lemonade. The lemonade flies up into his face and hair. All eyes again turn toward him and all the mouths break into laughter. The whole room has turned into giant, laughing mouths.

'What happened to you?' asks Miss Gute, coming to his side and trying not to laugh.

Frightened, confused, and sick with shame, he whispers:

'Nothing happened to us. It's nothing.'

Then the ambassador says in French,

'That's enough now, Alex. Tell him to leave.'

The girl says:

'Is the heat perhaps bothering you? Do you want to leave?'

Stephanos raises his eyes and looks at her. Out from under the spilt lemonade, out from under the sweat and the dripping pomade, pure as new metal, darts the look of suffering.

'I will leave,' he says.

She saw him to the door. There she said to him:

'Tonight there were a lot of people. Come back tomorrow, when I will be alone. I will wait for you.'

That night Stephanos did not sleep. He didn't even lie down on his mattress. Alone, his eyes fixed on one spot, he went over one by one, and back over again, everything that had happened at the mansion by the sea. Around him, silent, all in a row, his saddles with their blue beads watched him, the ones he had once fashioned with such light-heartedness and such confidence in himself. They watched him in bitter grief because he had denied them. Outside in the night, the olive tree with its coloured votive offerings, the friend of his childhood years, sees the light keeping vigil, hears the heartbeats that come from inside.

'Why?' it asks him. 'Why are you leaving us?'

But he can no longer hear the voice of the olive tree. He no longer has the privilege of speaking with the humble beings of the earth.

'My lady,' he murmurs. 'How I have waited for you!'

HE WENT THE NEXT EVENING. The young lady was indeed alone and was waiting for him. She didn't have the slightly teasing air of the previous evening; she was sweeter and spoke to him the way people speak to sick children.

'What do you want from me?' she asked. 'What can I do for you?'

Then he got up his courage. He forgot everything he had practiced the night before to say to her: beautiful words in puristic Greek from the *Amaltheia*. He simply told her how he wanted nothing else, only this: that she let him come sit there in a corner and watch her. He wouldn't say anything to her, only listen to the strange sounds of her music.

'How is that possible?' asked Miss Gute. 'The ambassador would get angry, and he could hurt you. He is my fiancé.'

Stephanos went white; he didn't know that the ambassador was her fiancé. He asked in anguish:

'And might you . . . might your ladyship someday leave with him?'

'Of course I might leave! Sometime I will leave with him.'

Oh, in the name of God, not that! Stephanos can't prevent the ambassador from being her fiancé. Only let her not leave!

'Don't leave!' he cried, and his tears flowed. 'What will become of me?'

Don't leave, he begged her. He said he could do the most incredible things for her ladyship. Only let her not leave.

At that point Miss Gute turned it into a joke.

'And what kind of thing could you do for me?' she asked, smiling.

Stephanos hadn't thought about it. But he promised her. At his house, he told her, he had old books. They told of magicians and wise men who spent all their lives trying to achieve the most unattainable things: how to make man fly, to make him never die. He would read the old books and see which was the most difficult of all the things that the wise men had tried to invent and not succeed. He would invent it himself for her sake.

'All right,' said Miss Gute. 'Do that, and I won't leave. And if I leave, I'll come back as soon as I hear that you have done it.'

THAT WAS THE PRELUDE to the 'Symphony of Perpetual Motion' that Stephanos played, that played Stephanos, a law-abiding citizen who once made saddles.

Where did he find the words 'Perpetual Motion'? He found them somewhere in his yellowed books. They filled his eyes instantly like a magic substance. Perpetual Motion! Yes! Yes! From now on, all his life would be for that: to find Perpetual Motion. What beautiful words! What a glorious achievement!

Miss Gute had already left. She left one Aeolian spring day, dressed in white. Her husband was dressed in white too, the new ambassador of his majesty. Stephanos watched them with misty eyes from an edge of the jetty where he would not be seen. When the boat had disappeared, he said:

'My love, goodbye... No one knows. But *I* know that you will return...'

HOW DO THEY BEGIN, those who want to find Perpetual Motion? Stephanos struggled as soon as he set out to be an inventor. He stayed awake for nights, wandering around in his workshop, continually whispering the magic words: 'Perpetual Motion... Perpetual Motion...' Daybreak came and found him with red eyes, exhausted. When the sun came out and cast peaceful light through his window, his silent companions from his carefree days, his humble saddles and blue beads, the witnesses of his anguish, begged him:

'Come now, lie down and sleep. Night will come again and you will begin again.'

Night came again, and he began again.

'Perpetual Motion! Perpetual Motion!' Alone, he would say the magic words again and again. Shadows would move in the half-dark space lit by his oil lamp. A hoop goes round and round and never stops; a tree starts growing and never stops, a star falls without stopping, a wave swells up, rises and then starts to travel without stopping through the seas of the universe. On the very top of the wave, in the foam, is an apparition in white; it is Miss Gute. She summons him.

'Will you send for me?'

'I will send for you,' he tells her. 'Don't worry. I will see to it.'

Perpetual motion.

And then the god of sounds took pity on him and helped him, and showed him how to begin. He was passing in front of a well-to-do household in the neighbourhood one day, preoccupied and absorbed in his thoughts, when he heard it: a sweet, soft melody from an unknown instrument was coming from the window. What was it? He stopped and listened hard. It wasn't really the same, but it was a lot like the music that ... Yes, it was like that music.

Hypnotized, he moved toward the sounds and knocked on the door. There was an old clock sitting on top of the household china cabinet. Two satyrs painted gold, held it upright, and the whole frame of the clock was painted gold.

As Stephanos moved closer to the cabinet, the melody stopped.

'What is that!' he asked, amazed.

'It's a clock, Mr Stephanos,' answered the lady of the house.

'How does it play music?'

'Just like that. You wind it up and it plays. Of course, it is a very good clock!'

Stephanos does not take his eyes off the gold satyrs. Sweat starts to bathe his face.

'It stops and starts up again?' he asks. 'Is that what you said?'

'Yes. It stops, you wind it up, and then it plays again.'

Stephanos does not hesitate. Light flashes in his eyes.

'How much would you sell it to me for, Mrs Kyriakoula?'

Ah, but Mrs Kyriakoula is not selling it! Her late husband, a sailor, brought it back for her when he made the great journey to Russia.

At that moment Stephanos grabbed her two hands and begged her passionately to sell him the clock.

'If I can't have it, I am lost. Lost!'

He offered her so great a sum and begged so much that Mrs Kyriak-oula finally gave in and accepted his offer. And so Stephanos sold many saddles with blue beads. He got the clock and brought it to his shop.

He spent the whole first night with the sounds. Stephanos wound and rewound the mechanism and the sounds rose and filled the bare room where the saddles had been. How beautiful it was!

Wind that blows over the Aegean, wind that blows through the great trees of Anatolia, quiet the bears and the wolves in her shadowy ravines. Quiet the blood from wild passion that is poured onto your earth, wipe the tears from the eyes of the mothers whose children were carried home dead from the windmills. Lay still the power that drives the smugglers to kill and be killed. Wind that blows, do all this tonight and then listen. Listen to the sounds that have filled the home of the saddles; take them and carry them to the girl of the sea. Tell her, wher-ever she may be, that Stephanos will do this thing that no other man was worthy to do in his life. Stephanos, the humble saddle-maker, will do it for her delight; because such is love. He will try to hold the sounds, to make the symphony unending. From now on his blood and heart and nerves are iron that burns, madness and passion for the chimera. What does it matter if in the end the sounds don't remain, if they always flee and are lost?

At daybreak when sleep came and closed his eyes, he was flooded with the happiness of a man who finally has a goal in his life.

EVER SINCE THEN, Stephanos, a law-abiding citizen who denied his saddles, seeks Perpetual Motion: to make the music from Mrs Kyriakoula's clock, the clock with the gold satyrs, never end.

He studied the mechanism for endless nights and days. He would take it apart and put it back together, always thinking he was nearing his goal, and that at last he was going to find the secret screw that would make the wheels turn continuously. In the beginning, his insanity made the rounds of the neighbourhood. Then rumour took it and spread it lower, to the smugglers and the urchins.

'Stephanos has gone crazy! Stephanos has gone crazy!'

'What is crazy Stephanos looking for?'

At first they all would stop in amazement before the mysterious words 'Perpetual Motion'. They didn't know how to get their tongues around them. But in the end they managed it:

'Stephanos is looking for Petual Motion! Stephanos the Petual Motion!'

Perpetual, illiterates! Stephanos corrected them, further broadcasting the extent of his insanity.

When he went out, he never left the magic clock in the saddle shop. Because he always thought he had somehow made some progress, that he was somehow nearing the solution, and he didn't dare to leave it unattended for fear of someone stealing it from him and breaking it. He put it in a bag made of coloured calico and carried it reverently under his arm. The street urchins followed behind and hooted at him, as they did to the other crazy people in town: 'Kambesa' and 'Erotokritos-with-wings-on-his-back'.* But Stephanos pretended not to notice. He walked haughtily, keeping his gaze high, confident that he was above mundane things.

One evening, outside the taverns of the Holy Trinity, the smugglers were carousing. They were Pagidas' men, the young bloods of the most famous smuggler in Aivali. They had been drinking since morning with their captain, and now that it was getting dark, they sat, half lying down, heavy and hardly speaking. Every now and then, they downed a glass of rum as they listened to the harsh rhythm of their primitive music — the drums and bagpipes that challenged their bodies to wake up and dance. At the front doors of the surrounding houses and at the windows, sat the girls. They spoke softly, and with flushed faces they watched the brave young men of their country.

At that point Stephanos appeared at the end of the road. The hooligans were running behind him, throwing mud and manure, and Stephanos was trying to get away like a hunted animal. At that moment, he came upon the smugglers' party. As soon as he saw this new danger, he lost his wits and began to turn. But it was too late. Behind him was a wall: the urchins with their mud clods prevented him from turning back. And in front of him was another wall: the bagpipes, the drums, and the drunks.

Stephanos stopped suddenly. He looked around him. He saw that there was no choice, he had to go forward. He clutched the magic clock under his arm. He stood up straight and proud. He advanced.

The shouts rose behind him again, they pressed him like a wave and pushed him:

'Stephanos the Petual Motion! Stephanos the Petual Motion!'

He arrived in front of the company of smugglers. The bagpipes and drums fell silent.

'Hey you, Stephanos, how are you?' asks one of them.

'Make him turn it on! Make him turn on the Petual Motion!' shrieked the chorus, the hooligans.

Then Pagidas shifts a little in his seat, Pagidas, the epic leader of the smugglers. He moves his hand and says calmly to one of his men:

'Tell them to beat it.'

After that, as it suddenly turns quiet, he turns to Stephanos.

'Come, you saddle-maker,' he says. 'Show me. What are you looking for?'

Stunned by the holy silence that spread out around him after so much shouting, Stephanos suddenly sees himself emerging as the protagonist in the theatre of the summer evening. He is choked with emotion because in the amphitheatre as spectator is the most sacred personage, the one of whom all the mountains of Kaz-Dak and all the seas of the Archipelago sing: Pagidas.

With trembling hands and with devotion, he unties his bag and takes out the clock. He puts it on the table of the arch-smuggler, next to the glasses of rum. The men's eyes look at the gold satyrs, they look at their leader who silently but without agitation, without impatience, is looking on.

'Listen . . . ,' whispers Stephanos. 'Listen, Andonis Pagidas!'

The melody gently flows through the moist eyes of the drunken men, through the open-air amphitheatre that smells of alcohol.

'I am listening!' says the harsh voice of the smuggler.

He listens devoutly. He is drawn into himself. Andonis Pagidas listens. The melody has ended.

'That's it . . . ,' whispers Stephanos.

Pagidas:

'What is it?'

Then the voice of insanity speaks again with deep emotion and tells of the chimera:

'That is it, Andonis Pagidas . . . I'm missing one screw. Only one screw, so I can hold the music, so I can make it never end. Then the wheels will turn without stopping . . . Then I will have found it . . . I will have found Perpetual Motion!'

He had hardly uttered the great words when the wild cry of an animal being slaughtered came from his mouth. He began to jump about as though he had been wound up, screaming:

'I'm burning! I'm burning!' while the smell of burnt cloth and flame sprang from his breeches.

Panic struck. Stephanos leapt about frantically, grabbing the parts of him that were burning, to put out the fire. His shouts filled the air. The girls were screaming, and the hooligans were guffawing and whooping. The *zeybek* drummer began to strike his drum wildly.

Then Pagidas stands up. He pushes through everyone and rushes to the saddle-maker. He kneels and puts his arms around the man's legs; he roughly grabs with his cupped hands the flames burning the madman's breeches. He squeezes hard to extinguish them. Not a sign of pain shows on his lips.

It's over. Pagidas stands up. He tells them to bring him oil. He kneels down, and he himself anoints the burnt flesh of the wailing man.

Pagidas stands up again. Silence. The madman, overwhelmed by the silence, stops crying out. Pagidas looks around with his stormy eyes. Slowly.

'Who did this?'

No answer. Everyone looks at him.

Now his voice speaks savagely:

'Which dog did it?'

Everyone looks him in the eyes. Only Miltiades, the barber, keeps his head lowered. He was a worm, an enormous hulk of a man, famous for his cowardice and dirty tricks. Whenever there was a party among the smugglers, he always came running, ready to do the most ignominious things to please the powerful. It was he who, thinking it would please Pagidas, had set Stephanos' breeches on fire at the moment that the saddle-maker, absorbed in his madness, was telling about what he was trying to find.

Pagidas looks at him steadily:

'Was it you?'

Suddenly he grabs his cup of rum from the table and throws it violently into the face of the barber, who starts to scream. Then he picks up a thick whip. He puts it in the madman's hands and orders:

'Beat him!'

Stephanos can't hold the whip properly; his hands are trembling and he is yellow with pain. Barely, lightly, he strikes him, as though he were caressing him. Then Pagidas grabs the whip violently from his hands and starts to mercilessly whip the barber, who is crying like a woman.

He has finished. Pagidas wipes his hands. He is breathing hard. He takes the clock and puts it into the hands of the madman.

'All right, saddle-maker!' he says. 'Get going now! From now on no one will bother you. Get going and look for your screw!'

And since he saw that Stephanos could not walk by himself on account of the pain, he took him by the arm and helped him. Everyone around them cleared the way. And in the silence that followed, they all watched in utter amazement, the women, the hooligans and the smugglers, and saw the two men walk between them and slowly leave, one leaning on the other, the two men of passion: one who hunted blood and death, and the other who hunted sounds.

THE SETTING SUN WAS ABOUT THREE MEN'S HEIGHTS from the horizon when he appeared, coming from afar toward the estate. Dressed in his felt clothes, black as a crow, enthroned on his donkey, Stephanos came. His donkey had blue beads on its bridle, and instead of a regular saddle, it had an aristocratic *tegki*, which gave a very official air to the traveller.

The first person Stephanos encountered at the farmstead was old Joseph, who did not know him.

'Is this the mansion of Yannako-Bibelas?' asked the stranger.

'It is.'

'Can a traveller stay here for a night?'

'There is always room for travellers here,' said the old man from Lemnos.

Stephanos dismounted, looked after his donkey and asked to wash himself. Then he asked to be taken to Yannako-Bibelas.

All of us children were playing around our grandfather when Stephanos appeared. He was walking proudly with his head high, a little to one side, and his eyes looked straight ahead. Under his arm, he was carefully holding the brightly coloured sack containing the clock with gold satyrs.

'Neighbour! Is it you? Is it you, Stephanos?' said grandfather kind-heartedly. 'What brings you to the Kimindenia?'

The saddle-maker made a deep Turkish bow, using his free hand.

'It is I, your lordship, and I bow to you. The road brought me to your parts, so I came.'

'You did well, Stephanos. Did they show you where you will sleep?'

Stephanos abandons his haughty air and a look of distress pours through his eyes.

'They showed me, your lordship. But I am scared. There are a lot of other strangers in there . . .'

And making his voice softer:

'I am afraid for this . . . ,' he says, and points to the bag under his arm.

Grandfather had heard about the sudden madness that had struck the saddle-maker. But since he had always lived in the Kimindenia, he didn't know the details.

'What's that?' he asks with curiosity.

'This? Oh, haven't you ever heard about this, my lordship?'

Then he tells him about Perpetual Motion: mixed up concepts, crazy ones, big words from the *Amaltheia*.

Grandfather hardly understands a thing.

'Won't you make it play?' he asks the madman.

'No, not now!' Stephanos begs.

Not now, he says. Night is the time when the spirit frequents the clock. He will make it play then. In the meantime, let him keep it safe. In the name of God, keep his treasure safe!

Grandfather thought he'd amuse us a little, the children and our grandmother.

He said to Stephanos:

'All right. I will let you sleep alone in a place where you will have nothing to worry about. For security, you will have beside you all the weapons that we have in the farmstead.'

And he gave instructions for them to take Stephanos and his clock to the Yellow Room. He sent him food from our own dinner and invited him to join us later.

All the family was there. Artemis could not stay still at her place for one second. It was as though she were sitting on nails. Grandmother smiled discreetly at the saddle-maker's regal manner. Grandfather was smiling too.

'Let us see it now,' he said.

With extreme care, the gold satyrs were brought out of their bag. Stephanos wound up the clock. And the Kimindenia mountains, which were listening, heard the sounds.

'I keep getting closer... I keep getting closer, my lord,' murmured the saddle-maker.

He keeps getting closer. It's just that he's missing that one magic screw. Then he will have found Perpetual Motion. He was toiling and toiling, he said, and was beginning to despair, when a vision of the Lord came in his sleep. The vision said to him:

'Why do you stay here with the smugglers, Stephanos? Here you will never arrive at your goal.'

And as Stephanos knelt and implored the vision to speak, it said this to him:

'Travel the great caravan road that is beyond the windmills. Take the road and go on and on. One day you will make it to the Holy Land, there where our Lord Jesus Christ was martyred. As soon as you step on the soil of Jerusalem, at that same moment the secret will be revealed to you: You will find the screw that you are looking for, you will hold the sounds forever.'

With these words, Stephanos roughly described his vision. A strange brilliance suffused his tired eyes. When he had finished, he turned his eyes and looked at all of us. What large, sad eyes they were. How large and sad!

At first grandfather was smiling. Then the smile disappeared from his lips.

'And your shop, old Stephanos, what did you do with that? What did you do with your saddles?' he asked.

'Oh! The shop and the saddles! Who cares about them now?'

'And what happened to your fiancée?' asked our mother, who knew the story of Alexandra Gute.

His fiancée! Stephanos searches his memory. Yes, yes, there *once* was a Miss Gute. She doesn't exist anymore. Stephanos barely remembers her, only dimly. Because now she has done her work; what she had to give, she has given. She gave the impetus toward the chimera, and she disappeared. The sounds absorbed her. She became one with them. Now only the pursuit of the sounds remains.

'But Stephanos,' says grandfather, and his voice is full of compassion. 'You were a good craftsman, Stephanos, and a good master of your house. Go back to your saddles!'

Go back to your saddles, he advises him. Where will it lead, and what screws are these that he is looking for? Does he know where the Holy Land is, where Jerusalem is? He will have to cross Anatolia, all of Anatolia to arrive.

'I will cross all of Anatolia,' echoes the calm and urgent voice of passion.

That night, when we children went to bed, strange feelings filled our hearts. We wanted to laugh at the madman. We laughed a little nervously and then stopped abruptly. Only Artemis, the most restless little deer who ever lived below the Kimindenia, was inexplicably silent. At last tiredness began to weigh on our eyelids. It became very still.

Then I hear Artemis' voice through the darkness, asking our big sister from her bed:

'Anthippe . . . What is it? What is Jerusalem?'

'You're still awake?' says Anthippe, scolding her. 'Go to sleep!'

'Tell me, what is Jerusalem?' says the child's pleading voice again.

'It's where Christ lived. Go to sleep, Artemis.'

There is silence again and then Artemis' voice again, trying to learn from Anthippe.

'Is it so far from here, Jerusalem?'

'It is very far, Artemis. Go to sleep!'

After a little while, when it seems all the other children have fallen asleep, I hear, muffled under the sheets, the deep sobbing of our little sister, who can't control herself anymore.

'Why are you crying, Artemis?'

But Artemis doesn't know why she is crying, she doesn't know how to say that she is crying because Jerusalem is very far away, and because the mad traveller with the sounds might never make it there.

It was a long time before Artemis calmed down. Then everything was silent. The Kimindenia mountains outside were silent and the jackals weren't howling. The night was alone. No, it was not alone. Suddenly, through the calm, it began to rise from inside the Yellow Room, soft and insistent, and to disperse like wind, to flow like the lightest of waves: the symphony of suffering. Stephanos, alone, surrounded by the swords and the rifles, was playing the clock with the gold satyrs.

'Artemis! Artemis! Do you hear?'

The little girl murmurs softly, so as not to disturb the magic symphony:

'Yes . . . yes . . . I hear . . .'

After a little while, I make out the very slight sound of her sheets moving. It's dark and I can't see a thing. But I sense her upright figure moving.

'What are you doing, Artemis?'

She comes close to me, feeling her way, and whispers:

'I'm going to go outside the Yellow Room to listen. Don't tell anyone,' says her trembling voice.

'You're going outside the Yellow Room? Aren't you scared?'

'I'm not scared. Go to sleep.'

I hear her leave, walking on tiptoe.

The music has stopped for a little. It begins again. And again. The Kimindenia mountains have never heard such a voice, so they have woken up to live this moment that was given them. The moon shone alone on the ravines and the oak trees. But when the sounds came out of the Yellow Room and went out into the night, the moist light began to tremble like a young heart. And Artemis is out there alone; she is living this exquisite moment that will never come again.

I open the door carefully so it doesn't creak, I try not to make any noise, and I go to Artemis. Her half-naked body hardly shows at all; it takes up the smallest amount of space outside the room of swords. She is on her knees, listening.

'Is it you?' she whispers, and her voice is distant, since it's coming from the world of magic.

'Don't say anything . . .'

I reach out my hands to find where she is. My fingers land near her chest, where her heart is beating very fast. She is kneeling there trembling. I kneel beside her and take her hand in mine. And tightly clasped together in this way, my little sister and I, suppliants outside the room of swords filled with sounds, we are gradually immersed in the enchantment that won't be silent. The madman inside keeps vigil; he makes the clock with the gold satyrs play over and over again. The moon isn't shining over the ravines anymore, since the night has filled with shadows. The under-ground veins of water have woken up in the Kimindenia, the oak trees have woken up, Little Red Riding Hood who turned into a deer has woken up, and so has Rose Slipper. They are coming, astride blue leaves. They open the farmstead's outer door, they go in the windows, they split open the stones of the walls and enter. They are there all around us, they are above us. They listen to the sounds and keep us company. They tremble and tremble so much that they all become one: the veins of water, the oak trees and the deer become one single shadow that weighs on our eyelids and closes them slowly, as the sounds gradually recede.

Two beloved hands nudge me, wake me, and pull me up. I hear frightened voices above us. I open my eyes. It is very early, and the sun has barely come up.

'My little children! My little children!' our mother is saying, terribly upset.

She holds Artemis with one hand and me with the other. She presses us to her. Grandmother is there too, that other sweet face of our childhood years. She doesn't know what to do; her eyes look around, and she moves her hands this way and that.

'Think of them staying up out here!' she says. 'Why did you do it, my children? Why?'

'Oh, that madman bewitched them!' says our mother. 'Why did we put him in the Yellow Room, so close to the children! At least nothing worse happened.'

Then everything comes back. The exquisite night with the sounds wakes up all at once. Artemis violently shakes free her hand from our mother's and asks in anguish:

'What happened to the strange man? What happened, Mother?'

Oh, luckily he has left by now, she assures her. By now he's far away. She says that when he woke up, he was the first to see us outside his door and let them know to get us.

Artemis rushes, and I also rush toward the farmstead's great door.

Far in the distance, on the caravan road, moves a black dot. You can't make out the mad traveller on his little donkey anymore: he's only a black dot. Speechless, with sad, wide-open eyes, we watch the dot as it fades and dissolves into the dust of the road that leads to far-away Jerusalem. We watch until it disappears behind the Kimindenia mountains.

≽ Chapter Seven ≼

GHOSTS COME TO THE KIMINDENIA

Below the Kimindenia mountains, the days dawn and set. The seasons pass. This year I will turn ten. What will I learn of this world this year? Let it come, whatever it may be. Just let it come.

ONE AFTERNOON, AUNT OURANIA, our mother's youngest sister, arrived unexpectedly at the farmstead. Unless she stayed in town, she always spent summers on her husband's estate, far from the Kimindenia. Because of this, we had never before had the opportunity to spend time with her. It was a sorrow for grandfather and grandmother that they never had both their daughters together in the Kimindenia. For us children, this was probably yet another reason why Aunt Ourania was a rather remote figure. Even in town, our two households had little to do with one another. Aunt Ourania was a very proud and haughty young woman. She had married for love one of the handsomest and richest men in the area; he was well-travelled and a partier. All this added a lot to her vanity. When they got married, they built a defiantly palatial house in the town with large marble staircases, heavy furniture, and lots of luxurious things. Almost every week they had parties, guests and music. Every now and then they travelled to the City.*

All this was in striking contrast to the unassuming and quiet life in our house. We would often hear conversations like this:

'I heard last night Theodore lost a fortune again at the club,' our father would say to our mother.

'Again? In the name of God! Where will all this lead?' said our mother, horrified.

'Where will it lead? It's obvious. They'll ruin themselves.'

'Oh my Panagia! What should we do?'

'What should we do? I think it's all Ourania's fault. If she wanted, she could turn him away from partying and the club. But would she?'

Then my mother would get up and go to secretly counsel her younger sister. She would find her around noon, still asleep, dead tired from staying up the night before.

'Ourania, my child, what are you doing? Where are you headed? Soon you're going to have children. Be sensible, my girl, get your husband off the wrong track!'

Aunt Ourania never liked to listen to a voice of reason advising restraint. She was a very pretty girl, with large almond-shaped eyes and an athletic body. She wanted to enjoy her youth for as long as possible.

'What do I care about what happens tomorrow!' she responded to her older sister's remarks. 'Today I'm living, and I'm happy.'

'But sensible people don't behave this way. In a few years, you won't have even a plot of land left to your name. You will have spent it all!'

'Poor sister! In a few years! What do you know about what will happen in a few years?'

'So you're not going to listen?'

'I'm not going to listen! Let us live the way we want to. And I give you my word, when we're poor in a few years, I won't come knocking at your door!'

Then the big sister would return home and start writing a long letter to grandmother telling her every detail and urging her to attend to the saving of her little sister, who was headed for disaster. When the letter arrived at the Kimindenia, grandmother read it secretly, so as not to upset grandfather. She cried inconsolably in secret and then began her preparations for the letter she would write to her younger daughter. She sharpened her pencils and racked her brain for the words to come. Her eyelids blinked incessantly from worry and distress.

Grandfather, seeing her preparations, would smile.

'What are you getting ready to do, Despina?'

'Well, I am going to write a letter to our younger daughter.'

Grandfather knew what a big proposition this was for grandmother, and he asked, smiling:

'Do you think you'll finish it today?'

'I think I'll be done by this evening.'

And when she was alone, she began to slowly draw large, childlike letters of the alphabet, round and carefully placed, one always spaced apart from the next. She kept moistening her pencil, bathing it with her tears. When the sun set and she had finished the letter, she took it to pass the night at the feet of the Panagia, placing it devoutly before the triptych icon that protected the Kimindenia. She crossed herself humbly and recited the Salutations.* Then the Panagia came in the flesh and stood there beside her. Bathing the ground with her tears, grandmother spoke to her as a mother to a mother.

'Protect my little one,' she begged her. 'She's on a bad road and doesn't know what she's doing. She is young and ignorant. She is also very pretty. Protect her so that she never learns what sorrow and tears are . . .'

Blessed in this way, grandmother's letter left the next day. When Aunt Ourania received it, she was very angry, not with her mother but with her sister who sent the reports to the Kimindenia. This led to coolness many times between the older and younger sisters.

FOR ALL THESE REASONS, the sudden and unexplained arrival of Aunt Ourania upset the serenity of the farmstead. Grandfather, grandmother, our mother and all of us ran to meet her at the main gate and find out what was going on. She stepped down, haughty as ever, from her covered *dalika* strewn with thick kilims. But she wasn't the Aunt Ourania we knew. Her face, which usually gleamed with the colours of perfect health, was now completely pale, and her large black eyes were tired and sunk deeply in their sockets.

'Ah!' Grandmother made a little cry, looking at her in alarm.

In the general silence, Aunt Ourania kissed her mother's hand, her father, her sister and all of us. She gave us bananas, a rare gift in our parts. She did all this with mechanical, distracted movements, as though we were not living creatures. Only when she had finished, as though she were used up, did she fall into grandmother's arms sobbing.

'What's the matter, my child?' grandmother asked, stroking her hair. 'What's happening to you?'

We only learned what was happening after we all went upstairs and sat down around her. What I understood from her words, which were drowned in tears, was that strange things were happening at Aunt Ourania's house. It seems that a ghost had come suddenly between her husband and herself and had turned their life upside down. Uncle Theodore would stay awake at night in a separate room with the ghost, and wild laughter would come at night from that room. Their life had become unbearable.

She would say to him:

'Come, Theodore, you shouldn't sleep apart at night and leave me alone.'

He would answer:

'I can't. I have to sleep alone.'

And he refused to give even the slightest explanation, or the slightest information about what went on in the closed room.

'I can't tell you, Ourania. It won't do for you to find out,' he said, and caressed her absently.

When Ourania finally got tired of asking him, she said:

'I'm going to go for a few days to the Kimindenia, to my father's. Why don't you come too, for a change of scene?'

'Go,' he said. 'I'll come in two days and stay at the Kimindenia for as long as I can.'

That was Aunt Ourania's account. After hearing what was happening in her younger daughter's house, grandmother began to tremble all over and make the sign of the cross.

'Christ and the Panagia! What are you saying, my child? Who told you it was a ghost?'

'It is a ghost, Mother! My husband locks the door of his room every evening and not a soul goes inside. So who is talking and laughing with him?'

In the general distress and amazement, none of the grown-ups had noticed that we children were there listening to what they were saying about ghosts. Only very late did our mother realize and turn in alarm to our big sister:

'Anthippe,' she said, 'take the children and go and play. Go and play, my children.'

We left. But our imaginations already had everything they needed. A new game had come from the world to the Kimindenia. It was dark and dangerous, and therefore sheer delight: ghosts.

Until then we had only heard about them. We had heard the strange stories told by the old men on the estate — sometimes scary, sometimes light — and our hearts took flight. Would it ever happen that we would see ghosts too? We trembled at the idea that it could happen. But stronger and more powerful than our fear was the desire that this blessing should not elude us.

Kosmas Livas, a ploughman from the Pontos region who had settled years before in the Kimindenia, had a lot to tell about ghosts. On rainy days, or late at night before he went to bed, chain-smoking by the light of the oil lamp, he would tell his story about the Moor. He told it every time the opportunity presented itself, identically and without variation. It had become necessary for him to relive it every so often, to relive it in his memory, to justify his life, to justify having ruined his life.

He was still a child when he saw the Moor for the first time. It was under a tree in the form of a snake. As soon as it saw the child, it slithered quickly up the trunk and hung from a branch. The child was terrified and stood there speechless, not daring to take a single step or tear his eyes away from the living line swinging in the wind. He kept them fixed on the snake's head and on its eyes.

Then the sky began to darken, the sun began to go out, and in the gathering dusk, the miracle happened: the long body of the snake began to grow stronger and to fill out. It gradually became thicker and thicker, like a tree trunk. And from that trunk, very slowly, a new human form began to take shape. First two arms emerged, as though from an elastic substance, then two legs, and then the head. It was a terrifying black head, with the face of a Moor whose eyes flashed as he hung from the tree, mouth closed, looking at the child rapturously.

This was when the ghost first entered the life of Kosmas Livas. From that time on it followed him until he was a young man. It appeared before him at unlikely times, especially times he was feeling happy, and froze his blood. If only it would speak and say something to him! But no, it never said anything. The Moor stood still and severe and took him hostage with his eyes. When he was sure that he had him in his power, he would lift his hand and gesture towards the west. Kosmas Livas agonized to find an explanation for this set gesture until at last he thought he had it: the ghost was gesturing for him to leave, to leave for the west! This thought entered his mind and moved around freely; it spread through every fibre of his body and into his blood. In that way, every other impulse inside him was lost. He could no longer work or get on in any way. He was overwhelmed by the urgency for flight. And then, unable to stand it anymore, he left his village and headed for the west. Every night of his journey the Moor appeared before him, always with the same, unalterable gesture: To the west! To the west! And every morning, obedient, Kostas Livas set out on the road, always for the west, further to the west. Only when he reached the border of his country, far-off Pontos, only then, the evening that he crossed the border, did the ghost not come. It didn't come the next night either, or the next, or any other night again.

Then Kosmas Livas understood that that was his fate, for the earth of his country not to want him. And he obeyed. He looked one last time at the trees of his ancestors' land that were disappearing in the distance. He looked at the clouds that were travelling in that direction, towards the east. He lowered his eyes and took for once and for all the road of exile, to remain a good-for-nothing all his life, without his own land.

'But do people from your part of the world expatriate themselves so easily?' the other ploughmen asked Kosmas Livas.

'Foolish Kosmas, perhaps the Moor was not really telling you to leave. And yet you left . . .'

Kosmas, without looking at the man who was speaking, asked:

'Have you ever seen a ghost in your life?'

'No, never!'

'Then how can you say anything? You can't judge me,' said Kosmas Livas with the unruffled expression of a man who knows better.

'And what about me who *has* seen one?' said Manolis Lyras, the man from Tenedos, one day. 'I have seen a spirit, and I tell you the same thing: you got scared and ruined your life for no reason.'

'Have you really seen a ghost?' asked Kosmas.

'I told you: I had an encounter with a spirit.'

'And you weren't scared?'

'No, I wasn't scared. Where I come from, near the sea, spirits don't frighten you. You just have to know how to talk to them.'

And the islander, Manolis Lyras, then told of his encounter with a spirit. It was a terrible moment on the Aegean, when the south wind and the rain were thrashing it. The sun was still far from setting, and yet the low clouds cast such an obscurity over the sea that you couldn't make out anything from stem to stern of the caique. The caique was a small lateen, whose captain was Lyras' father. Manolis, then a boy of ten, was on his first trip together with his father.

Things were deteriorating from moment to moment on the little caique from Tenedos, which was flirting with death. The captain called for his son, and they brought him from the hold, where he had settled down. With rapid movements of one hand, and without lowering his eyes, which looked straight ahead at the sails and the waves, he tied the child beside him with the same rope that kept him from being swept overboard. He did it to ease his heart a little. Whatever was going to happen would happen to them both. The storm kept getting stronger. The rain turned into hail that struck the deck and bodies violently. The clouds grew lower; you couldn't make out anything even a few metres away. Only the terrible roar that came from behind through the fog told you that the sea was there.

At that moment, a huge wave struck the caique and swept over it. Then a second wave, and another. The tied-up boy let out one, two, three heart-rending cries. He turned his eyes to his father, looking for help. But all he could make out was a hard face streaming with water, struggling to escape the enemy before him, the wave. Then the child, abandoned, tried to cry and shout. But he couldn't make a word come from his mouth. By then the Great Fear was in his heart. And when it comes, men don't cry out the way they do in small sorrows and small fears. The sailors, enveloped in the storm, ran like dim monsters from stern to bow to ease a sheet, to prop up the mast, to throw cargo overboard so that the boat could stay afloat. They shouted and screamed. But when the crucial moment came on the Aegean, which was playing the game of death with that piece of wood from Tenedos, all the voices were silent like the voice of the boy. The piece of wood leaped to the top of a wave, to its very summit, and was about to dash down into the lacerating chaos, when suddenly a clamour was heard through the roar of the storm. Then came the voice of the captain shouting, speaking to the wave:

'Does he live? The great king lives! Alexander the Great lives!'

And again, in anguish, while with one hand he held the tiller tight, and with the other he clasped the head of his child to him, as though to protect him, he cried:

'The great king lives. Alexander the Great lives!'

The little boy, the young Manolis Lyras, remembers how he then saw a fish tail like a dolphin's in the murky water by the boat's prow. Then he saw the whole fish. From the waist up it seemed to have the body of a woman. Two eyes shone like fire. The body sprang upright to the height of the wave and then suddenly dove head first, not to reappear. Black hair, like the tentacles of an octopus, blew in the wind for a short while when the Mermaid's head came up. Then the foam enveloped the hair and took it away.

All at once the wind dropped, the storm subsided, and in the sky, the rainclouds withdrew to the west.

Evening came. The stars came out, and on the Aegean, there was not a ripple. The boat's crew rested, exhausted from their struggle with death. Only the captain stayed awake. His boy, the little Manolis Lyras, was upset and stayed awake beside him.

'Remember what you saw, son,' murmured the captain, gazing at the sea with a rapt and ecstatic expression.

After a while, as though a sudden fear had to be dispelled, he asked: 'You did see it? You didn't miss it, did you? Were you able to see it?'

'What was it father? It was like a fish with hair . . .'

'It was the spirit of our sea. It was our mistress, the Mermaid,' said the captain.

Clasping the child's head, he caressed it with the harsh tenderness of simple people and said:

'Remember her and love her. She saves sailors if it is their fate for her to appear to them.'

And under the stars that shone on that serene Aeolian night, the captain of the caique, which was built with wood from Kaz-Dak, spoke to his son of the Mistress of the Aegean, his Mistress. From the old days of the Greek Archipelago came the shapes, the colours, and the magic of myth to become, in his telling, the motion and quivering of the heart.

A young king once lived in the land of Greece, Alexander the Great. He had a sister; they called her Gorgona. Alexander the Great travels to distant countries, he crosses mountains and seas, and when he returns, he brings the water of immortality with him. He would have drunk it when his time came, and he would never have died. He would have taken all the fortresses on earth and ruled until the end of the world. But he didn't do it in time. His sister saw the water of immortality and drank it without suspecting what it was. Alexander the Great got very angry. He grabbed her by the hair and threw her into the sea. From that time Gorgona lives in the sea. Her eyes are round; she has snakes in her hair; she has copper arms and gold wings on her back. From the waist down, she is a fish, and all the other fish in the sea consider her their queen. She always remembers the great king, her brother, who died young.

She always asks to find out from sailors she encounters on her way:

'Does Alexander the Great live?'

'He lives and rules!' they answer her.

Then Gorgona, upon learning that, is very happy and orders the waves to let the caique pass. If, however, some mariner happens not to know and tells her that the king died, then there is no escape: Gorgona raises a whirlwind and takes both the boat and the sailor down with her. Afterwards she rises high on the wave to find another sailor to tell her, to reassure her that her brother lives, that no, Alexander the Great did not die.

Finally, after we had waited for him for two days, Uncle Theodore arrived.

He was a tall, handsome young man with curly hair and cinnamon-coloured eyes. He was known as one of the best horsemen in the area, and it showed in the horse he rode. He loved horses with a passion. Once, when his horse died — a white thoroughbred with gray spots on its forehead — he didn't eat for three days but closed himself in his room to grieve his lost friend.

After he dismounted nimbly, with his tall boots, his leather riding breeches and the jovial expression that never left him, everyone waiting for him at the farmstead's great gate looked at each other in surprise. They were expecting to see a silent being with the agony of ghosts written on his face. There was nothing of the kind, only a little paleness and some tiredness in his eyes, that was all.

It seems that he read the confusion in everyone's faces. So he looked at Aunt Ourania and smiled, then turning to grandfather and grandmother, he said:

'As you see, I am just fine. How are you?'

The way things had turned out, for grandfather to have both of his children and their families with him, he very much wanted to give a celebratory tone to this happy chance. However, the worry over Uncle Theodore's condition had been holding him back. But now that he saw him in such a good mood, he thought everything was all right. He gave orders to slaughter a choice lamb, set up a big table and bring aged wine. Then a look appeared on his face, as if he wanted something but didn't know how to say it. Finally, he asked what had become of the good clothes he'd worn when he was a bridegroom. Since then he had worn them only on important days like Easter Sunday or New Year's Day.

'Why don't you get them out, Despina,' he said hesitantly, as if he were afraid the reason for his question would be understood. 'The moths will eat them.'

'I'll get them out, Yannako.'

After a pause, grandmother smiled slightly and said, without looking at him:

'Might you want to wear them tonight, Yannako?'

'What do you say?'

'I say you wear them.'

'Well, since you say so, I'll wear them,' said grandfather. 'It's been such a long time since I've had my whole family around me.'

He put on the clothes of his youth. And grandmother wore her simple and lovingly preserved wedding dress so that no one could say she didn't honour her children too, as was fitting. It was a little tight at the waist, and the long black jacket was also a little tight. She fixed her white hair prettily. And she was sweet, so sweet!

This formality made a big impression on us children. At one point Agapi said to Artemis:

'How different everything is tonight! It must be because of the ghosts that came here.'

'Yes,' said Artemis. 'It must be because of the ghosts.'

When we were seated at the table, grandfather looked around him. We were all there. Then grandfather stood up. His black felt waistcoat contrasted with his white head and made it strangely bright. He stood up straight like the trunk of a tree. He lowered his eyes and crossed his arms.

Slowly, in a clear voice, he began the prayer:

Our Father who art in heaven, hallowed be Thy name. Thy kingdom come, Thy will be done, on earth as it is in heaven. Give us this day our daily bread . . .

We all crossed ourselves, and grandfather sat down. Then he cut the large dark loaf of whole wheat bread and gave some to everyone. Then he said:

'May my children be welcome in the Kimindenia!'

Then Aunt Ourania, our mother and Uncle Theodore all responded: 'Blessings to us all in the Kimindenia, Father. Blessings, Mother.'

Grandfather took the lamb's shoulder on his own plate and cleaned the scapula, but for as long as we were eating, he didn't look at it.* Only when the food was finished did he lift the thin bone to the light. Then there was silence. First grandmother's eyes, then everyone's turned soberly to grandfather. It was that solemn moment when man tries to speak with God, to read omens, to prepare himself for the good or bad fortune of the land. Grandmother remembered the trepidation in her heart, for as many years as she'd lived in the Kimindenia, every time that her husband, in a moment like this, had silently studied the messages from heaven in the bone of a slaughtered animal. In the time of her youth, when there were difficult years, it wasn't just trepidation, it was agony. For as long as her husband was studying the bone, since there was nothing else she could do to help, she murmured a prayer to herself, an appeal to the Panagia that the omens be good:

Under thy protection, O Panagia our lady, do all thy servants unworthily run and supplicate thee . . .

Tonight it is not for the earth. Grandmother senses that tonight the omens will speak through the bone of something more precious and more dangerous: their younger daughter's future, and what this dark power, these ghosts who have come, have in store for her. And so grandmother prays again, as she did in the time of her distant youth when they were battling with the land. With the same powerlessness, she prays again now for her child:

Under thy protection, O Panagia our lady . . . *

It's clear that the others, Aunt Ourania and our mother, also sense that the lamb's bone will speak tonight about the ghosts. The deep throbbing of their hearts shows clearly in their faces, which are unable to stay composed. And grandfather is solemn; he is taking a long time tonight. He looks insistently at the bone as though there is a force in it that is resisting.

Then, finally, his face becomes serene. He puts the bone down slowly and lowers his eyes as though they are exhausted from the effort.

'Everything will go well this year too,' he whispers.

And then, looking slowly at Aunt Ourania, he says:

'Everything will be fine, younger daughter.'

Then light shone in every face.

The table was cleared. We sat a little longer. Then, at a signal from grandmother, the women and children stood up.

'Anthippe,' said grandmother to our big sister, 'the children should go to bed. And we have a little work,' she added, and took her two daughters with her.

Only the two men remained, grandfather and Uncle Theodore. For a little while there was silence. Grandfather put his hand to his head and stroked his white hair. Then he looked at the young man and said, as though making an effort:

'Do you have anything to tell me, my son?'

He thought this was all he had to do, all he had to say. Two men don't have another way of talking, they don't have much to say when the gap between them that needs filling is a dark, unknown world.

Uncle Theodore looked absently at a fixed point on the wall:

'I don't have anything to tell you, Father.'

The old man spoke again:

'You don't have anything to ask of me? You don't want me to help you with anything?'

Now uncle's cinnamon-coloured eyes had grown dark and were staring motionless at the fixed point on the wall. A fleeting hoar frost passed over them; they closed and then opened again. Then the will and desire for submission were written on his face; it was that extraordinary power that compels people to refuse to escape from what torments them, because its taste is irresistible and unique.

'I have nothing to ask of you, Father. I don't want you to help me with anything.'

'Very well.'

After a pause, grandfather said:

'Let's do something to pass the time. Shall we play cards?'

'Let's play.'

They called the women in and played *pastra*. Grandfather and my mother were one team, Uncle Theodore and grandmother were the other. This family game of *pastra* was always a great amusement to Uncle Theodore. With various sleights of hand, he stole the jacks and kept increasing his points. Grandfather didn't notice what was going on at his expense, but grandmother was paying attention. Her eyes looked nervously from left to right, and she kept moving around in her seat. Even now, her kind heart was watching over her husband to protect him from anyone who might do him harm. As soon as she noticed some foul play, she turned bright red and began by signalling to Uncle Theodore to say, 'For shame!' Uncle, amused by her childlike goodness, would continue. Poor grandmother couldn't sit still on her chair. She kept moving as though it were burning, until finally she gave voice to her protests:

'Theodore! Come on now!'

Tonight, too, Theodore began to amuse himself with this game with grandmother. But as time went on, he gradually became distracted. He forgot not only to steal points, but even to play his card. Grandmother, accustomed to seeing him play differently, gave him looks filled with puzzlement, as though something was missing, as though she were begging him to steal the jacks and the points to tease her. She divined the enemy that was disturbing the old harmony. Whether the demon that circled over her head would win or lose was about to be expressed in the bright colours of a stolen jack.

The demon won.

Uncle Theodore quit the card game abruptly.

'I have go to bed,' he said, 'I'm tired.'

Alone in our own room, it was impossible for us children to settle down. We knew that all around us, in the air that trembled inside the rooms of the farmstead, in the thickening silence, there was something new. It had travelled, wrapping uncle somehow in a mist, and now it was here and was going to appear. How could we be still?

We heard, just barely, the grown-ups' conversation coming faintly from the other room. That comforted us with the idea that we weren't missing out on anything special. But how slowly the time was passing, how very slowly! Every so often a veil passed over my tired eyes from sleeplessness and worry. Then I thought shadows were quivering in the dark: horses and boats and trees. But later the veil would lift again, and I saw nothing was there.

At last we heard Uncle Theodore stand up and say:

'I have to go to bed. I'm tired.'

'Your bed is ready,' said grandmother. 'We gave you and Ourania the north bedroom.'

Uncle hesitated a little, then he asked:

'Don't you have some single bedroom?'

'What for, my child?' said grandmother solemnly. 'We gave you a room with your wife.'

'Very well.'

We heard the doors open and close. After that it was quiet. A little time passed. It seemed the whole farmstead had gone to sleep: the people, the things. Only we were staying up and waiting — even our big sister, Anthippe. It was the first time she lived through our agonies with us. In the distance, through the cracks in the door of the north bedroom, we saw a light keeping vigil. What was happening in there? Had the ghost come? We were afraid to venture out, to be separated from each other. We sat gathered there at the door and, with eyes full of anguish, we watched. What was going on through the bright cracks in the distance?

Until Artemis had had enough of waiting. She couldn't hold out any longer.

'Come!' she whispered to me. 'Come there with me.'

She pulled me, and we went. We bent down to the keyhole and saw: Uncle Theodore was sitting at a little table near the bed. The lamp shone beside him, and he was wide awake. He was reading a book, but it was clear that his mind was elsewhere. Every so often he lifted his eyes from the book and fixed them penetratingly on the wardrobe that was opposite him. He waited like that, watching for a long time, then lowered his eyes again to the book. His eyes did not shine with their cinnamon-coloured light; deep lines slashed his face.

'Come, Theodore, come now,' said Aunt Ourania every so often, half-lying on her bed. 'It's very late.'

Uncle didn't even move. It seemed he didn't hear her voice.

'Come now,' his wife implored. 'What's the matter?'

Then she stopped begging him. There was silence. After that we heard Aunt Ourania's soft, persistent sobbing. She cried piteously, like a child. The lament seemed to reach uncle. It was as though he were surprised, as though something were happening that he hadn't expected. He stood up nervously and went to his young wife's bed. He stroked her hair.

'What's the matter?' he asked. 'Go to sleep. I'm going to read a little more.'

And then again, more softly, with a voice that came from the deepest part of his being, he said:

'Go to sleep.'

We went back to our room and told the other children, who were waiting for us, what was happening in the north room. We were almost disappointed. Fatigue and drowsiness weighed on us heavily. We agreed to lie down in our beds but not to sleep, and to go back in a little while to see if anything was happening. But deep sleep took us as soon as we lay down, and all our plans came to nothing.

THE NEXT DAY UNCLE THEODORE seemed terribly tired. It was certain he had stayed up all night. He said he wanted to take a long ride on his horse in the Kimindenia mountains and was gone all day. He returned when the sun was just about to set. He said he was exhausted and would go to bed immediately.

He told our aunt in a tone that did not allow for objections:

'Ourania, you will sleep with your sister tonight. Why should you also stay up whenever I don't sleep?'

'But . . . ,' his wife started to say.

'Then I'll leave the Kimindenia tonight!' he told her abruptly.

'All right, Theodore, all right,' said his wife submissively, holding back her tears. 'Stay by yourself.'

We were sure now that the big moment was tonight, that tonight the ghost would come. Our secret premonitions told us so, and our deep longing. Everyone went to bed early. In a little while, all the rooms were plunged into silence. But through the calm we divined a spirit that was staying awake. We sensed that the grown-ups, safe behind their doors, were waiting for it. Outside, too, the night was quiet. The Kimindenia were resting. No wild animal was heard. A cold, solitary moon hovered above.

In the north bedroom, alone, Uncle Theodore was staying up with the light of a lamp. None of us dared to go there tonight. Our hearts were pounding. It was close to midnight.

Artemis was again the first to make up her mind.

'Will you come?' she said. 'I'm going.' Her voice trembled.

Holding hands, my little sister and I stepped out into the corridor. The light of the moon was coming through a window that faced the courtyard. Suddenly, an unexpected dark cloud passed beneath the moon and covered it. Then everything became very dark. I felt Artemis' hand trembling in my palm. I wanted to run and flee, but my legs wouldn't let me. And that silence! The terrible silence that surrounded us! Just to hear a human voice, just to hear my own voice, I whispered:

'Don't be afraid, Artemis.'

'I'm not afraid,' she said softly.

We advanced, trembling, and reached the door of the north room. We bent down to the keyhole and looked.

Uncle Theodore was sitting in the same place as yesterday, next to the little table and lamp. The book was on his knees, and his eyes were fixed on the wardrobe opposite him. I saw three quarters of his face. Nothing recalled the bright, cheerful, smiling face of the uncle we knew. His eyes flew savagely from their sockets in their desperate attempt to see something, to make something come out. Under those straining eyes, his cheeks seemed to have gone in the opposite direction and were deeply sunken. Behind his tightly closed mouth, his teeth must have been clenched and grinding. And only his dark hair, motionless and undisturbed, weathered the storm on his face with indifference.

Suddenly a violent gust of wind came down from the Kimindenia, chilled by the sunless forest. We heard it hit the nearby trees, and we heard the branches creak like bones. At the same moment, we heard the howl of a jackal in the distance. I tightened my hold on Artemis' hand as she stood bending over, looking through the keyhole. I wanted to tell her we should leave, but it was too late.

Wild, and hard as a knife, laughter came from inside the room. Uncle Theodore was laughing with all his might. He stopped for a moment to catch his breath and began again, as though someone were tickling his feet, his armpits and his whole body. But it was nothing like a laugh of joy; it was as though he were being torn apart.

Artemis, trembling all over, had dropped my hand, placed both her hands around the keyhole and was looking, looking, unable to tear her eyes away, as though drawn by the light. Bewitched by the same force, I pushed her aside suddenly and leaned down and looked. Uncle was still sitting in the same place. He had crossed his arms over his chest and was squeezing them hard as though he were trying to prevent something from flying out from inside. His eyes were still looking at the same place, the old wardrobe. The more he looked, the more he shook with laughter. I turned and looked there too. Nothing! I didn't see anything! But suddenly I noticed: the doors of the wardrobe were wide open. Were they open before, when I first looked, before the laughter began? No, I remember clearly, they were not! And Uncle

Theodore kept looking there, his face unrecognizable from the convulsions, and he kept laughing as though he were looking at something indescribably comic. Flooded with fear, all my tiny being was concentrated in my eyes, so they might see it. But I didn't see anything. The room was empty. Only a slight breeze trembled; it must have come in through the shutters.

And yet we sensed that something was in there, something was in the wind in the room. Artemis was about to take her turn bending down to look. Her face leaned on mine. It was icy. I was about to pull away when suddenly the wind from the Kimindenia blew again. It flew through the shutters and struck the light of the lamp. Suddenly it was pitch black, and the laughter stopped as though cut with a knife. At the very moment, we heard footsteps in the corridor and recognized them. It was grandfather, feeling his way as he came.

I grabbed Artemis and pulled her to the wall. From there we slipped into our room. The other children fell upon us and asked us in anguish:

'What did you see? What did you see?'

We were both shaking and couldn't answer.

'Nothing,' stammered Artemis.

'Nothing,' I stammered.

'And uncle's laughter? What was it?'

'Who knows what it was. It wasn't anything.'

At the end of the corridor, at the north room, we heard the door unlock, then we heard grandfather's voice and then uncle's voice saying something. Footsteps. Then silence.

WE WENT TO BED. In a little while the other children fell asleep. Only Artemis and I were awake. Our beds were next to each other.

I hear her voice whisper:

'Petros, are you awake?'

'I'm awake.'

'I'm cold,' she murmured. 'Can I come close to you?'

'Come.'

I made room for her, and she came. She squeezed tightly against me. That made her feel better, and in a little while she was calmer.

'Did you see anything? Did you see it?' she asked me softly.

'Ah no, Artemis. I didn't see anything. Did you?'

'Nothing!' she said in despair. 'And yet . . . it was there.'

After a while she said:

'I saw the doors of the wardrobe open by themselves, but nothing else.'

'Really? Did the doors open by themselves?'

'They opened by themselves.'

The memory of that moment makes her tremble again. Her teeth chatter violently. But her body is warm now. It is still pressing against mine. I open my arms to embrace her, for her to know I love her, that I am beside her and for her not to be afraid. She is wearing a light nightgown that has ridden up above her knees. Unconsciously, my hand slips underneath her clothing to find the trembling flesh and to calm it. How warm it is there! How warm it is. A strange, unfamiliar sensation passes through my touch. From the tips of my fingers it enters my veins and slowly pours through them. It fills them with their first stirring; it fills them with trembling.

'Do you feel better now, Artemis?'

Her body seemed to be calmer now and had stopped shivering.

'Yes,' she murmured.

'Do you want . . . Do you want me to take my hand away?'

The new, unfamiliar world that was trembling there in my fingers, pressed against her smooth body under the covers, waited in suspense for the answer. Ah, what if Artemis were to say no. It is so sweet . . .

'No,' whispered Artemis. 'Hold me like that . . .'

We fell asleep that way, in each other's arms, on that great night. The wind outside passed through the deserted ravines in the Kimindenia and whistled frightfully. In a distant swamp the frogs, emerging from the water, gazed at the night with frozen eyes and croaked, looking for love. In the body of a plant carried by the wind, the pollen stirred and trembled, trying to bind and fertilize. The closed wardrobe in the north room opens by itself again. But now my time had come, and I could see the ghost. A little priest, about half the span of a hand in height, comes out from within, with his beard, black cassock, priest's cap and boots: everything. How funny he is! With his little hands, he lifts his cassock a little and jumps out of the wardrobe. Afterwards, he lifts his eyes, looks at me and smiles. I convulse with laughter and shake with fits — like Uncle Theodore — while the little priest smiles. He doesn't say a single word or take a single step. I do not dare to move. I only sink my hands into the warm substance I am holding. I tremble, and I cry out with laughter.

A powerful shove, and it's all gone.

'Why are you hurting me like that? Why are you shouting?' asks Artemis, on the verge of tears. 'Your nails made me bleed.'

Confused and drenched in sweat, I know nothing.

'I didn't mean to hurt you, Artemis.'

⇒ Chapter Eight ⇐

Very early the next morning, Uncle Theodore left with my aunt. Some urgent business called them back to their estate.

Artemis is pensive. She doesn't want company, doesn't want to play with boats. And I just want to lie under the trees alone. The air is still full of the ghosts. Everyone is talking about the extraordinary night that the Kimindenia has passed.

'Are they still here?'

'Did they leave with Uncle Theodore?'

Ghosts are spirits and they depart. They leave traces of their passage within us, in the depths of the closed space that is set apart for the world of miracles; but they are spirits, and they depart. But in the hands that touched Artemis, in the fingers, at their very tips, there is substance. A drop of blood moves silently under the skin. Curious about what it heard, it stops and strains to hear again. 'What could it be?' Behind it, the other blood, the other drops stop too and are silent. 'What could it be?' they all ask, and they throb in agitation. They distinctly hear the beating under the light covering that envelops the blood, under the skin. And then the vibrations move away from their source to become a force that begins its own independent life. The skin trembles, the desire to learn and to hold moves over it like light.

When night comes, and the other children go to sleep, I call to her softly:

'Artemis . . . Are you awake?'

She is slow to answer and then whispers:

'I'm awake.'

'Are you scared?'

Again there is a little pause before she answers.

'Why do you ask?'

I say:

'If you're scared, come close to me . . .'

'No!' she says abruptly. 'I'm not scared.'
'All right.'
What a shame that Artemis doesn't want to come close to me! I would have hugged her again and warmed her if she were cold. But why doesn't she want to come? Why?
Artemis is already thirteen; I am younger than her.

THE SUN PLAYS OVER THE LEAVES of the olive tree. The light flows. It is a fertile substance, a greedy substance, overflowing with curiosity, like the veins of water in the bowels of the earth, like people's fingers on flesh. It slips through the leaves. At one moment, it pours through the cracks in the trunk and rummages around. It doesn't find what it is looking for, it doesn't find release. Again it glides down lower, to earth. Each drop of light is a being that lives independently of the others — alone it must discover the magic of the earth. It must hurry before night comes and it dies. It is a painful struggle, flooded with the feeling of panic:
Will it be able to find out? Will it find out in time?

WHEN THE WIND BLEW A LITTLE, it took a grain from the pollen of a plant, carried it a short way through the blue void, then let it fall. The fertile seed falls in vain, it falls to no avail onto the earth where a worm is going along, writing its fate. Worms are blind, they are creatures that crawl on the earth. Things that crawl have no curiosity, no anguish. But the plant's pollen came from up high, it saw and heard the wind, it saw and heard the sound of insects and sap, it saw the stars and the night. It would have learned much more from the shining world, but now its fate is sealed: it must die on the earth. Yet even at that last moment, the moment of its death, it still wants to learn, to learn as much as possible:
Why are there worms that crawl on the earth? Why are there creatures that drag themselves along?

I wandered far from the farmstead. I crossed the olive grove and entered deep into the kingdom of the oak trees. I was tired. I lay on my back under a tree and listened to the leaves whispering. After a while Artemis came from another path.
'You're here too, Artemis? Where are you going?'

Artemis sat down to rest. She stretched out her legs and looked at the sky.

'Do you know what a hoopoe is?' she asked after a while.

'No, I don't know what a hoopoe is.'

'Of course, how could you know!' she cried sarcastically. 'But I do!'

She tells me about a strange, beautiful bird with a wonderful crest; it is chestnut-coloured and yellow on its head and breast, and has black wings with white stripes. It flies low among desolate rocks and moves crazily, left and right; it catches insects and flicks them up high, opening its beak to swallow them. It's a very beautiful bird, but it never sings. Whatever it had to say on earth, whatever it had to do in its life, it did with its colours. That's why God took away its voice — it would be unfair to the other birds in the forest for it to have everything: a voice and such colours.

'Who told you all that, Artemis? Where did you learn about the strange bird?'

'The hunter with the yellow stars told me. He knows the stories of all the birds in the forest.'

There is the sound of a horse's hooves. Who is it? We both jump up to see. A small-bodied white steed runs in a lather under the foliage that covers the path like a green cloud. As soon as the hunter notices us, he pulls hard on the reins. He is suntanned, tall, about twenty years old. Knotted on his head is a white kerchief embroidered with yellow stars. His cartridge belts are crossed on his chest. The afternoon light illuminates his eyes in a strange way: the colours of the forest play inside them.

'What are you doing here?' he asks, looking at us. 'How are you, little roe deer?' he says to Artemis familiarly.

Little roe deer? Oh, so he is such good friends with Artemis? And I didn't know about it! How did they become friends? He is not one of our men; he works at the estate near the sea. So Artemis hobnobs with everybody, with every strange hunter?

'How are you little roe deer?'

Artemis springs towards him. Her eyes don't have tree branches and leaves in them like people of the forest. They have dolphins and waves, because Artemis is from the Aegean. Their eyes meet there in that small space: the green leaves meet the waves.

'I walked a lot today,' says Artemis. 'I went deep into the oak forest without realizing it.'

'What were you looking for,' asks the hunter, surprised. 'Weren't you scared?'

'What should I be afraid of?' says Artemis proudly. 'I was looking for hoopoes.'

'You were looking for hoopoes?'

'Yes. Didn't you tell me about the birds with colourful wings? I really wanted to see them.'

'Oh, I forgot I told you. And did you find any?'

'No, I didn't.'

'And how could you find any there where you were looking!' says the hunter teasingly. 'You don't find hoopoes in the forest; they fly around pasturelands where there are no trees.'

'I didn't know,' whispers Artemis, and she blushes a little. 'You didn't tell me. Tomorrow I'll go to the pasturelands . . .'

'Hmm . . . I still don't know if you'll find any,' says the hunter.

Because by now, he says, the hoopoes have passed through our land and left. They will come again with the first rains. Then they'll start their strange antics again: they'll screech and hunt insects in the hollows of trees, the branches, and in rocky crags.

'So,' says Artemis sadly, 'you say that I won't find hoopoes, that there aren't hoopoes anymore, that they're all gone?'

'You can always find a few. Who knows why they don't leave with their flock,' replies the hunter. 'But you're not going find them! I flushed out two today, but I didn't shoot them.'

'You didn't shoot them?'

'No, I didn't shoot them. I left them for her to hunt, my young mistress who is coming from far away, from the islands of the Ocean.'

Who is this young mistress who is coming from far away?

Artemis asks in astonishment:

'Is some mistress of yours coming from the islands of the Ocean?'

'Yes, she's coming.'

'She's coming here, to our part of the world?'

'Yes, she's coming here.'

'What's her name?'

What did they call her? She has a foreign name. He struggles a little to remember it.

'Her name is . . . Her name is Doris.'

'Doris . . . ? What does Doris mean? Is she a Christian?'

'No, she's English.'

'And she's coming to the Kimindenia? What's she coming for?'

'Oh, don't you know? She married the son of my master, Vilaras, who owns the estate by the sea, the son who studied abroad.'

'Her name is Doris and she's coming here?'

The hunter is very amused by the insistent questioning. He smiles.

'Her name is Doris and she's coming here.'

'And she'll hunt our country's hoopoes?'

'That's what they say. She's a good shot. She'll hunt deer in the Kimindenia and she'll hunt hoopoes.'

'And that's why you didn't shoot them?'

'That's why I don't shoot them, so she'll see that we have hoopoes too.'

Artemis' voice and lips tremble slightly.

'And that's why you didn't shoot anything else today?'

No, that wasn't why. Today he had gone for big game. He had gone for wild boar and killed three. He had left them high up in the forest. The Turkish servant boys from their estate would bring them down.

'And now you should be going!' says the hunter suddenly, in a protective tone. 'You better go back, the sun is setting.'

'We'll go back.'

'All right then! And don't go looking for hoopoes, little roe deer.'

The small-bodied white horse dashes under the green cloud again and disappears. For a while we can still hear the hoofbeats. Then that sound dies out too. Only the whispers of the forest remain.

'Artemis, aren't you ashamed to have friendships and conversations with strangers?'

'Let me be!' says Artemis abruptly. 'Why should I be ashamed?'

True, why should she be ashamed? What I said was crazy.

'And furthermore, he's a hunter!' adds Artemis. 'You saw how handsome he is!'

After a while she continues; her eyes shine as she looks up at the clouds:

'He's a hunter! I love hunters that kill wild boars in the Kimindenia.'

What is she saying? How much time, how many years had passed since we used to cry, and Artemis along with us? How long had it been since we used to pray for the hungry jackals of the forest? Artemis is a despicable creature for loving hunters who kill birds and wild boars.

'How can you love hunters now?'

Artemis looks me straight in the eyes:

'You say that out of spite!' she says. 'Because you'll never become a hunter! You would never be able to.'

'*I* can't be a hunter?' I say, choking with indignation. 'I don't *want* to be one!'

'No, it's that you can't.'

I have my rubber slingshot in my pocket. I had made it in the town since the other children had them for shooting sparrows. But until then I had never tried to aim at a bird. I only shot at leaves.

My fingers slip into the pocket where the slingshot is. They stroke the rubber band. Artemis is leaning against the root of a tree staring straight ahead of her, completely absorbed. Beyond the oaks, beyond the Kimindenia, beyond the mountains of our land and beyond the windmills, travels the great sea. There is the dark country that they call the Ocean. There is always fog over the water; there is no gold sun there, no azure clouds. Only murky fog. And from that place, from the land of mist, she is emerging slowly. Wet as rain, she emerges from inside the fog and keeps coming, keeps getting closer. She is the girl from the distant islands, the girl of the Ocean. They call her Doris. What does Doris mean? Her hair is damp as though she had lived in the sea all her life. It flows like watery tentacles. And her eyes? Do they shine like the eyes of the luminous girls of the Aegean? Do they have dolphins and blue waves in them?

Artemis' eyes, with dolphins and blue waves in them, remain fixed for a long time, motionless. When they suddenly begin to move, they lose their silence. It is as though Artemis is coming to her senses. She sits up very carefully, so as not to make any noise.

What is it?

I turn my eyes to where Artemis is looking: it is a weasel, a tawny little animal creeping up the trunk of the tree a few metres away. It stops for a moment, as though to smell something in the air, to search for something, then it moves again. Its lithe body makes soft, distinct movements against the trunk.

My fingers still touch the rubber band of my slingshot, hidden in my pocket. They keep touching it. They tighten. Their touch is flexible and light. But suddenly it becomes hard. Right there, opposite me, the tawny body of the small animal stands still and waits.

Slowly, softly, I take out my slingshot. Without changing my position, I pick up a stone from next to me and put it in the sling. Only then does Artemis turn her eyes toward me, alerted by the shadow of my movement. At that critical moment, her eyes are filled with contempt and the certainty of my weakness: 'You can't do it! You'll never be able to! You'll never be a hunter.'

I pull the rubber band back and aim at the tawny target. At first my hands tremble, but then they become steady. I sense Artemis' eyes on me, still watching with the same contempt.

'You can't do it. You'll never be able to.'

The whole space under the foliage has become eyes, all the branches and all the leaves. 'You can't do it.'

In one final effort, I pull back the rubber of my slingshot. The stone flies. I don't expect anything. And yet for that slightest of moments, how clear everything is, everything is a vision! Through the azure air, I follow the hard substance that leaves my hands and shoots like a bullet. My heart beats so hard, almost breaking, until its turmoil takes over, and I close my eyes.

'Ahhhh!'

I hear Artemis let out the piteous cry. I hear the noise she makes as she stands up and rushes forward. What happened? I jump up too and run to the place under the tree where Artemis runs. What happened?

The tawny little animal, struck in the head by the stone from my slingshot, is squirming on the ground. A little blood runs from its wound — it gives a strange accent to its sleek fur. At first I don't understand. I could not have imagined or expected it. But as soon as the amazement of the moment passes, I feel the wave swelling, I feel a wild joy in shouting:

'You see, I *am* a hunter! I killed it! I killed it!'

At that moment, Artemis rushes at me. She has never been so wild. She scratches my face with her fingernails and hits me with her fists. She is beside herself, shrieking:

'You brute, you brute!'

I don't understand and try to defend myself, crying:

'What do you want? Look, I'm a hunter! Look, I killed the weasel!'

'Brute! Brute!' she keeps shrieking. 'The poor little animal! The poor thing! It was just standing there and didn't know...'

Finally I gather all my strength and push her so violently that she falls on the ground. She makes no effort to stand up, but stays where she fell. Her face is pressed on the ground, near to where the weasel lies, now dead, no longer squirming. The blood runs slowly from the open hole and drips onto the earth drop by drop. Drop by drop Artemis' tears flow and water the earth.

A long time passes. Artemis doesn't move. I sit apart and look away. Slowly Artemis puts her hand on the dead animal. She strokes it lightly, as though she is afraid to wake it up. She looks at it. Then with her finger-nails she begins to dig the earth. First there is a layer of rotten leaves that keep the ground moist. Artemis removes the leaves and afterwards, when she reaches the fresh soil, she begins to dig with her fingernails until there is a shallow, hollowed out place. Artemis takes the tawny body in her two hands and places it in its grave. Then she takes new green leaves from a cyclamen plant and covers it. Afterwards, she puts the moist earth on top.

The sun has set. It is starting to get dark. Without speaking, Artemis gets up and takes the path home. She speeds up her pace and soon is running. The shadows thicken around us as though they are trying to take us with them. I run too, behind Artemis.

By the time we reached the farmstead, it was already night and everyone had begun to worry. When my mother saw the blood and scratches on my face, she asked in alarm what had happened to me.

I told her that I had climbed up a rock to find eggs in a bird's nest and had slipped and fallen. It was nothing.

END OF PART ONE

PART TWO

SYMPHONY OF THE DAWN

≫ Chapter One ≪

Winter of 1850. Night. In Scotland, in the region of Loch Lomand, the storm comes in waves from the frozen North Sea and tears over the trees and land. Not a light is seen keeping watch on this furious night to show that living creatures inhabit these parts. The people are lying low under their wind-beaten roofs. Surrounded by darkness, they hear the howling outside while Fear, the ancient divinity of the land, stands over them and oversees the story of their souls.

And yet one light, one single light, has not gone out tonight in the country of Loch Lomand. Sir Arthur Castibel is staying up alone in the library of his ancestral tower. Lying in an armchair in front of the large fireplace, he follows the shadows that come from the fire and dance on the walls. The years weigh heavily on his white-haired head. The shadows weigh heavily too. The only things left that can lighten this wintry loneliness and make it a little less painful are memories. They aren't memories of the outside world, of actual things. They belong to a journey that took place in an unmoving landscape: inside the four walls of the tower.

From birth, he was a sickly and weak child, and now it has been twenty years since he was overtaken by the paralysis that has kept him bound to his armchair since then. But within his sick body there stirred a strength that, fed on immobility, became in time like an ocean wave. It was the blood of his race and his ancestors that boiled inside him, the love of adventure, travel and life's difficult moments. Having no other outlet, this indomitable strength poured out from his books: out of books of voyages, stories of corsairs, memoirs of travels in foreign lands, and the logbooks of explorers. The paralyzed lord gradually learned to live the foreign stories as though they were his own, because he was ready to feel their true quality, the quality of intense passion. And so that weak frame, pinned to an armchair in Scotland, shared a perfect understanding with Magellan, Marco Polo, Bering, and Vasco da Gama. In his imagination, he travelled every ocean, carried out every act of piracy, discovered every mythical island. He lived all the adventures of the corsairs of the Empire; he crossed the Indies, the Red Sea, and further south he rounded Africa by the Cape of Good Hope. He had reached the Strait of Gibraltar and was about to complete his return voyage when temptation drew him in: he entered the Mediterranean. After everything he had experienced, after the fortunes of the oceans, this sea was like a lake, like a game. He planned to breathe its air for a short while and then go back out through the strait without worrying too much about this new sea. But confused winds blow in the Mediterranean, powerful currents flow. They drew him further down, further and further down, until they had brought him to the land of the Aegean, the land of myth.

Reader, you who asks what the imagined journeys of a paralyzed Scottish nobleman have to do with the story of Aeolia, with this simple story that tells of a land bathed by the Aegean, you will now understand the web that gradually envelops the stranger from a strange land. The man had come to Greece, and once he had entered the land of the Gods and Satyrs, the Naked and Azure Land, he was unable to leave it. He had sailed every ocean and had been able to leave every land he had reached because they all had something unfinished about them, something that wasn't complete. But Greece doesn't leave room for desire or chimera. Greece is the Chimera.

From that time on, Sir Arthur Castibel made Greece his life. He learned all her tales and discovered all the islands of her Archipelago. Where he travels most, almost every night, is to the islands of the Cyclades. The *meltemi* carries him with it; the waves carry him. He listens intently and hears the sounds that come from the depths: from the depths of time, from the depths of Myth. They tell of nymphs and satyrs, of gods with passions and weaknesses, fears and schemes — the only real gods who ever came to earth and understood man, because they were the most human. They made nature their friend — Thunder, Rain, Lightning and Wind — useful companions in their passions and their joys, not weapons for the oppression of man.

The waves tell on and on . . .

A SERVANT WHO ENTERED AT THAT MOMENT shook him from his thoughts. 'The young lord asks if he can come in,' he said, and he stood waiting for an answer. The flame which suffused the face of the paralyzed old man shone more brightly...

'Have him come in.'

The 'young lord' who came in was a youth about fifteen years old; a tall, blond boy.

'Shall we continue tonight, Uncle?' he asked, after greeting him.

'Sit near me, Robert.'

The boy sat on the floor at his uncle's feet. He leaned his head of fair, wavy hair against the armchair. The old man put his fingers on the young head and caressed it silently.

'Let's continue our journey to Greece,' he said.

And while the storm howled outside and the waves raged on the ocean, while trees fell, struck by thunderbolts, the serenity that comes from the Aegean's ancient days entered the wind-beaten Scottish tower and filled it with light and poetry.

> *I speak such mournful melodies*
> *shrill and heavy with falling tears,*
> *alas, alas, worthy of lamentations,*
> *though I live, I sing my eulogy.*
> *I beseech the mountain of Apia,*
> *O earth, you understand*
> *my barbaric speech.*
> *With my nails, again and again*
> *I shred the linen*
> *of my Sidonian veil.*[1]

Slowly, the storm outside abated; the wind died away, and the trees stopped groaning. Peace passed through the doors and walls; it came in and stayed. And from this peace came shadows that began to stir in the half-dark room. They were women. They were young women dressed in yellow chitons that came down to their feet. Their loose black hair fell over their bodies, while the Desert walked slowly behind them, close and unperturbed. They were suppliants pleading. But in their faces, the agony of supplication, passed through the distance of time and the space of poetry, lost its rending power, became inspiration. It lost its hard lines and

---

[1] Aeschylus, *Suppliant Maidens,* 112-12, translation Therese Sellers.

became only light. And the waves of the Greek Archipelago were moved; they walked beside the desert of Egypt, then they passed over the desert of Egypt — and everything turned blue.

The reading lasted for a long time. When the boy grew tired, he stopped reading. The suppliants slowly dissolved and left.

Then the storm returned, and again the roar of the wind could be heard howling in the forest.

'How strange all those things are,' whispered the boy. 'What strange fairy tales.'

Then, after a short while, he asked about Greece, as though he were talking to himself:

'But does this country still exist?'

The hand of the old Scotsman moved again through the boy's hair.

'It does exist, my child,' he said. 'That country doesn't die.'

'But does it exist in that way, like a fairy tale?'

'Yes, it exists like that, like a fairy tale.'

Then, after a while, the old man said:

'Lord Byron went there to die.'

He said that for an Englishman to be able to leave his island and go to another country to die, only to die, this magic must be alive.

Again he was silent. Then he said:

'You will go there some day, Robert. It is your destiny to go. It was not mine.'

And in the silence of the tower in Scotland, the paralyzed Scottish lord, closing his eyes, took the child and travelled. He described the journey to the islands of the Cyclades to him as though he saw it. The sea of the Archipelago is not a calm and expressionless sea. The *meltemi* always blows hard. The azure water drinks light from above, from the shining sky and the shining sun. And to dissolve this light, to set it in motion, to turn it into harmony, the sea summons the *meltemi*, and the waves are born. They are not great mute waves like those of the Ocean — dark forms that labour aimlessly — but small waves, fitting the country, just big enough to leap up from among themselves and balance the bare, austere, sharply cut rocks of the islands. The light strikes the rocks and they vibrate. The waves vibrate too, and the dolphins come out joyously to play with the foam. When evening comes, the sun goes to sleep behind the islands' mountains. It sets. Then in the distance, the forms begin to reveal their different layers with unexpected clarity. Where before there was only one line, a single mountain, the individual mountains' imposing forms are now visible, one behind the other. The first is drawn in a rich, deep colour, while the others in the background are still bright. It is as though for them the sun has not set, as though it were setting between them, going into their ravines to sleep.

'You will go there sometime, Robert,' whispered the old Scotsman with emotion.

⇒ Chapter Two ⇐

HOW A FISHERMAN'S DAUGHTER FROM MYKONOS
BECAME A NOBLEWOMAN IN SCOTLAND

Summer of 1866. The young man of that winter's night in Scotland is sitting on a rock on Mykonos. Entranced, he is watching the sunset in the Cyclades that the paralyzed lord, now dead, described to him with such clarity sixteen years ago. Delos is directly opposite.

Delos. Hera, enraged, was pursuing Leto, whom Zeus had fallen in love with, and who was about to become a mother from that illicit love. What should the king of the Gods and Men do to help his mistress give birth to their child in peace? What country should he take her to? Hera had spies all over the world. So Zeus thought to himself, 'What if I were to find an unknown island, a tiny island solely for that purpose: for Leto to give birth, and for my illegitimate children to be born there without fear?' He asked his friend Poseidon to help him. Poseidon thought about it. He remembered the small island that had broken off from Sicily and had been floating and travelling through the waters ever since. He ordered the waves to stop the traveller, and they stopped it. And the island went from being unmanifest to being manifest. It became Delos, which means Manifest. And Leto went and gave birth there to Apollo, the god of light.

Delos: an island for a god's love child. The stranger hears steps behind him. A small path passes that way, leading to the nearby well. Robert turns and looks. Through the golden light comes his fate, making strange harmonies, uniting the waves in the Aegean with those outside it, the waves of the Ocean. A strong, suntanned young figure is walking along. She is a brown-eyed daughter of the Aegean, ripened by the brine of the archipelago. On her shoulder, she holds a jug she is taking to fill with water.

Dazzled, Robert watches. What is coming through the golden light is a figure from this ancient, sacred land, lifted from the old vases that the earth preserved inside itself for thousands of years. And now she is walking and approaching, wrapped in the sea and the azure light.

She is coming. She has arrived. She turned and looked at the stranger. She looked steadily, deep into his eyes. Confident of her distant past and her history, she looked at him without fear. Then she smiled at him.

'Good evening,' she said.

'Good evening.'

Then the girl disappeared, running hastily down the path to the well.

The foreigner waited for her to come back. What is this thing that comes suddenly like a light wind, like the gusts that blow on the peaks of the Aegean islands and make waves where it was perfectly still? Delos. The little island that travels. Zeus stopped the island's journey to help Leto, whom he loved. He made it manifest, there opposite . . .

The shadows thicken with the approach of evening. The foreigner waits and waits. Then he hears her footsteps. It couldn't be anyone else's. From now on he would be able to distinguish those footsteps coming towards him from all the footsteps of mankind.

'Goodnight,' she says.

But he can no longer make out whether she is smiling at him.

'Goodnight.'

That night Robert stays awake and waits for the dawn. When dawn comes, he sets out and wanders around all day making inquiries. Towards evening he finds out which house the Aegean girl lives in.

He goes to her father, a fisherman of Mykonos.

He finds him cleaning his fishing nets and says to him:

'I'm not from here. I come from the British Isles and have much wealth there. I want to take your daughter as my wife.'

Confused, the fisherman of Mykonos leaves his nets and asks:

'Where did you see my daughter? How do you know her?'

'I saw her yesterday. Didn't she go yesterday, around sunset, on the path to the well to fetch water?'

The fisherman scratches his head. All the tricks and suspicions of his seagoing ancestors wake up inside him.

'Where did you, a foreigner, learn to speak our language? And how do I know what kind of a man you are? How can I give you my daughter to take to a faraway country? Let me think about this.'

'I will marry her no matter what!' says the Scotsman, with the stubbornness of his race. 'But think it over if you want to. I'll come back tomorrow.'

The next morning the Scotsman goes back and finds the fisherman.
'What did you decide?' he asks him, his eyes red from lack of sleep.
'Nothing yet. I don't know,' says the fisherman, trying to avoid giving a straight answer.
'Where is the girl so I can see her?' asks the foreigner.
'She isn't here now. You can't see her. Come tomorrow.'
The foreigner goes the next day. But the fisherman's house is closed. Not a soul is there. A neighbour who sees him says:
'He went on a long fishing trip. He went with his daughter.'
'They went on a long fishing trip? Has that happened before?'
'Of course, that's how it works. On our islands the fishermen don't stay in their own area year-round. They travel sometimes to one place, sometimes another, depending on the season and where the fish are, and depending on the markets. My husband is away now too. I think he's fishing in the waters of Crete.'
The woman from Mykonos talks on and on, looking at the foreigner out of the corner of her eye as though she's making fun of him.
'Tell me, my good woman!' He cuts her off and grabs her hands impetuously. 'Tell me! Did you by any chance hear where the fisherman and his daughter would go first? Here, take this,' he says and puts a gold sovereign in her hand.
'Why are you doing this, young man?' asks the woman, and her teasing expression vanishes at once. 'Why are you doing this?' she says and looks now with fear and pity for the passion that burns in the foreigner's eyes.
And after only a moment of hesitation:
'I heard they were going to Syros,' she tells him in a confidential tone. 'Take back your sovereign. Goodbye!'
Robert leaves two sovereigns with the woman and chases the fisherman and his daughter from island to island through all the Cyclades. The fisherman doesn't stop anywhere; he wants to save his daughter from the evil he thinks awaits her. It is not only the foreigner that pursues him. All the memories of the ancient people of the Aegean, passed down by word of mouth from generation to generation, are chasing him too. Memories of the corsairs who ravaged their islands, who killed their men or threw them in the galleys, who took their daughters and brought them to Anatolia and Arabia to sell as slaves. The memories

and the eras get mixed up. A foreigner, from you-know-not-where, comes without any warning and says to you: 'I'll take your daughter, the light of your life. I'll take her to the Ocean. You'll never see her again.' Isn't it the same as when there were corsairs? He says he's English. So much the worse. How can a poor fisherman from Mykonos take on England?

The fisherman keeps fleeing from port to port, trying to lose the 'pirate'. But he chases after them with stubborn persistence, with blazing eyes and an anguished heart. The fisherman sees the islands running out. He decides to make a leap and cross to the land opposite, to Anatolia. He crosses the sea and comes to the Moschonisia, the ancient Hundred Islands of Aeolia. There, at last, the 'pirate' finds him. The fisherman is alone in a foreign country. He has no more strength. The wedding took place in a country church in the Moschonisia.* The Scotsman took the girl with him, and they left for his country.

Since then, what stories they tell of the thrice-blessed life that the two of them lived, the foreigner from Scotland and the girl from the Aegean. Their love became legendary in the whole region of Loch Lomand. He didn't let her lose any of the magic that she brought with her from her bright country. He didn't teach her letters or anything else of the foreign world. That way, she stayed as simple and natural as she was when she came from the Aegean. And yet they said she had so much nobility inside her and was so strikingly beautiful, that she magically commanded the respect of all. They received her like a divinity, come from the land of Myth.

She had a son and a daughter. When the son grew up and married, he had a daughter. This daughter had blond hair and brown eyes, the eyes of the children of Greece. She loved horses, and all day long she rode around in the forest.

One day a foreigner passed through those regions of Loch Lomand. He had gone to England to study, and now that it was summer, he was hunting with his friends in the woods around the loch.

He meets the girl on horseback.

'Good day,' he says to her.

'Good day. Are you a foreigner?' she asks, seeing his black hair and dark face.

'Yes, I'm a foreigner. I'm from Greece. My name is Vilaras.'

'Oh, from Greece!' cries the girl in delight. 'I am too! Do you see the chestnut colour of my eyes? It is from Greece! I know how to speak Greek. My name is Doris.'

The Aegean isn't only light and sea. It enters men's hearts. First it is one beat, then another, until it becomes every heartbeat. It enters the veins and becomes blood. It burns the blood. It enters the memory, and from then on nothing can erase it until the hour of death. The Aegean always calls and beckons you.

That's how it happened that, after many years, the daughter of a Mykonos fisherman who had left for Scotland, sent back another girl to the waters of the Aegean that were calling her. So as not to leave her place empty, she sent back another girl of her own blood to the land of Aeolia: Doris Vilaras.

⋙ Chapter Three ⋘

DORIS

The hot days of summer have come. The sun sends waves of light to the Kimindenia and the olive grove. I always want to stay outdoors during the midday hours, close to the earth and exposed. This is the time when the sun burns and the season is living its greatest hour. I don't want to go out only in the morning or the evening when it's cool, but in the middle of the day. That way I feel that I'm living the summer deeply, that I'm becoming one with it. I am a molecule of its substance, of the earth, the leaves and the rocks, which, unable to absorb all the light inside them, send it back with a spasm that lashes their surface.

The ants and I live the great hours of summer together. Lying on my stomach, my mouth biting the black earth of Anatolia and chewing it, I watch them near their ant hole at their monotonous labour. A hawk, fixed to the sky, keeps watch for a lizard or a salamander, but she, unsuspecting, cannot foresee the journey on high that is being prepared for her. A frog, somewhere in the distance, cried out, then was silent. A camel caravan passed by. It added a few sounds, then was silent. Everything happens with a heavy, slow rhythm below the Kimindenia. Summer shows the true face of Anatolia.

I move a little and turn my head to one side. Something's happening. It's Artemis. She doesn't see me since I'm half naked, one with the earth. She comes cautiously out of the farmstead's big door and looks behind her as though she's doing something secret. Then she takes off at a run.

I jump up and run after her:

'Wait!'

She is startled and about to run away, but then she stops. She's wearing her best dress, blue with white polka dots. She has a red ribbon in her hair. She looks beautiful.

'Where are you going?'

She stands there for a moment as though she's preparing the lie she's going to tell me. But quickly her face recovers the proud expression that sets her apart from the rest of us children.

'She is coming today,' she says. 'I'm going to see her.'

'She is coming? Who is coming?'

'*She* is coming,' she says, 'the little mistress of the estate by the sea. The girl from the Ocean with the strange name. What did they call her? Doris.'

Really? Is she coming?

'And how did you find out?'

'The hunter told me. I saw him this morning on the path through the oaks. He had been on an all-night hunting trip for her.'

'And why do you want to go there?'

'I want to go!' says Artemis decisively.

'Do they know at home that you're going?'

No, they don't know. They wouldn't have let her. She is going secretly.

'And what if he tricked you? What if he's telling you lies?'

Artemis stamps her foot hard on the ground. The hunter with yellow stars never tells her lies. He never deceives her.

'Come, little roe deer,' he said to her. 'It will be like a festival today at our estate. I'll lift you up in my arms so you can see.'

'And what if grandfather finds out. What if our mother finds out that you went out alone like this? Do you know what they'll do to you?' I say to frighten her.

She comes close and looks me in the eyes. How beautiful my little sister's eyes are, so wild and determined!

'Will you tell them?' she asks. 'Could you?'

'Why couldn't I? I'm telling!'

'Tell! Tell them! Fink!' she screams furiously and turns her back. 'I'm going anyway.'

Artemis will go. How can she do otherwise? Come roe deer, he said to her.

I see her disappear with bounding steps down the path that leads to the estate by the sea.

'Bad girl!'

Should I go home and tell them? The hours pass. The sun is lower. The hawk doesn't keep watch anymore, and the salamander has closed the circle in the story of the heights. The day she was born, under a hot crag in the Kimindenia, her mother, the big salamander, said to her: 'Learn not to look up high, not to dream. Always look at the earth. The earth is our fate.' 'Why did she tell me that?' thought the little salamander to herself. 'Can't salamanders dream? Are they creatures that can only creep along and that's what they will always remain?' And yet, today her time came. And the little salamander ended her story up high, all illuminated with sun and blue, making a line that writhed as it ascended, hanging from the hawk's mouth. And so there: even for the creatures that creep along, there is sometimes hope; it exists outside of their will, in the powers of on high.

EVENING COMES. No one has wondered about Artemis yet. Grandfather and grandmother have gone out for their daily stroll and are sitting alone on their bench under the oak at the big door. Quiet steadily descends. It advances slowly with the shadows coming down from the Kimindenia. It drips into the earth and the trees.

Suddenly distant sounds disturb the calm.

'Listen!' says grandmother to grandfather. 'Where is it coming from?'

He strains his practised ear to find the direction of the sound in the air.

'It's coming from further down, from the sea. What could it be?'

They hear happy voices, the voices of people celebrating; they hear drums. Suddenly, over the sounds, a bright rocket shoots up impetuously, as though moved by an excess of passion.

'Oh!' says grandfather, 'that's a big celebration!'

And then it suddenly occurs to him:

'That must be it! Vilaras' son will have come from abroad with his foreign wife. That must be it.'

'Oh, do you think they've arrived? All the best to them!' says grandmother. 'May they be happy in our neighbour's house; may those good people be happy.'

And as they think about them, they recall the events that bound the Vilaras family to the neighbouring land.

'We spilt a lot of sweat over our land too,' says grandfather. 'But old Vilaras! Do you remember what the land he bought was like when he first came from Greece? Water, all water. And yet, they drained it.'

Vilaras had come from Greece as a young man many years before. Everyone learned at the time that he was from a rich and important family of fighters in the War of Independence.* He studied agriculture in Europe, and when he returned his father said to him:

'I gave you the means to become a man. You learned the science of the earth. Now you can be useful. Go to Anatolia and make your life there. There are Greeks there. You will be useful to yourself and to Greece. Go and teach the Christians what you learned abroad.'

The young Vilaras came to our area by chance. To establish a large estate and to work it with his expertise, he would have had to buy land from many different owners. It would have cost a lot, but then the work would have been easy. This didn't suit Vilaras. He had a demon inside him that told him to struggle. That's what he listened to. He bought up all the *ghiolia* for a song, all the infertile swampland that lay in the coastal area below the Kimindenia. He struggled for years. His hair turned white. But his estate came into being. It was the richest, noblest and largest estate in the region. A whole village arose for the men who worked year-round on his property. At the edge of the village, in the middle of a large garden surrounded by tall poplars, the Vilaras tower was built. He built it when he was about to bring his wife there. He went to his native land, to Athens, to marry her. Thisbe Vilaras was the daughter of a Phanariot* family, full of refinement and nobility. It seems that when she first came, Thisbe Vilaras suffered a lot before she got used to the isolation. The ploughmen heard her play that strange instrument with white keys for hours and heard the strange music that came out of it. The men of Anatolia understood nothing of those sounds, but secretly they sensed it: they contained suffering and homesickness. In the afternoon, on summer days, they'd see her sitting on the veranda for hours looking at the sea and the tranquil lines of Lesbos opposite.

'It's as though she were speaking to the sea,' they said. 'What is she telling it?'

Other times she'd sit there reading, bent over her book for hours on end.

'What's she learning from that book,' asked the villagers. 'Do sheets of paper have so much to say to a person?'

Once, a small French warship came and anchored there. They gave a large reception at the Vilaras mansion for the French officers. The next day all the ploughmen were saying with amazement:

'Did you hear? Our mistress spoke to them in their language. Imagine that!'

The next year an English ship came. Again there was a reception for the British officers at the Vilaras house.

The place was buzzing now:

'What is this! She was speaking to the English in their language too! Is it possible for a woman to know so much?'

Later their only child came, their son. Then the strange music tapered off and was heard very rarely. Then the years followed and did their work. Thisbe Vilaras adjusted.

'It seems the Vilarases have it in their blood to bring wives from far away,' said grandfather.

'Where do they say their daughter-in-law comes from?' asked grandmother.

'From far away. From England. I wonder how...'

'How what?'

'How she will get used to our country, this girl who comes from such a foreign land.'

'Thisbe Vilaras will teach her,' grandmother says. 'It is our lot as women to learn to get used to things. As long as...'

She hesitated for a moment. Then she said:

'As long as she loves him,' and looked at grandfather straight in the eyes as though she were confiding in him her own secret.

'Yes, Despina,' he says, and strokes her hand. 'As long as she loves him.'

By now it was the time when their evening journey ended. It was the time for everyone to go inside and close the big door.

I was there near them. I saw them stand up and my heart pounded. Now what would happen to Artemis? What had happened to Artemis?

Grandfather goes to the door. He stops. Grandmother goes inside. Grandfather stands there a little by himself. It is the time of his silent prayer; for the people, for the land, for the animals, and the day that has passed, blessed, and is done. He has finished. Now he is getting ready to close the door and bolt it. I hear his voice calling out loud, saying our names, the names of all the children, as he was in the habit of doing whenever we were staying at the farmstead.

'Anthippe! Lena! Agapi! Petros!'

Everyone:

'Here we are, Grandfather! Here we are!'

'Artemis!'

Only Artemis does not reply.

'Artemis! Artemis!'

'Where is Artemis?' asks our mother anxiously. 'Has any of you seen her?'

'Where is Artemis?' asks grandmother.

'Where is Artemis?'

I jump up and shout:

'I know where she is! She went to lie near a hollow tree on the path to the sea! She is waiting there for a nightingale to sing.'

And before they have time to ask me anything else, I rush out of the door.

'I'm going to call her. She's nearby!'

I run down the path to the sea. By now the stars are shining. It is a very clear night. It's a little cool, but my body is burning. Deep inside, at the bottom of my heart, a powerful tightness disrupts the calm rhythm of my heartbeat. The shadows, the trees, the solitude. I am scared. Where am I going? Will I reach the estate by the sea? It is so far away! I had only been that far once.

'Artemis! Artemis!'

A jackal howled in the distance, in the Kimindenia. A nightingale sang nearby, then was silent.

'Artemis! Artemis!'

At first I say her name to myself, then I call it softly, then louder, so that I can hear a voice, my own voice, and not be alone.

And gradually my voice is getting louder until it becomes a wail, until it becomes the voice of panic.

'Artemis! Artemis! Come here, Artemis!'

Come, Artemis. I give you my word, next time I won't leave you alone in the night. I'll come with you wherever you want, wherever the hunter with the yellow stars tells you. I'll never leave you alone again. Just let nothing to have happened to you now. Let nothing have happened!

Is that footsteps I hear? I freeze and strain my ears. From further down, from the direction of the sea, steps are coming. Who could it be? Could it be Artemis? What if it's some brigand or bogeyman? What if it's a ghost? My heart beats hard. Instinctively, I move off the path a little. I draw aside into the clumps of earth, the small ridges made by the ploughed earth. I kneel. And there, one with the earth, my eyes wide open, I watch to make out the shadows that move as the steps approach.

As soon as I recognized her, I jumped up.

'Ah!' bursts out a frightened voice.

'Artemis! Artemis! Is that you?'

I hug her and kiss her head with emotion. Her heart beats like a wounded bird.

'For God's sake, run!' I say. 'Everyone's in a state. What happened to you?'

She doesn't answer; she just starts to run. I run, too, alongside her. In the green light that the stars send down, I can make out her face; it is unspeakably silent and closed to the outside world, closed to me and to the stars.

'Why were you so late? What did you see down there?'

I try to get a single word out of her. Nothing. She only runs and doesn't answer.

Now the farmstead's blue walls can be made out. We're almost there. The austere mass of the great oak becomes visible.

'I told them you were after the nightingale,' I tell her. 'They don't know anything.'

'What nightingale?' she asks, out of breath.

'A nightingale. I said you went to hear it.'

She stops suddenly, takes my hand and looks me straight in the eyes.

'Really, you didn't tell them anything? You really told them about a nightingale?'

'Yes. I just told them about a nightingale.'

She starts to say something to me. I feel as though she's about to rush to me and throw her arms around me. But she doesn't do anything. She starts running again.

They are all waiting at the big door of the farmstead: grandfather, grandmother, our mother and my sisters. Artemis stops for a moment in front of that wall without saying anything, then she starts to go and run right past it.

'Where were you? Where were you?' many angry voices cry.

'Didn't I tell you?' I say loudly. 'She was listening to the nightingale.'

'Naughty girl!' says our mother. 'For grandfather and grandmother to have to wait for you here at this hour! Aren't you ashamed?'

She stands there sweet and upset, powerless to defend herself. She stands biting her lip not to cry. How beautiful she is now, because she has seen, she has lived, she has suffered. She is beautiful because she is coming from the exquisite story of the land near the sea where his voice beckoned her, his voice crowned with stars. She is beautiful from fear of the night, and from the voice of the nightingale.

Mother goes on and on.

'And wearing your blue dress! And your best ribbon in your hair! You're wearing them for that? For sitting on the ground at night in the hollow trees listening to nightingales?'

'Come, come, that's enough now,' says grandmother in a kindly voice. 'Come, Artemis, come, my child.'

She takes her by the hand. Then she changes her mind; she drops her hand and puts her arm around the girl's shoulders. They go slowly, the two of them, with their arms around each other. The chorus follows silently.

'Hush, little child,' grandmother says, and gently strokes her shoulder.

And then, as though she senses something:

'Now don't go and cry when you're all alone,' she tells her. 'Tomorrow, come and tell me about it when it's just the two of us. Tomorrow, come and cry by my side.'

The dinner table that night did not have a happy tone at all. Everyone was silent; grandfather most of all. Artemis wasn't there. She had said she wasn't hungry, and they let her go straight to bed.

When only grandfather and grandmother were left:

'What's going on with that child?' he said pensively. 'Do you know what the matter is?'

'She's thirteen years old now,' said grandmother. 'I think I know.'

A little later he said:

'We will have to help her. You will have to help her,' he corrected himself.

'Let's not speak of this anymore.'

LYING ALONE IN OUR ROOM in the dark, Artemis went back over the extraordinary hours that had passed.

When she arrived at the estate by the sea, she found it in a flurry. The whole village, all the ploughmen with their wives and children were gathered in the large garden talking in small groups. They were wearing their best clothes. The women had on brightly coloured dresses of yellow and red. The children were making a terrible racket. The young women, tanned by the heat of the sun and the sea's salt, ran to and fro setting the tables, preparing the food, and pretending to ignore the young men's teasing, and becoming more flushed the more they heard.

'They're still not here?'

'They'll arrive any minute.'

Every now and then, Thisbe Vilaras came out onto the large veranda, went down to the tables and checked on the preparations. Her white hair, done up with care, wreathed and illuminated her face.

'That's what the queen must be like, like our mistress!' said the girls, admiring her.

'Do you think they'll be much longer?' asked Thisbe Vilaras, wringing her hands anxiously.

'I sent our hunter up the avenue of poplars. As soon as they arrive he'll bring us word,' said old Vilaras.

'Did you hear?' said the girls. 'Andonis Pagidas' men are accompanying the newly-weds! The smugglers of Aivali are coming!'

'Why are the men from Aivali coming?'

'To honour our master, who stands by them. They're bringing his son and daughter-in-law.'

Artemis hides so that no one will see and recognize her, and her eyes search for the hunter. Then suddenly, galloping astride his little *mintili*, his white stallion, the hunter comes shouting:

'They're in sight! They're in sight by the poplars!'

There was a great stir. Everyone ran towards the garden gate. Old Vilaras, dressed in his black frockcoat, with Thisbe Vilaras at his side, came out onto the veranda. They looked around them. Dressed as they were, they stood out among the crowd of their men, who were all wearing their black felt trousers, and the women with their striking colours. The Vilarases stood motionless, side by side, smiling benevolently.

Then the shouts of the crowd stopped.

'Here they are!'

The procession was entering the long avenue of poplars. First, astride their horses, came the company of Pagidas, the bravest youths of all the smugglers of Aivali. Their cartridge belts were strapped around them, and their brightly shining rifles hung from their shoulders. On their head, they wore black velvet caps wrapped with colourful kerchiefs. They pulled hard on the bridles. And the stallions, foaming at the mouth, reared up before submitting to the terrible force that tamed them. There were about fifteen riders. Behind them, at some distance, came the newly-weds. The man was astride a gray horse, the woman, a white one. Her golden hair fell to her shoulders in tresses, and her face shone. Behind them, astride his cinnamon-coloured horse, came Pagidas himself. Silent and serious, he alone was unarmed and wore a kerchief on his head. He looked around slowly, sometimes to the right, sometimes to the left. Behind them followed the caravan, the camels laden with the newly-weds' possessions. The first *deves* — the first female camel — adorned with beads and shining bells, was enormous. She foamed at the mouth and all her bells rang. The bells on all the other camels rang too. The whole place was filled with their sound.

The smugglers, riding in two lines, reached the stone stairs to the mansion. There they parted, half stood to one side, the other half to the other. The youths and their horses that neighed and foamed became like a river. Through that river the young couple advanced. He dismounted first and helped his wife get down. He took her by the hand, and they walked up the stairs. Pagidas reached his hand out silently to a man near him. He took his rifle. The other men took down theirs. Old Vilaras embraces his son. The young woman bends down and first kisses the hand of Thisbe Vilaras, then falls into her open arms. Next she kisses Vilaras' hand, and he kisses her on the forehead.

'Welcome,' he says, 'to our land and to our country. Welcome, my children!'

A servant woman standing nearby holds a large silver tray with a pomegranate on it. Old Vilaras takes it and throws it hard against the ground. The pomegranate breaks open. Large red pomegranate seeds scatter about. At the same instant, Pagidas and his men fire their rifles with the muzzles turned up to the sky. The air fills with the gunshots and the frightened voices of the women.

'May you be strong and bound together like the seeds of this pomegranate that came from our land,' said old Vilaras with solemnity. Then, with his son and new daughter beside him, he turned to look down at the crowd. There was silence.

'I give thanks to God that He willed me to live to see this moment,' he said. 'I thank you too, who look after the happiness of my house. Eat and drink from what is mine for three days and three nights. I will give dowries of land to whichever of your daughters marry this year, and I will give a horse to the young men who take them. May this summer day be blessed!'

Then all the people, the young women, the men and the children, cried out:

'May you live a thousand years, Master. May you welcome your children with gladness! With gladness may you welcome them!'

Everyone settled down at the tables and started to eat and drink.

As if lost, Artemis goes around through the crowd looking for the hunter. She finds him in a corner priming his rifle. The fuzz that shades his upper lip is damp. He seems to be trembling, and his eyes blaze.

'Ah, it's you, is it?' he says. 'You really came?'

'You see, I came.'

'Did you come by yourself?'

'By myself.'

'Did you see? Did you see her?'

Sparks fly from his eyes.

'I saw her,' says Artemis.

'Did you see how beautiful she is? Like the angels in icons. And how well she rides!'

His eyes shine.

'I will learn to ride too,' says Artemis. 'It's nothing.'

The hunter grabs her with his hands around her waist and lifts her up roughly.

'Oh, where will you learn to ride? You will never be able to ride like her!'

Artemis shakes her legs and body hard, gets free of him and falls to the ground.

'Let me go!' she tells him. 'It's time for me to leave!'

'You're leaving? You haven't seen anything yet. Stay and see the men dance! Stay and see the camels fight! Stay and see . . .'

Doris appears again on the top step. Her husband is coming behind her, and behind him the old Vilarases. Doris has changed. Now she's wearing a white dress that comes down to her feet. Her hair is fresh and shiny, like cascading locks.

'Look at her,' says the hunter softly, dazzled by the white magic in the distance. Look what she's like .'

With that, he rushes to the veranda where Doris is standing. He passes between the revellers, holding his rifle in his hand while his kerchief with the yellow stars flutters on his head. He stops, out of breath, on the first step. He stands, turns and looks around. At the garden gate, entwined in a poplar tree, climbs an enormous rose vine. It has white roses. One rose, the largest, is hanging up high, begging to be picked, as though it was offering itself. The hunter lifts his rifle. He aims at the high stem. Doris watches with curiosity, everyone watches. The clean crack of the rifle is heard. The bullet flies with assurance, like an act of fate. The rose, struck in its stem, falls. The women screech at the death that passed over their heads. Voices full of admiration are heard from all sides.

'Bravo!' says Pagidas, without any expression on his austere face.

The hunter rushes forward, picks up the rose and places it in Doris' hands, while looking down at the ground.

'Thank you,' she says, and smiles at him.

She said it like that, '*efharisto*', in Greek. But the sounds were different in her mouth, like in the mouth of a small child who is first learning to talk.

Doris comes down the stairs and passes among the tables. The drums and bagpipes begin to play the harsh dances of the region. The sounds of passion and longing tremble in the air. As Doris passes, everyone stands up and drinks to her health. She smiles at them. She reaches the table of the smugglers. Only their leader stands up. He wants to look her in the eyes and to greet her. She looks at him evenly and intently. Andonis Pagidas makes as if to return her gaze, to look at her. And then everyone around him sees with awe: he, Andonis Pagidas, can't do it. He lowers his eyes to her hands. He raises his glass. She takes another glass and they clink their glasses. They drink. His men empty their rifles into the air joyously.

Old Vilaras gives the order:

'Let the camels begin! Let them fight!'

Then the whole crowd shouted:

'The camels are going to fight! The camels are going to fight!'

Everyone runs to the big open space next to the mansion. The Vilarases and Doris sit in the first row. Pagidas' men stand behind them.

And all around, in the improvised open-air theatre, shine the colours of the crowd.

'Now you'll see something you've never seen before,' says old Vilaras to Doris.

'I warn you, my child,' says Thisbe Vilaras, with the expression of someone who is bothered by this spectacle, 'what you are about to see is barbaric.'

'I come from a rough country that knows how to look things in the face,' says Doris. 'Is what I am about to see "Anatolia"?'

'One hundred percent,' says Vilaras. 'That's why I wanted you to see it.'

In the middle of the theatre, the drums begin, deep and slow, played by the *zeybek* drummers wearing short breeches above their knees. The first camel appears in the back. The camel driver is holding it by the bridle and begins to bring it in a circle around the whole theatre. It is an enormous animal, freshly groomed. Its coat shines in the setting sun. Around its neck it wears a red amulet from which hang small, jingling bells. They have put an expensive saddle on him, embroidered with colourful beads. He walks slowly and formally. Bits of foam fall from his mouth. From the other side comes the other camel, the rival he will fight. It is also led in a circle around the arena. As the two camels come close, the camel drivers holding them stop for a moment. The two proud male animals look each other in the eyes. A deep lowing comes out of their mouths along with the foam, and their heads shake nervously. The drums resound. One more time they pull the camels to make a second round of the theatre. Afterwards they hold one of them at one side of the circle and the other opposite.

Then they bring out the female camel. Next to the huge male camels, the female seems ugly and miserable. And yet it is for her sake that they will fight. First they bring her close to one male and leave her there for a minute for him to smell her. The male stomps his hoofs nervously and shakes his head. Then they take the female and bring her to the other male. The same again. Then back to the first one. And again. The dark force floods their veins and blood; it floods their trembling hides. Then they put the female in the middle of the open space and bring the two males close to her from one side and the other. They hold all three tightly by their bridles. The males are trying with all their might to break free and charge. The drums play maniacally:

Doum! Doum! Doum! Doum! Doum!
Doum! Doum!

The dark voice has reached its limit. It can't hold out anymore. The foam runs continually from the mouths of the two males. The drums resound. For the last time they inflame the males by bringing the female in front of the nose of one and then pulling her away abruptly to take her to the other while the first is lowing. The drums resound.

Then they abruptly pull the female from between them. They drag her away and hide her. The drums are suddenly still. There is a deathlike silence. The two males are let free. One looks at the other. Then, with maniacal rage, they rush upon each other. It is a terrifying and savage battle; it is the culmination of instinct that rages and bellows. It is the dark divinity of Anatolia that knows no measure, that knows only passion, leavened with foam and blood.

Covered in blood and utterly exhausted but still savage, with only a little needed for death to come and finally silence the passion — only then do they pull apart the two males who fought and spilled their blood but were not satisfied.

'I warned you, my child,' says Thisbe Vilaras to Doris. 'It is barbaric.'

But the brown eyes that came from the Ocean are bright and wild. Her whole face shines.

'I liked it very much.'

It has started to get dark. Everyone hurries back to the laden tables and the celebration. The girls' cheeks are flushed, and the young men watch them darkly. The bagpipes and the drums begin to play again, breathlessly and hard. The sound trembles under the leaves of the trees where large lamps with coloured glass have been hung.

Where is the hunter with the yellow stars?

Artemis, upset, alienated, alone, looks for him in vain.

Suddenly, a clear and bright voice is heard from up high. It silences all the others. Everyone turns their eyes upward.

'Who is it? What is it?'

Only Artemis recognizes the voice at once. But where is it? Where is it coming from?

It comes from high up, from the highest poplar in the garden. Hot, inflamed, it passes through the leaves, through the air, through the people to bring its message. But the message is not for Artemis. It is not.

'For my little lady who came from abroad!' shouts the voice from high up.

And he immediately lights the first rocket and lets it fly. It is a violent line of light that flies out of the tree and rushes to meet the stars.

'Bravo!' shrieks the enthusiastic crowd from below.

'Another for my lady who came from abroad,' comes the voice from the poplar tree, and a second rocket explodes.

Artemis is a shadow that wants to disappear. With frightened steps, her small heart trembling, she emerges from the sounds of the crowd, and alone in the night, she takes the path homeward, while behind her the rockets merge with the stars.

WHEN WE CHILDREN WENT UP TO BED that night, we found Artemis motionless. It seems she has fallen asleep. I sink into my bed, which is next to hers, and I close my eyes. But sleep doesn't come. What did Artemis do down there? What did she see? What did they do to her? I am overcome with boundless rage. My nails dig into my palms. I hate all the hunters of the world.

Quite some time must have passed. All the other children have gone to sleep.

Then I hear the faintest of sounds coming from Artemis' bed. There is half-darkness. A small oil lamp burns before a triptych of the Panagia that is in our room to protect us. Artemis gets up very slowly and comes near me, walking on her tiptoes. She thinks I am asleep. I hear her breath.

She leans over and kisses me on the forehead. Then I reach out my hand and take hers.

She is startled.

'Oh, you're awake!' she says.

'What is it, Artemis?'

'Nothing. Nothing. I just wanted to tell you that . . . you, Petraki, you are the only one who loves me.'

≋ Chapter Four ≋

A JOURNEY INTO DREAMS AND TO THE STARS

Agapi is fifteen years old this year. During winter in the town, she goes to the classes for older students at the girls' school. She's a thin girl with dark hair, a pale face and plaits; and she's clever. She sits alone for hours reading and solving problems. This year she did cosmography and algebra for the first time. Numbers became her passion. Ever since she was little, she never liked to play with us; the older she gets, the more she avoids us. She doesn't know how to play with dolls or toy boats. She is withdrawn and melancholy, with large, dark eyes full of daydreams. She always liked to look at the stars, but now that she's learned to use cosmography to bring the stars down onto paper and measure the distances between them, it's gone to her head.

I say to her:

'Do you see what I brought here? They're eggs from a hawk's nest. Do you know how to find a hawk's nest in the Kimindenia? And are you brave enough to take its eggs?'

Artemis says:

'Why are you asking her? Of course she couldn't. She can't do anything.'

I climb up high, following the bed of the Jackal River that comes down from the Kimindenia. I know the place where the tortoises are: where they come to feed, and where they have their young.

I choose a small baby tortoise with a shiny yellow shell and bring it to Agapi.

'Take it!'

'Leave me alone!' she says with annoyance. 'You horrid boy! What are you going to do to it?'

She knows what I'm going to do with it. I want to have it during the winter at our house in the town. I turn it upside down, put it on the ground and weight it down with a stone. The small, defenseless being, sensing the terrible death that awaits it, sticks its little head and legs out of the shell and waves them in the air. But who will take pity on it? I'm beginning to enter the phase when children, following the traces of the world around them, don't have mercy, don't know how to feel pity.

'Tomorrow I'll take it to the wild boars' cave. That's where it will die,' I say.

I follow the hares' tracks. I know how to find them. One day I come across one of their grass nests. I come back triumphant. I'm carrying a small baby hare.

'Look at this!' I shout to Agapi. 'This is something that even the greatest hunters would have trouble finding.'

Even though she's so grown up and shouldn't need to compete with me — so much younger — Agapi feels the need to defend herself. She wants to preserve her pride.

She says to grandfather:

'How many stars are in the sky, Grandfather? Do you know?'

'Who knows that, my child? I, for one, don't know!'

'I know!' cries Agapi, and her dark eyes grow larger.

'You know how many stars are in the sky? How can you know?' he asks, smiling.

'I learned it from my books! Listen, Grandfather.'

And she starts spreading out her calculations in front of him. She tells him:

'This is how many stars there are. This many.'

The old man's smile is gentle and accommodating. There is no show of irony.

'Why shouldn't it be that number?' he says. 'If that's how Agapi wants it, that's how it must be.'

'And do you know where the North Star is, Grandfather?' says Agapi, referring to Polaris. 'You must know that.'

Yannako-Bibelas knows the North Star. He has consulted the stars on many, many nights of his life in the Kimindenia. He has consulted them about rain and wind, and to divine their messages, to know if the trees will bear fruit in good or bad weather.

'But Grandfather, do you know how far the North Star is from the earth?'

'No, Agapi. That I don't know. Who can know that?'

'I know!' says the girl, her eyes flashing. 'I know how to figure it out!'

She does her calculations again, her cosmographic charts, and again she comes up with a number.

'That's what it is!'

Grandfather smiles again obligingly. But he is thinking to himself. He is simple, illiterate and wise. He reflects:

'Why do they teach children to leave the earth? Why do they teach them to fly to the clouds? And what will happen when that time comes that they need to return to earth?'

'As for me,' says Artemis, 'I want to have a yellow silk dress. When I grow up, I will wear all yellow — not lemon yellow, canary yellow. I will wear chaste tree blossoms in my hair. My hair makes waves. I will put chaste tree flowers in the waves of my hair.* When I get married, I'll take my husband with me and we'll go to the islands of Greece. One day I'll fall into the sea, just as I am, all in yellow, with the flowers in my hair. My husband will throw himself in at once and pull me out of the water. But the flowers won't be in my hair anymore. They'll float on the waves . . .'

'Why should I go to the islands of Greece and fall into the waves?' says Lena, the youngest of us all. 'I'll stay here and get married. I'll tell grandfather to give us the land that's near the Jackal River. The soil there is red. The sun sets more quickly there, falling behind the mountains, and the temperature is cooler. I'll learn to knead bread dough and make well-risen loaves. And we'll have rabbits, doves, and horses. I want to be like grandmother.'

Lena speaks of her dream, and the roses in her cheeks bloom even more from joy than from health.

'I will go beyond the islands of Greece,' says Artemis. 'I will go to those seas they say are always covered in fog. I'll go to places where there are lots of deer. I'll go deer-hunting there with my husband.'

'What kind of work will your husband do?' asks Lena. 'Mine will be a man of the land. He'll know how to sow seeds better than anyone else in the area. He'll know how to graft trees like Uncle Joseph and make good fruit come from wild olive trees and wild pears. What will yours do?'

'He'll be a hunter,' says Artemis.

'Stay with us, Artemis,' pleads little Lena. 'Why should you leave here? Why should you want to go to a country with deer? Here in the Kimindenia we have wild boars.'

'It's what I have to do, little Lena,' says Artemis, and her eyes look far away, in the direction of the sea. 'I'll go to the islands of the Ocean to see what that place is that she came from . . .'

It's what she has to do. She will go to see what this place is that makes girls' hair look like cascading water, girls who inspire hunters with yellow stars to pluck roses for them with their rifles and climb high poplars to hurl rockets into the night.

'Who is the one you're talking about who came?' asks Lena, confused.

'Oh, you don't know,' Artemis answers. 'Poor thing, you are so young . . .'

OUT OF BREATH FROM RUNNING, I come upon them suddenly — Lena, Agapi and Artemis — telling their dreams for their futures. It isn't midday yet. Artemis is torturing a cicada she's caught and pulled one wing off. She's tickling it on its belly, while it continues to chirp. Lena is kneading mud; she makes it into a loaf and puts it into her small earth oven. Agapi is writing numbers on a piece of paper with a pencil.

'I saw her!' I shout, with a triumphant voice and bright eyes. 'I'm telling you, I saw her!'

Only Artemis guesses. She turns suddenly and looks at me searchingly.

She's the first to ask:

'What did you see?'

'I saw *her*! The one who came from foreign lands. How beautiful she is!'

'Where did you see her?'

I tell them in a rush: she was coming back along the path through the wild oaks. It seems she had been hunting in the Kimindenia. She was dressed strangely, like a man. She was wearing leather riding breeches and a red leather jacket; her cartridge belts were wrapped around her waist. She was astride a white stallion and was holding her carbine rifle together with the reins. She had a hard, white hat on her head with a wide brim. Her blond hair fell over her cheeks.

'And how does she know her way around our mountains?' asks Artemis. 'How did she learn about the paths through the wild oak forest?'

'But she wasn't alone, Artemis! She was . . .'

'She was . . . ? '

'Of course! She was with him, the hunter with the yellow kerchief.'

Artemis' fingers slacken and open. The captive cicada struggles to fly with its one remaining wing but can't; it drags itself along the ground and escapes.

Lena stops baking her little loaves out of mud.

She asks:

'Is it true that she's beautiful, Petros?'

'Oh, I can't tell you how beautiful!'

'I want to see her,' says Lena indifferently and again bends down over her game of housewife.

'They'll come and pay us a call some time,' says Agapi, in the same indifferent tone of voice. 'If I can, I'll show her my exercise books.'

And she leans back over her paper and the numbers.

'As though she would want to see them!' says Lena, mockingly.

Only Artemis is silent. She looks at her fingers, open and empty without her cicada. How sad her eyes are! I am disappointed at how small an impression my news has made on them. And yet my own cheeks are burning.

'And do you know what? I hid and saw what they were doing.'

'Stop bothering us, Petros!' says Lena, annoyed because one of her little loaves broke in the palm of her hand and fell apart.

'What were they doing?' asks Artemis.

I tell her. I tell how, as soon as I saw them, I hid without knowing why. It was where the grave of the weasel that I killed is. Does Artemis remember? When they got near me she said: 'Let's stop here for a while. It's beautiful.' I heard her voice and understood the words, but she spoke differently, very differently. The hunter jumped off his horse. He ran and caught hold of her, helped her dismount. She took off her hat with the wide brim and lay down on her back. She closed her eyes. The hunter sat down beside her cross-legged, and all the while his eyes never left her. At one point her hands began to idly dig the earth a little. I wanted to shout out to her: 'Not there, that's where Artemis buried the weasel.' But they weren't speaking, not a word, and I was afraid even to breathe out loud for fear they'd notice me. A little time passed. 'Let's go,' she said, and stood up. He wanted to help her to mount, but she said: 'I don't want any help. I know horses as well as you do.' They mounted their horses and took off. How beautifully she rode! How beautiful she is!

'Aren't I prettier, Petraki?' asks Lena. 'Look at my cheeks!' And she smiles naively.

'What nonsense!' says Agapi.

And right away, not having anywhere else to display her knowledge at that moment, she says:

'Listen to something! It's like a riddle! Can you figure it out? Let's say there were some jackals and some wild ducks here, all mixed up. Together they have twenty-three heads and fifty-six legs. All right, can we find out how many jackals there are and how many wild ducks?'

Lena, finding it strange at first, listens to the riddle and tries to think about it, but gets confused right away. She has a comical, naive expression on her face. She says a random number and then another. But Agapi shows her that the heads and feet don't match up with the numbers that she tells her.

'Look how I'll work it out,' says Agapi, excited that she has a rapt audience.

She starts to write strange signs on her piece of paper, her simple algebraic equation, the knowledge of the few years by which she surpasses us.

She writes, articulating her reasoning out loud:

$$\chi = \text{wild ducks}$$
$$23 - \chi = \text{jackals}$$
$$(23 - \chi)4 + 2\chi = 56$$
$$92 - 4\chi + 2\chi = 56$$

Agapi stops for a moment to think. Absorbed, she says her calculation out loud again:

'Ninety-two minus four χ plus two χ equals . . . Ninety-two minus four χ . . .'

Then Artemis jumps up and rushes at her. She snatches the paper from her hand, makes it into a ball in her fist and throws it on the ground angrily. She's never been this wild.

'You fool!' she screams at Agapi in a rage. Then, to get away before she starts to cry, she rushes down the path that leads to the wild oaks.

Lena's hands have dropped to her sides, and her kind eyes are filled with utter amazement as she watches our sister go. Motionless, I watch her too.

'What's the matter with Artemis?' says Lena with sudden gravity.

'Nasty girl!' cries Agapi angrily. 'You're a beast and you'll always be one!'

'What's the matter with Artemis?' murmurs Lena to herself again, incapable of guessing.

'She's jealous of me!' cries Agapi. 'Don't you get it?'

She retrieves her crumpled paper from the ground and unfolds it. She smooths it out to make it flat.

'Come, Lena, come and see.'

Again she begins to lay it out, uttering out loud the incomprehensible symbols:

$$- 4\chi + 2\chi = 56 - 92$$
$$- 2\chi = - 36$$
$$2\chi = 36$$
$$\chi = \frac{36}{2} = 18$$

'That's it!' cries Agapi triumphantly. 'There are eighteen wild ducks, which have thirty-six feet! And there are five jackals, which have the other twenty feet. Do you get it, Lena? Do you get it, Petros?'

'Oh, leave me alone!' I say from where I'm sitting watching the flickering sun.

'Do you get it, Lena?'

But Lena has fixed her eyes on the Kimindenia as though she is trying to grasp what she can of an unknown world whose existence, by intuition, she is just now beginning to suspect.

'What's the matter with Artemis?' she keeps murmuring. 'What's the matter with Artemis . . . ? '

Agapi's voice, softer now and more desolate, falls into a void:

'χ is equal to . . .'

THAT NIGHT THE JACKALS HOWL. Their familiar voices, the wild divinity of our mountain, comes from way up high. Memories and fears surround me. Who can I talk to? Artemis is sleeping next to me. Should I share my thoughts with Artemis as I always did? 'Artemis, listen to them! They're coming! The voices are coming. Protect me! Come here to me. Come so I can protect you. We always helped one another . . .'

That's what I would like to say to her. But I don't say it. What has happened to me? Artemis is disappearing. She is becoming air. In her hair she's wearing a wreath of chaste tree blossoms and lilies from our seashore. And she leaves like that. The voices take her with them; the howls take her. No, tonight I can't hold Artemis. I don't want to keep her from going. The head adorned with chaste tree blossoms dissolves slowly in my clouded eyes. And where the beach lilies were, now there is cascading hair.

'I will remember you. You who came from far away. Don't go by yourself into the Kimindenia. Listen! It's the jackals howling. We have a lot of wild animals in our region. They could tear you to pieces. They will know that you are foreign and helpless, and they will tear you to pieces. How can the hunters help you? Don't go alone into the Kimindenia, don't go with them. Take me with you . . .'

In the lamp light, I see Anthippe standing over me. Woken up suddenly, I rub my eyes.

'Who are you talking to?' says our big sister.

'Was I talking to someone?'

'It was a dream, my boy. Go back to sleep, don't be scared . . .'

'I'm not scared, Anthippe.'

'Yes, my boy.'

GRANDFATHER PUT ON HIS EXPENSIVE FELT BREECHES, and grandmother wore her black silk dress with a high collar. She fixed her hair beautifully. There are little curls over her forehead.

'Why did grandfather and grandmother put on their best clothes?'

'They're going to the estate by the sea. They're going to welcome the newly-weds who arrived and give them their blessing.'

They sent their present in advance. It was a small white calf with brown spots. Around its neck they hung blue glass beads, and on its forehead they put a talisman, a heart embroidered with small stones. They also sent a basket of fruit and a basil plant in a pot.

They yoked the best white horses to the *dalika*. They lay a thick kilim inside. Grandfather got in first, then grandmother. The *dalika* with the white horses set out. All us children stood at the gate and saw them off.

When they came back, grandmother said to mother:

'The poor girl! Her husband has already left.'

'Her husband left? Where's he going?'

'He went to Greece. He had to do his military service. Now the girl will have to get used to our mountains by herself.'

'What a shame!' said the young woman.

'What a shame!' said the other.

⋙ Chapter Five ⋘

I left early in the morning. I set out on the path and go deep into the land of the wild oak trees. I'll stop here. From here I can hunt mountain birds with my slingshot, sitting down. Above me our blue sky shines. The earth is dry. It is red earth, sprinkled with leaves and acorns: the earth that Lena loves. I'll dig it up a little. I thrust my nails in and dig hard and long until they find coolness. Let me take aim at that passing bird. The slingshot lets the stone fly. But the bird escapes, and the stone vanishes into the blue heights. I watch it disappear. Ah, this is the best game: to shoot without a target into the azure depths and measure which stones go the furthest, as we do when we skip stones over the sea.

'Will she pass by today...?'

The hours pass. This year, when winter comes and we return to the town, I'll go and find my father in his study, there where he shuts himself in the evening to go over his work.

'Haven't I grown up a lot, Father?'

'You certainly have grown up a lot, Petros! You're ten years old!'

'Well, Father, I need a gun. I have to become a hunter.'

He'll look at me strangely. He has blue eyes and always wears gold-rimmed glasses. I'm very scared of the eyes of people who wear glasses. You can't see into them clearly.

'Did you say you wanted to be a hunter? I hadn't realized that's what you wanted to be.'

'No, Father, you hadn't realized it. But that's how it is. I didn't know it either. But I *must* become a hunter.'

Will she pass by today?

I hear the hoof beats of two horses. My heart starts to pound. Why is that? For a moment, it occurs to me to hide. But I don't make it in time. They catch me there, sitting down with the band of the slingshot in my hands.

The foreign girl says to the hunter:

'Who is this child? What's he doing here by himself?'

'Oh, he's from the neighbouring estate. He's the grandson of Yannako-Bibelas.'

And then, turning to me:

'Say good day to my mistress!' he says, in a tone which is both commanding and patronizing.

I am not used to being spoken to in this way by any old hunter I don't know. I tighten my fist angrily around my slingshot and look stubbornly at the ground.

Doris takes a few steps with her horse and comes close to me.

'What a beautiful slingshot!' she says. 'Have you shot any birds?'

Then for the first time I turn and look her in the face. The azure light of our sky above her head dissolves. In its place only golden light remains.

'No,' I tell her shyly. 'Today I wasn't hunting.'

'Ah, so you are really a hunter?'

'I know how to shoot birds,' I tell her, gaining courage. 'And once . . .'

'And once?'

'It was a little while ago. I killed a *nyfitsa!*'

'A *nyfitsa?*' says Doris, not knowing what the word means. 'Is that a wild animal?'

The hunter laughs wholeheartedly, and again I feel the wave of hate for him boiling inside me.

'It's not a big wild animal,' I tell her. 'But it lives in our woods.'

'Ah! And you do all that with your slingshot? You don't have a gun?'

What should I say? Should I tell her that when winter comes I'll go to my father, shut in his study, and I'll beg of him: 'Look how I've grown up . . .'

'Let's go, my mistress,' says the hunter to Doris, as though he wants to be done with my little story.

Then my pride, which runs through my blood like light through air, rushes out and shouts.

'I don't have a gun,' I say to her. 'But I know how to find eagles' nests in the Kimindenia that he doesn't know about. He only knows how to kill wild boars. Do you want me to find you eagles' nests?'

And before she has time to laugh, before they have time to laugh, I say:

'Take me with you, and you will see!'

It seems that fire is burning in my eyes. Doris loves eyes that shine. She looks at me in surprise.

'Really, little boy? Do you know the eagles' nests that are in your mountains?'

'Take me with you!' I say, pleading with her. 'Take me and you will see!'

'Come on, then!'

And turning to the hunter:

'Take him on your horse!' she orders him.

No! I'm not getting on that horse, not his horse. I'll go by foot. I can run like a hare.

'What a strange child!' says Doris. 'Come, get on my horse!'

I jump onto her horse and sit astride the saddle in front of her. In front of me are her hands that hold the reins; a little beyond is the horse's head; a little beyond that is the green sea: the wild oak trees. And behind me, pressed against my back, is the warm body wearing cartridge belts and crowned with cascading hair. It comes gradually: a numbness that flows from that other body passes over me, passes through me. Everything is moving, everything is shaking: a horse's head, two hands, and a green sea . . .

'Hold on tight!' shouts Doris and kicks the horse, letting the reins out free for him to run

At first the horse runs slowly, then suddenly he charges like lightning. I tighten my fingers' hold on the horse's mane. The hot wind beats my face and the trees disappear, the lines and the shapes vanish, everything is waves. And behind me Doris' hair, blowing in the wind, becomes waves.

Suddenly waves of clouds fill the sky too. They burst from behind the Kimindenia, mute and dense. The sky has turned black. A storm is coming!

Summer storms in the Kimindenia are terrifying. The startled birds hurry to find cover in the hollows of rocks or in their nests. Their shrill cries can barely be heard over the thunderbolt that booms high in the mountain.

'Let's turn! Let's turn back,' shouts the hunter. 'The storm is going to break any minute!'

I hear Doris' heart beating. The beating passes through my back and runs into my body. At one moment I turn back and look at her as we gallop furiously. Wild delight shines in her eyes, the lightning that breaks in the Kimindenia shines in her eyes.

'I know where we'll take cover!' I shout to her. 'In the caves where the eagles' nests are! Don't stop!'

Doris doesn't stop, and the hunter, like it or not, gallops after us. Doris must be thinking: where is this boy taking me in the height of a storm? Close to the nests of fierce eagles sitting on their eggs? That's what she must be thinking, because she doesn't know. She doesn't know what suddenly came into my mind to show her, something that surely neither she nor the hunter has ever seen before.

'Faster! Faster!' I shout, burning with excitement. 'Faster, so we get to the great eagle in time!'

The wind takes my voice and dissolves it, turns it into incomprehensible sounds.

'What did you say? What did you say?' I hear Doris' voice behind me as she tries to understand.

'Faster! Faster! You'll see!'

All the while the dark clouds are hurtling down from high in the Kimindenia towards where we are. But they still haven't reached us. I can imagine the rain that's beating the mountain like a waterfall higher up. But above us the sky is still clear. Soon. Soon the clouds will make it here.

Is it too late?

Wild birds fly all around us, screeching terribly as they rush in flocks to find cover.

Is it too late?

'Faster! Faster!'

We make a turn on the path. Now the two gigantic rocks I'm taking them to are visible: the eagles' domain. The horse is out of breath and has cut his pace a little. I raise my eyes to the sky anxiously. Above the two rocks, the sky is still clear. It will be for a little while yet. Did we make it? I fix my eyes intently on the crest of the cliff, there where I know that the eagles have their nest. It is still at some distance from us, way up high; I can barely make it out.

Suddenly my hands clutch Doris' hands violently, and with all my strength I pull on the reins. The horse stops short.

'Look!' I shout triumphantly to Doris, pointing high above the cliffs with my hand. 'Look there!'

First I look at her eyes, then I look at the cliff. Her eyes are burning from the lash of the wind. They are not brown anymore, they are gold.

'What is it? What is it?' she cries, not comprehending.

'Don't you see? Don't you see the great eagle rushing to get above the clouds during the storm!'

Majestic and precipitous, a large spot detaches itself from the rocks and rises like a bullet against the deep backdrop of the mountain.

'What did you say?' asks Doris, not understanding.

'You see! You don't know about it!' I cry, shouting in triumph. 'But I know. I've seen it.'

I try to explain it to her in a rush. It is the great eagle's exquisite and unique game. When the other birds so much as suspect a storm, they rush in fright to find cover on land, in caves and in trees. The great eagle, and he alone, leaves his haunt and rushes to the sky. Is he going to hurl himself at the thunderbolt and the rainstorm? That's what I thought the first time I saw it, when I was watching the eagles during a different spring storm. But I asked Uncle Joseph, the wise old man at our estate.

'You saw that?' he asked me in amazement. 'You saw the great eagle at such a moment?' and he patted my head as though he were blessing me. 'I've only heard about it. No, my son, he doesn't go to hurl himself at the thunderbolt. He is taking himself above the clouds pouring rain to the place above, where the sun is still shining. Eagles love the sun. That's what they say.'

I try to explain all this to Doris, who is listening to me, radiant. Then I turn suddenly to the hunter with the yellow stars. I'm excited and happy, and every pore in my body is shouting with joy.

'Did you know that?' I say to him. 'Did you know that?'

Now Doris is looking at him.

'Did you know?' she asks him, and at the same time turns her eyes and fixes them again on the black mark in the distance, which keeps getting smaller and disappears in the sky as the storm comes closer.

'No!' says the hunter. 'This is the first time I've heard of it. What hunter sits watching what eagles do when a storm comes?'

He says this in a tone of voice full of contempt and indifference.

'So then you didn't know?' asks Doris again, and her eyes, fixed on the black mark in the sky, are flashing.

'No! I didn't know it!'

Then Doris impetuously takes my head in her two hands, looks me straight in the eyes and kisses me on the cheek.

'Will you teach me about other things like this, my boy?'

I am bright red with embarrassment. A strange confusion, a strange warmth . . .

'I don't know anything,' I murmur. 'What I know in our mountains, I will teach you.'

Doris laughs aloud, delighted. The first drops of rain are beginning to hit us. The hunter looks around. It seems he's never come to these wild places before. This is the domain only of the eagles. He hunts deer and bears and wild boars.

'Let's go under some big tree!' he says.

'No!' I shout. 'I know. I know where we'll take cover.' And I shake the horse's reins.

We go up towards the cliffs. There is no path, and the horses are making their way with difficulty. The storm is getting more powerful. Thunderbolts tear the clouds, making a furious noise that becomes even more terrifying as it hits the sides of the cliffs. But everything inside my small body feels warm and calm. A little further. A little further . . .

The landscape around us now is bare and wild, without trees, and covered by the black clouds. Not a soul can be heard, not the cry of a single bird. We are alone, astride a horse, Doris and I. Even the great eagle is high above the clouds and doesn't see us.

The horse stops in front of the two steep and enormous cliffs. There, at the base of the cliffs is the large vault of the cave. The downpour is hitting us now with unbelievable force.

'Here!' I shout to Doris, as the rain drenches me. 'We'll take shelter here!'

We dismount and pull the horse quickly into the cave. All is well. It is dark. The thunder roars frightfully through the cave. Our eyes, turned to the mouth of the cave, can't make out a thing, only the dull sheets of rain coming down. I am shivering. I put my hands under the horse's nostrils to try to warm them a little.

'If only we had a fire!' says Doris.

The hunter always looks her in the eyes like a faithful dog. He gets up and goes towards the mouth of the cave. He pauses a moment, then plunges into the storm.

He comes back soon, loaded down with branches and holm oak, dripping with rain water.

'They won't light!' I say resentfully, since he is going to do something for Doris that I didn't think of. 'They're too wet!'

'You be quiet!' says the hunter. 'They will light.'

He had a little trouble, but the fire took.

'Thank you,' says Doris, and lies down on her back.

Sitting next to her, the hunter on one side and me on the other, we stoke up the fire. The flame illuminates Doris' face in a strange way. Her hair has gone from gold to red. It's become waves of blood, like the leaves of bushes in the autumn.

'I only know about sea eagles,' says Doris. 'We have a lot of those in our country.'

'Does the sea have eagles?'

Indeed it does, says Doris. They also love the sun. As soon their young are hatched, the big eagles force them to look straight into the sun. Any baby eagle that can't endure it, whose eyes fill with tears from the light, they kill. They are savage birds. They can even get into a fight with an ox. They dive into the sea, and while they're wet they go and roll on the beach until their feathers are covered with pebbles and sand. Then they fall upon the ox, throwing sand into its eyes, while attacking it wildly and drawing blood with their beaks. The ox runs around stupefied, trying to escape, while the sea eagle keeps attacking him and blinds him, until he falls down, exhausted.

With eager eyes, overflowing with enchantment, I hear about the eagles in the land that Doris comes from.

'Is it true? Is that what your eagles do?'

'Our fishermen,' says Doris, 'have often seen eagles fighting with seals in the sea. They dive onto them furiously and drive their claws into their bodies so hard that they can't get them out. Then the seal dives under the water, dragging the bird attached to its body to a watery death.'

How strange all those things are! Doris' eyes rest on the dome of the cave without moving. The way she looks at this moment is like a child making a wish and dreaming.

'I would like to have a baby eagle to raise,' says Doris, as though she is talking to herself.

'Would you like to have a baby black bear from our mountains?' asks the hunter, hanging on her words. 'I know the big bear's lair in the Kimindenia. She will have given birth by now. I'll kill her and bring you her baby.'

'No,' says Doris. 'I don't want a bear. I would have to put a chain in its nose and lead it. I don't like wild animals that are chained and dragged around. I would like an eagle that wouldn't cry when he looked at the sun. I wouldn't put him in a cage. I'd teach him to follow me, flying high above my hair.'

Is it true? Does Doris want a baby eagle? My heart pounds. What, I wonder, has become of the eggs that the female eagle is sitting on in their nest up there? I know that was happening at the nest recently. I saw the great eagle flying around alone above their nest without his mate. I told Uncle Joseph. He told me that when this happens it means that the female is sitting on her eggs. But now it's been days since I last came here. Have the baby eagles hatched? And if they have hatched? And if . . .

The rainstorm is gradually moving off. The black clouds, after passing violently over us, are withdrawing now towards the west. The rain is diminishing.

The hunter stands up straight and shakes his arms to get his circulation going.

'I'll be gone for a moment,' he says, and goes out of the cave.

Doris is still lying on her back beside the fire with her eyes fixed on the dome of the cave. She's opened her jacket a little in the front since she's warmed up. The light passes through the scattered clouds, through the drops of rain and comes to rest on her skin. It's a strange light made of rain and blood. Ah, Doris should stay here, safe from the rain and the wind, and desire nothing. Whatever she might want should come here, to be placed between her and the fire — so that she might reach out her hand and take it. Even if you have to seize it from inside the eagle's nest, from the claws of its mother: a baby eagle.

I stand up, take a few steps towards the mouth of the cave and look up. There is nothing to be seen. The big eagle must not have come down from the clouds yet. Who knows? Maybe the female is away too. A few drops of rain fall into my eyes. I make the sign of the cross. Now, now is the best time!

I start to climb the huge rock. I grapple with the wild undergrowth that sprouts out here and there from the heart of the rock and keep going up. I was always afraid of heights. I don't turn and look down so as not to get vertigo. Behind me in the distance, I hear the thunder in the west as it rumbles and moves further off. The branches I'm grabbing are wet and slippery. They have sharp thorns. My hands are bleeding. Doris will sit beside the fire, and she won't know. I keep going up. Her eyes will glow strangely and she'll kiss me on the cheek.

'Thank you, my boy,' she'll say, and take the baby eagle I will give her. I keep going up. Will the female eagle be in the nest? Will she not be? Will the other eagle get there before me as he comes down from the clouds?

What a strange stillness this is that slowly starts to enfold me as the crowning moment draws near, the moment of danger . . . All around, the rain has grown silent. In the distance, the lightning from the storm only flashes; you can't hear it. The branches that break under my feet, and the rocks that roll down, fall without a sound, as though they lived in a silent world. I keep going up. What a strange stillness this is! Nothing exists anymore. Even Doris' hair, even her eyes lit by the rain and the fire, even they fade away.

For one moment, for one moment only, I turn and look up. Suddenly the silence is broken by a violent beat of my heart. There! Only a few yards away, there it is! The goal! The nest! I gather all my strength and grapple at the rock with my two hands and make the final effort. A little further! A little further!

'Ahhh!'

It is as though it comes from very far away, from very low down, the rending cry. Is that Doris shouting?

I don't have time to turn and look down. Above me I feel a powerful gust of wind: a flapping and a fearful shadow coming near me.

'Don't move! Don't move!'

I hear Doris' desperate voice coming from below. At the same moment I hear above me the savage cry like a dog's, the familiar voice of the eagle. A blurry shadow passes quickly before my eyes, and suddenly everything starts to tremble and blur. I know nothing now, nothing is holding me up. Barely, in that blurred chaos, just barely, I sense the metallic sound of a rifle, the shot that puts my own life in the balance as Doris shoots at the eagle, aiming just a few inches above my head. Then I feel as though everything is toppling down. As though I'm falling. I fall.

Below everything is dark.

MUCH LATER, WHEN I OPEN MY EYES, I see that I'm lying at the base of the rock. The hunter is standing above me, and Doris is bending over me.

She keeps wetting her handkerchief and cooling my brow. I feel a strong pain in my forehead. I try to bring my hand up to it and find that they've bandaged my head. Another cloth is beside me, drenched with blood. I'm afraid of blood.

'It's nothing,' says Doris, following my gaze. 'You hurt yourself a little. But look over there!'

I look towards where she's pointing. Shot down, the bird of the heights lies a little to my side, motionless, with his enormous wings folded. When the storm came, he rushed up high, just as his ancestors had done: he, the great eagle, alone among other birds. He did it so that no creatures of the underbrush might tell him later that he had been conquered by the clouds, that he couldn't find the sun when the earth had lost it. And so, wrapped in the sun, wrapped in triumph, he can lie motionless now. All the other eagles in the Kimindenia, when they learn, will say that he died like an eagle.

'What were you looking for in the eagle's nest and giving us such a fright?' says the hunter angrily. 'And with me gone, and my mistress all by herself! What if she hadn't seen you? What if she'd missed and hadn't hit the eagle with the first shot? What if she'd shot you?'

Doris turns and looks at him severely, gesturing for him to stop. I am just regaining consciousness, just beginning to remember. The time on the rock is coming back. I start to understand what had happened.

'Are you feeling better, my boy?' asks Doris, and her voice is so different, so tender. 'Can you ride?'

'Yes,' I tell her. 'I can.'

'We have to go back quickly,' says Doris. 'Don't be scared. You hit your head a little when you fell. You fell on soft ground. I'll take care of it.'

'How were you not killed, falling from such a height?' says the hunter.

The horse gallops as though possessed on the return to the estate by the sea. Now the sun is shining again. The drenched earth gives off a powerful odour. The cool light wind hits my face. Everything is clean. Everything is beautiful. Doris is behind me. The way she holds the reins in front of my chest, it is as though she is embracing me.

I will tell you, I will tell you, girl who came from the foreign land:

'I went to get you the little eagle that you wanted . . .'

The wind carries my voice away. Maybe she heard it, maybe she didn't. But I can't say it to her again. Her arms tighten around me more, and the wind that surrounds us is singing.

AT THE SEASIDE ESTATE, the Vilaras family were frightened when they saw us. The blood had seeped through the kerchief that bound my forehead. Doris took me quickly to her room and lay me down on a settee. She rolled up her sleeves, washed her hands carefully and then cleaned my wound and put on iodine and gauze.

'Rest a little,' she said, and went out.

In a little while she came back.

'Are you all right?'

'Yes,' I tell her. 'I have to go home to our house. I have to go to my mother.'

'I'll take you.'

She mounts again, takes me close to her and brings me to our farmstead.

It was midday and they had begun to worry. My mother let out a cry when she saw me with the bandage. All my sisters ran over. So did grandfather and grandmother.

'In the name of God! What happened? What happened? Is he seriously hurt?'

They all were seeing Doris for the first time dressed that way, like a man. Their eyes were dancing with fear and surprise.

'In the name of God, what happened! What happened, daughter?'

'Nothing! Nothing!' Doris calms them down. 'He slipped a little and fell. Where is his bed?'

She asks with assurance and holding my arm, she leads the way to where they point. All the others follow behind, as though she's the one in charge.

She singles out my big sister, Anthippe.

'I brought you bandages and gauze,' she tells her, 'in case you don't have any. That way, you can change the dressing. But let him rest now.'

I look at her one last time before she leaves. She looks at me too. I see her come close to me, lean over and, in front of everyone, kiss me on the forehead.

THE SAME EVENING THE HUNTER COMES. They bring him to our room where I'm lying.

'My little mistress sends you this,' he says. 'It's for you to keep.'

It's a small child's gun, a rifle. It had been at the estate by the sea since the time when Vilaras' son, Doris' husband, was a boy. This was the explanation that the hunter gave.

Among the cliffs in the Kimindenia, Night, the Deity of silence, descends, slowly. The stars come out. Beside the great eagle that lies motionless with open wings, the spilt blood stirs, the blood of the eagle. The earth took inside her as much as she could, together with the water from the rain. But one drop, saved upon a leaf, remained. And another drop from the blood of the boy, which had spilt during the storm, also remained. The body of the dead eagle separates the two drops; they are separated by his silenced feathers.

When night comes, the drops awaken.

'Come,' says the first — the eagle's blood. 'Come and let us go into the earth together.'

'No,' says the second drop — the boy's blood. 'I am going to wait for dawn. A wild bee or the hoopoe will come to take me. I want to soar into the sun.'

'As for me,' says the eagle's blood, 'I have lived the hour of sun. I have the sun inside me. Now I want to return to the earth.'

'We will meet sometime,' says the boy's blood. 'But not yet. It is not my time yet. I am waiting for the dawn.'

⇒ Chapter Six ⇐

The hunter is riding at a gallop when Artemis jumps out in front of him.

'Stop!' she cries.

The horse stops suddenly. The hunter's face has lost its usual calm. It is yellow like the stars on his kerchief.

'It's you, is it?' he says angrily. 'What do you want?'

'Take me on your horse!' says Artemis. 'I want to go to your mistress!'

And before the hunter has time to say anything, Artemis throws her arms around the horse's neck and leaps on like a deer.

The hunter helps her get astride in front of him. The horse takes off. He gallops at full speed.

'What do you want with my mistress?' Artemis hears the hunter's voice behind her ask. 'Did your family send you?'

'No, my family didn't send me!'

'What do you want with her?'

The summer wind, the *meltemi* from the sea, is blowing hard.

'What did she do to my brother?' shouts Artemis into the *meltemi*. 'What happened with my brother? I want to ask her.'

'And why don't you ask me? I was there, too.'

Artemis pulls suddenly on the reins.

'Oh, you were there too? You were with her again?'

She looks him hard in the eyes with a savage intensity. And he understands, the hunter who hunts wild boars and black bears in the Kimindenia, that he has such a terrible weight inside him that he can't even withstand the gaze of a little girl, not even the gaze of Artemis.

He lowers his eyes.

'I am with her every day,' he says. 'I go around in our mountains with her every day.'

And suddenly he seizes the reins and kicks the horse's belly with his feet to make it run.

Again nothing exists but the wind that beats their faces.

'What happened to my brother?' asks Artemis again in a savage voice.

'The eagle would have taken him and killed him,' says the hunter.

'The eagle would have taken him and killed him? What eagle?'

'Your brother wanted to raid the eagle's nest. My mistress killed the eagle. What she did, no woman in our country would have been able to do. If her aim had been off by even a little, she would have killed your brother.'

The sun is setting. The hunter's voice has a strange, deep tone. Artemis guesses that at that moment, the same deep expression is in his eyes. But she doesn't want to turn around and see his eyes that way. She could bloody his face with her nails to kill that expression.

They pass through the avenue of poplars.

'We're here!' says the hunter and dismounts.

He helps Artemis get down.

'Are you going?'

'I'm going.'

They proceed. There is a dense stillness under the imposing poplars. The only sound is the roar of the waves, lashed into turbid froth by the *meltemi*. They will wait for the night to come and take the wind from above them and bring the blue light of the Aegean at dawn.

Suddenly the hunter stops.

'Listen!' he says to Artemis, holding her back forcefully by the arms. 'That's her!'

The sounds are slow and weak at first, with strange pauses, then they are violent and hard. Doris is playing the piano.

'That's her!' says the hunter, and his eyes are clouded like the waves, while the fingers holding Artemis tighten around the girl's arm.

'It always happens at this time of day,' says the hunter. 'If she's not riding around the Kimindenia, she is playing her instrument. Nobody's allowed to see her now. She wants to be alone.'

And then:

'You'll have to wait,' he says to Artemis.

Silently, they go below the window from which the sounds are coming. They sit at the base of a tree. What is this music? It's as though horses that are out of breath are passing by, trees are being uprooted, drowning men are asking for mercy. Then everything gets mixed up: the horses, the trees, and the waves. Then they all stop at once. All that's left now is the light sound of the wind.

'Did you hear that?' says the hunter, his eyes ecstatic.

Artemis doesn't understand this foreign music. It doesn't touch her, and she hates it.

'Why are you acting like this?' she says. 'As though you've been bewitched!'

'That's a fine thing, you not liking my mistress' music!'

Then the anger rises until it chokes Artemis and turns her face red.

'And you like this music!' she shouts. 'How can you, a hunter from the Kimindenia, like such strange things?'

And then, looking up at the tree's foliage, she says:

'I only like the tunes of our country. I like the clarinets, the drums and bagpipes. I like it when the smugglers play and dance, the young men of Aivali.'

'Be quiet!' says the hunter angrily. 'Shut up now and listen.'

Artemis is not used to being spoken to in that way. She jumps up suddenly.

'I'll go inside and stop her!' she cries. 'I am not a servant who has to wait. I want her to tell me what happened to my brother! I want her to tell me what happened to my brother!'

But the hunter jumps up too.

'I won't let you make my mistress angry, whatever else happens! Be quiet and stop shouting! Be quiet!' he says harshly, and pulls her by her arms to get her away.

'Is that *you* saying this to me? Is that *you* speaking to me this way?' Artemis' angry voice trembles on the verge of tears.

'Enough of that! Come on!'

And he keeps pulling her, running, until they reach the entrance to the garden.

'You have to leave now,' he says sharply. 'It will get dark soon.'

He drops Artemis' arms and stands in front of the gate with his feet spread apart, resolved not to let her come back in.

Artemis bites her trembling lips, and no longer able to keep from crying, she slaps the hunter hard on the face. Then she rushes up the path towards home.

I WAS RACKED WITH FEVER. It seems I had caught a cold in the rain.

Lena doesn't want to leave my side. She stays and takes care of me. She looks me in the eyes to divine what I want. She puts covers over me, and every so often she moistens my forehead with water.

'Won't you play with your oven today, Lenaki?'

'But I am playing here,' she says. 'Don't you want me to?'

'I do.'

She says it so simply, but it's the truth. Lena is playing her favourite game, the one it seems she'll play all her life: to give, to offer of herself, and to care for others.

'Give me my rifle, Lena.'

I stroke the slim black barrel and examine the letters on it, the foreign letters of the make. I don't know how to read them.

'How did you get hurt?' asks Lena, who still could not understand what had taken place from what she'd heard. 'What happened during the lightning?'

'Nothing, Lena.'

'We're not friends anymore,' says the girl. 'You always play with Artemis. Aren't you two afraid when you go into the Kimindenia?'

'Artemis and I haven't gone anywhere together for days. We're mad at each other.'

'You're mad at each other? Why?'

'We just are.'

'We two won't fight,' says Lena. 'Threshing time is coming up. If you like we'll go and make a hut out of wheat sheaves on the big threshing floor. We'll play grandfather-and-grandmother there. I'll be grandmother, and I'll wait for you outside the hut. When you come, I'll stand up, and you'll stroke my hair.'

'No, Lena. I don't want to play grandfather-and-grandmother. I don't want a hut out of wheat sheaves. I want to get well and go into the Kimindenia. I'll go to the cave where the wild boars go away to die when they grow old. I have a little tortoise there and a green lizard. I caught it with my slingshot and tied it to a cross of reeds, just like they crucified our Lord Jesus Christ. There is the bat there that Artemis and I caught. We have them all there to die. I want to show it to her.'

'How can you go to caves where wild boars die and not be afraid? How can you kill little tortoises and bats and green lizards?'

'But I've grown up now, Lenaki. Don't you see? All grown-ups do that. They kill.'

'You said you wanted to show it. To whom?'

'To the foreign girl who came from the faraway country.'

'What does she want, wandering around like a man in the Kimindenia? Grandfather doesn't like her, and neither does grandmother. Yesterday they were saying that this is odd behaviour. They were saying that in our country the women stay at home and have children and make bread.'

How wrong they are to say bad things about Doris! But what do they know? Have they ever been beside her in a cave during a storm, when Doris is lying down and the flames from the burning branches light her face? Then you resolve to do anything for her to have what she desires. You resolve not to fear the eagle, but to go and bring her its baby eaglet. And at the critical moment, Doris' hand does not waver. If this shot fails, you are lost. Doris shoots and doesn't miss. What other creature in the Kimindenia other than me has ever lived such a moment?

I stroke my small rifle.

'Why are your eyes like that?' asks Lena in astonishment. 'It's as though you were stroking a living thing.'

A vague worry crosses her small, round, kindly face. It reminds me of grandmother's and mother's faces when they're overcome with tenderness.

'Listen,' says Lena thoughtfully. 'Do you like the smell of incense? Do you like it? Tell me.'

'I like it. Why do you ask?'

Lena goes away and comes back a little later. She's holding grandmother's yellow copper censer. It has one or two lit coals inside. In her hands she's holding leaves from the 'flowers of Christ', from dried roses and rosemary.* She puts the leaves on the coals. She stands at my head, and her hand holding the censer draws circles. The smoke makes bluish circles, and all the while Lena's face is silent and concentrated. That's what grandmother's face looks like when she's afraid that the evil eye has befallen us and she burns incense to drive it away. Then grandmother's lips move in a mystical prayer, a secret magic that strikes the dark spirit, and the peace of God is restored inside us. None of us has ever been able to catch a word of that strange prayer, not a single word. 'What are you saying, Grandmother?' I asked her the first time she burned incense over me. 'Shh! Shh!' she said fearfully, and closed my mouth with her fingers. 'Children must not know what grandmother says in this prayer. No one should listen at this moment when grandmother talks to God.'

It's an exorcism that comes from the old days, passed down from generation to generation. When her time comes to die, grandmother will make her last requests and wishes; then she will ask to be left alone with her eldest daughter. To her alone of all her children and grandchildren, will she pass on the secret exorcism — its dark words — just as she received them from her mother. Later my own mother, when her time comes, will pass it on in the same way to her eldest child, the custodian of the family. In this way, this secret voice becomes the most imperceptible and reliable bond between the generations of our ancestors and of those who are to come: a resonance that will remain when the memory of the people themselves is lost.

The bluish circles fill the room. I take pleasure in breathing the wonderful fragrance of the dried leaves of the roses and rosemary that adorned the body of Christ. Lena puts the yellow copper censer on the small table. The sacred gravity of the moment lingers on her face. She is so beautiful with that childlike seriousness of hers.

'What were you murmuring, Lena, when you were censing me? Do you know grandmother's prayer?'

'Shh! Shh!' says the little girl. 'Children shouldn't talk about those things!' she says now with genuine solemnity, since now the game that she was playing, the game of grandmother-burning-incense, has entered into her like the truth. She has assimilated the realms of both fantasy and reality.

➢ Chapter Seven ⪦

IN THE WILD BOARS' CAVE

The next morning, the hunter with the yellow stars dismounts outside the big door. Artemis is waiting for him there. Her intuition told her he would come. His sunburned face is pensive and his eyes are red. It seems as if he hasn't slept.

'Why did you come?' asks Artemis, looking him straight in the eyes.

'Oh, are you here?' says the hunter. 'My mistress sent me to ask about your brother.'

'Oh, that's why.'

The hunter makes as if to go in through the big door.

'You don't need to go in!' says Artemis and stops him. 'My brother is fine. My grandparents and I don't want anyone worrying about my brother!'

'Did the grown-ups tell you to say that?'

'Yes!' says Artemis, lying.

'All right.'

The hunter is getting ready to leave when Artemis goes up to him and begs:

'Take me with you. Are you going to the Kimindenia?'

'I'm going to the Kimindenia with my mistress! I'm taking her to the wild boars' cave. What business do you have with us?'

They're going to the wild boars' cave? To the wild boars' cave? A surge of anger reddens Artemis' face.

'You're not taking her there! You're not taking her there!' cries Artemis in a rage. 'That cave is mine. Mine alone! That's where my brother and I keep our tortoises and our lizards and the eggs that we take from birds' nests. That's where . . .'

But the hunter isn't listening anymore to what his silly roe deer is saying. He takes off on his horse at a gallop.

Artemis runs to the stable and takes her grandfather's horse. She is friends with the horse. Every day she gives it sugar. She jumps on without saddling him and rushes down the path that follows the *Tsakal-Dere*, the Jackal River.

The sun is burning. Far away, at the end of the great road, the camel caravans advance slowly. There is not a breath of wind. A fruit ripened, let go of the tree, fell. Everything is happening slowly. Only Artemis gallops madly on the horse, with her hair loose. Her hair is not wreathed with wild chaste tree blossoms. It floats in the light, shaken out wildly behind her, as though the light wanted to take her hair with it.

She comes to the source of the Jackal River, goes through the dense wood and crosses the large ravine. Frantic, she finally reaches the wild boars' cave. She dismounts, looks around anxiously and then looks inside the cave.

She takes a deep breath.

'Ach!'

There is not a soul. Thank God! They haven't got there yet!

Artemis gathers up her hair a little and ties it with her red kerchief. The deep crimson of her face is balanced now by the brightness on her head. Her eyes are wild. She sits down on the ground. There is not a sound.

Her memories flow freely. How long has it been since then? It was the very beginning of spring this year. Artemis had gone one day to gather blackberries in the ravine. The hunter with the yellow stars found her there. He found her there for the first time.

'Give me some blackberries to eat, little roe deer, I'm hungry,' he said.

She picked fresh blackberries, filled her hands and gave them to him.

'Here. Eat.'

She ate too. Then she said to him:

'I'm thirsty. Do you have a flask of water with you? The spring is far away.'

'I'll take you somewhere nearby to drink water,' said the hunter. 'I'll take you to the wild boars' cave.'

'I haven't been to that cave. I don't know it. Is it far away?'

'You don't know the wild boars' cave? Come and see.'

He lifted her up on his horse, and they went to the cave. There was deep darkness inside. The hunter cut some dry holm oak, made sparks with his flint and lit the branch. And in this way, accompanied by the flame, they went deep into the cave. Above them hung thick stalactites, the dome's invocation to the earth that she take them with her.

'Listen!' whispered the hunter.

Amazed, the girl fell silent and listened. There was a very soft sound: damp, persistent and solitary.

'It's the Kimindenia. The Kimindenia are sweating, and they're dripping,' murmured the hunter.

The rock was soft where the water was dripping. After years of doing this work, from time immemorial, the dripping dome had formed a small hollow in the rock on the ground. When this filled with water, it overflowed and trickled slowly down towards the mouth of the cave. The drops, asleep for years inside the heart of the mountain, now fearfully began their journey towards the light: their final journey. They would proceed a little, then they'd hesitate. A little more again, then hesitate. And so, in addition to the big hollow, the place was full of other, smaller memories of fear and hesitation. From generation to generation, the drops that come follow the tracks of their ancestors. They stay there a while, for as long as their ancestors stayed. And in the fullness of time, when the drops that follow come looking for space, the first ones leave. Above them the stalactites, the steady voice of the mountain, send the drops on their way and bless them for what they did in their lives, for the tenderness they gave to their great mother, the Kimindenia : 'Farewell! Farewell!' A hoopoe passed and took one drop. A wild boar passed and took the next one. Another travelled lower down. It went to the root of a blackberry bush close to the banks of the Jackal River, and became blackberries, blackberries for a girl to gather and give with her hands to a hunter. Yet another drop made its way to the bed of the river, became one with the rainwater and reached the sea. An eel that was in love found it there and took it inside him.

The flame of the holm oak branch was getting weaker. The wet earth in the cave showed its colour more clearly now. It was green. The light from the flame fell on the green water, stayed there for a moment, and then turned green itself.

'Look over here!' said the hunter, and pulled Artemis to the left.

And then suddenly he said:

'Look out!'

They stopped above an underground chasm. The hunter lowered the burning branch towards the bottom. Nothing but silence and darkness like a dense substance came from there. The girl's fingers trembled in the hunter's hand.

'This is their place,' he said, and his voice had a deep tone as though he were performing a solemn act. 'The wild boars come here when they grow old and sense their death approaching. They come here to die.'

'Have you seen them come yourself?' asked the girl, enchanted.

'No! I haven't seen them. I am still young. But my father has seen them, and so has my grandfather. All the old hunters in the Kimindenia know about it. And it was here, they say, that the gray stag came to die many years ago, the only stag that ever lived in the Kimindenia mountains.'

'Then why don't they set up an ambush and kill them, the way hunters always do?' asked Artemis.

The other voice came through the darkness with even more solemnity:

'No hunter kills an animal when he knows that it's going to hide itself to die.'

'Why not?

'If he does, he himself will die in the same year,' said the hunter.

THE SOUND OF HOOFBEATS is heard from the ravine. Artemis realizes they are coming. Her heart pounds. She gets up and goes to the entrance of the cave. She makes sure she's in the centre of the opening. She stands there and waits.

Doris isn't wearing her white sun helmet anymore, as she did when she first came. She's wearing a scarf in her hair like the local women; a scarf with blue flowers.

'What are you doing here?' says the hunter to Artemis, taken aback. 'When did you get here?'

'What is it to you?' she answers boldly, looking him straight in the eyes. 'This is my place here!'

'Who is she?' asks Doris.

And turning immediately to Artemis:

'What's your name, little girl?'

Artemis' eyes turn on her now, wild and hard.

'I am not a little girl! I am from these parts! The Kimindenia are our mountains!'

Doris dismounts and comes close to Artemis.

'Why are you speaking to me like this? What have I done to you?'

'What do you want in the Kimindenia?' says Artemis, and she bites her lips. 'What do you want with the hunter? I used to be the only one to go around here with my brother and the hunter.'

'Really? I didn't know.'

'What did you do to my brother?' asks Artemis, and the anger that boils inside her turns her cheeks bright red. 'Why did he want to fight with the great eagle? My brother is a timid child. What did you do to him to make him want to go and get hurt by the great eagle?'

Doris is starting to enjoy herself. She smiles slightly and takes a step towards Artemis.

'Oh! The boy is your brother?'

'He is my brother!'

And then, still fierce, she says:

'What did you do to him?'

The smile on Doris' mouth takes on a playful expression. She says in a comically serious manner:

'Don't you understand? I bewitched him!'

'Don't make fun of me!' cries Artemis furiously and waves her arms. 'People don't make fun of me! What you're saying is true. You bewitched my brother. And him . . . ,' she says, pointing in the direction of the hunter, but she doesn't finish what she's saying.

'Why are you talking like this?' cries the hunter, unable to control himself any longer. 'Why are you talking like this to my mistress?'

And turning to Doris he says:

'Let's go. Let's go into the cave.'

Then Artemis, standing in the mouth of the cave, shakes and opens wide her arms. She is like a wild bird that has stretched out its wings.

'No! No!' she shrieks at Doris. 'You will not go into this cave.'

'Why?' she asks, more and more amazed. 'Why can't I go in?'

'You won't go in! You won't go in!' shouts Artemis.

And she keeps saying frantic and crazy words:

'This is where the old wild boars of our mountain come to die! This is where my brother and I have our secret cemetery. Our lizards and our bats and our tortoises are here. Here . . .'

She stops abruptly. And then she says it:

'We came here the first time I met him,' she shouts, and points at the hunter. 'No one else should go in here! No foreigner! No woman!'

Doris looks inquisitively at the girl's face, which is stamped with despair. Then she looks the hunter in the eyes.

'Oh, I understand,' she says.

And suddenly her expression becomes hard; a wave of cruelty floods her face. Her bottom lip trembles slightly.

'Get out of the way!' she says imperiously to Artemis. 'Let me pass.'

'You will not pass! You will not pass!' wails the girl. 'This is where . . .'

Doris moves to grab her and pull her out of the way. But she stops. She turns to the hunter. Now her eyes are even more hard and wild.

'Throw her to the side!' she orders, looking at him insistently, straight in the face.

As though pulled by a magnet, he moves towards the girl. Artemis has also fixed her eyes on him now. They are flooded with agony and an awful question. 'Will he do what the foreign woman asks him to?' It is a wave of agony and supplication. 'Will he be able to do it?' The very moment, the very light, are trifling with the first fantasies and dreams of a young girl who is about to learn whether you win or lose when you give so much, when you dream so much.

The hunter's hesitation lasts only as long as a gunshot. Then he goes towards Artemis.

'Get out of the way,' he says harshly.

The resolution in his eyes burns like hot iron. Artemis isn't ready to receive this blow; she had not expected this. Her legs tremble. The tears are ready behind her long eyelashes, and they wait.

'You?' she stammers. 'Are *you* driving me away from here?'

'Come on! Come on!' cries the hunter nervously. 'Get out of the way!'

The tears have now soaked her quivering lashes. Behind them, memories are at play. The same memories play for one very slight moment in the hunter's eyes. Is this the roe deer who used to follow him wherever he went, who always looked at him like a faithful dog, the one he took for the first time to this place of the wild boars? And now he has to drive her out of his sanctuary.

The hunter lowers his eyes for one moment.

'Come on! Hurry up!' shouts Doris, walking towards the cave.

Artemis rushes at her to grab her by the hair, the cascading hair. But she doesn't make it. The hunter seizes her with both hands and throws her down hard like an inanimate object. The girl falls in a heap on the ground.

A sharp rock cuts her cheek, and it starts to bleed. Doris and the hunter go into the cave.

Artemis stays there, unable to recover from such a blow. She doesn't move. Only her heart pounds. It pounds harder and harder. Very slowly, Artemis stands up. Something hotter than fire burns her cheek. She slowly brings her fingers there. They are covered in blood.

There is not a sound from inside the cave. The girl strains her ears to hear. Nothing. It is as though the wild boars' cemetery had swallowed up Doris and the hunter. A whirring sound comes from a long way off. It must be the cicadas down in the olive grove. There are other sounds too: a camel caravan going down the great road of Anatolia. The gray form of a lizard looking for sun emerged hastily. It saw Artemis. The thorns rustled as it passed. It disappeared. 'Now she'll be looking at our dead lizard. Now she'll be touching our nailed bat. Now she is defiling our sanctuary. Now she and the hunter . . .' Her heart beats violently. A lightning flash passes over Artemis' eyes and face. The lightning doesn't go away but leaves a deep mark. 'Ah, if only she would die! If she would die and never come back! She who took the cave, who took the hunter, who took her little brother.' Nearby, Doris' horse is stamping the ground with his hooves. It seems he's thirsty. Unconsciously, Artemis' eyes pass over the horse. She sees his colour, his saddle, the strap that fastens the saddle around the animal's belly. The mark from the lightning that is still in Artemis' face grows deeper. She takes out her knife with the bone handle and approaches the horse. She strokes him. She knows how to get along with horses. Then she bends down under his belly and starts to cut the saddle's girth. She leaves only a narrow strip, half the width of a finger.

She looks around. Not a soul. Full of fear, flooded with awe for the death that Doris will meet in the ravine when the saddle breaks and she is hurled from the bolting horse onto the rocks, Artemis mounts her own horse and disappears like lightning.

THE EELS IN THE JACKAL RIVER understand that the time has come for their great journey of love. They were born far away in the depths of the Ocean, in the place where all the eels in the world go to mate. When they turned two years old, they left their cradle in the depths of the Ocean and followed the road of their ancestors. They crossed all the seas and came one winter's night to the Jackal River. There was a moon over the

Kimindenia. It was peaceful. Now and then the jackals howled in the thick forest, but the eels, safe in the water, were not afraid. They were dazzled by the austere tranquillity of the Aeolian land and the desolate moon. 'How beautiful the land of our mothers is!' they said. 'How beautiful is our fatherland!'

They stayed and lived there happily for six years. Then a certain night came again. Again the moon shone high above, again the jackals howled, and a young girl named Artemis, a child of those mountains, experienced in the cave of the wild boars the first story of her heart, the first that spilt blood. From deep inside them, the secret voice came to the eels of the Jackal River: a strange voice that told them to leave, to go far down the river and out into the sea. All the eels woke up; they heard the voice's command; they went far down the river and found the sea. At the shores of the Aegean, they found a strange commotion. They looked around in the water and were amazed at what they saw. All the eels from all the rivers of Anatolia were gathered there.

'How do you come to be here, companions?'

They answered:

'The voice spoke within us. We are going on the long journey.'

'Oh! You too? We are going on the same journey. The voice spoke to us too.'

And the river eels kept on talking happily, and they got to know one another. Only one eel, covered with strange silver skin, did not move from his place. He did not want acquaintances, did not want chatter; he wanted to be alone with the joy that was flooding him. Another eel with shiny skin that had also begun to turn silver saw him alone and thought that he was sad.

'What's the matter,' she asked him, 'for you to be alone like that? Do you have some secret that is tormenting you?'

'Where do you come from?' asked the solitary eel.

'I come from the Meander. That's the name of the big river where I used to live.'

'Come close to me,' said the other eel, 'you who comes from a big river. Lean against me. Do you hear?'

The eel from the Meander presses against the eel from the Jackal River and listens.

'What is that which is calling out inside you?' she asks, amazed.

'It is the voice of our mountain,' answers the solitude-loving eel with the silver skin. 'The river brought it down today from the cave of the wild boars, a single drop. And I swallowed it. Now it will travel with me. Now I'll have it inside me: the voice of my country. Come along with me.'

That is how it came to be that the two eels travelled very close to each other, together with their swarm, and reached the bottom of the distant Ocean. They lost many companions on the way in battles they had with other fish. But nothing happened to the two companions, because they helped one another. When they reached the place in the depths where they would mate, they chose a spot at the root of the coral to make their nest. Then the other eels in the swarm began to change their skin and be dressed in silver — their wedding clothes. But the two companions of the coral didn't need to wait. They had been ready since the beginning of the journey. They fell in love sweetly, and when they were tired, they waited quietly for the children that would come. Every so often the male eel would bend over the body of his wife, and when he heard heartbeats, he would ask impatiently:

'Have they come? Is it our children?'

'No,' she would say. 'Not yet. That is *that other heartbeat*. It is the voice of our country.'

But when the children formed inside her, the heartbeats got mixed up. And then even she could not tell them apart.

ARTEMIS DOESN'T LEAVE MY SIDE in our room where I'm lying. She sits with Lena and they keep me company. She doesn't talk at all. She seems distracted, and she's very pale.

'Are you sick, Artemis?' Lena asks her every now and then. 'Should I tell mother?'

'There's nothing the matter with me,' says Artemis.

'Do you want me to burn incense over you?' asks Lena, in a comically serious way. 'Ask Petros too . . .'

'Oh, leave me alone!'

Every now and then she turns and looks fearfully at the door as though they are going to come for her any minute to ask her to confess.

'Do you know what I was thinking, Artemis?' I whisper to her at one moment. 'Our bat in the wild boars' cave: we should go get its bones now and put them on us. Then everyone will love us. As soon as I get well . . .'

On hearing the mention of the cave, Artemis shudders. She's about to say something, but at that moment the door opens suddenly. It's Anthippe, our big sister, and behind her is the hunter with the yellow stars. His face is radiant; it shines with a strange joy as though something wonderful is in store for him.

Anthippe says to me:

'The foreigner from the sea has sent the hunter again to learn how you are. She asked him to see you. Tell him you are well.'

'I am well,' I say happily. 'In a few days they'll let me go out.'

The hunter walks towards Artemis, who is sitting there on the floor beside my bed huddled up and trembling with distress.

'And she sends you this!' says the hunter, and he gives her the scarf that Doris was wearing at the wild boars' cave.

Artemis is lost. She stammers:

'Then didn't . . . didn't anything happen yesterday?'

The hunter looks at her with a smile.

'Nothing,' he says. 'What should have happened? Only that as we were crossing the Jackal River, the girth of her saddle broke. But it was nothing. The horse was walking on sand at that moment, on a dry part of the river. It was going slowly. My mistress didn't even get a scratch. Goodnight!'

Artemis stays there speechless while conflicting waves of emotion come from opposite directions and collide inside her. And the colours in the scarf that Doris sent her struggle to find movement in her frozen fingers.

⋙ Chapter Eight ⋘

A BEAR FROM LEBANON, A BEAR CUB, AND MEN

Beyond the place where the beech trees grow, at the summit of the ravine — which is the most untrodden place in the Kimindenia — the great bear has made her den between two rocks. She has covered it with branches of dense foliage; with other branches, she closed the opening. After she gave birth to her small cub at the beginning of the summer, she uprooted wild shrubs and used them to block the entrance to her den even more. This way she thinks she is safe from the eyes of man.

The little bear understands many things now. He understands that the honey his mother brings him, plundering the hives of wild bees, tastes better than acorns and worms. He understands that outside their den, in which he has been enclosed since he was born, there must be a strange world, a world made of beautiful and terrifying things: trees, rivers, dogs and men. But he has never seen them. And every day, now that he's bigger, he begs his mother, the big bear:

'Take me with you. When can I come with you to see it?'

'In a little while,' she says to him. 'When you're a little bigger.'

Only on moonlit nights does the mother bear grow bold and take her little one out to the mouth of their den. Then they sit, wrapped in the green light, at the top of the great ravine, and the bear tells her cub the story of their ancestors.

In the old days, she says, they used to live in the mountains of Lebanon. They were living there peacefully when herds of men sniffed them out and started to kill them. There was lamentation every day, and their race dwindled. Then with heavy hearts, the bears that were left said: 'The mountains of Lebanon are no longer ours, we will have to leave our fatherland.' Saying this, they bid farewell to the country of their birth and set out on the road to the west. They travelled night after night and kept moving towards the west. They travelled until one day they knew from the smell in the air that winter was coming. In the good old days in Lebanon, when that message came, they would lie down in their dark dens and sink safely into their long winter sleep. Now that winter found them on the road as refugees without dens, they prayed to the white snow.

'You, protect us,' they said to it. 'We are desolate and without dens.'

The snow answered their prayer; it fell very heavily that year and covered them. They went to sleep and woke up when spring came. Again they set out on the road, heading further down, further and further from the men of Lebanon. They were crossing the mountains of Kaz-Dak when one morning they suddenly reached a high peak. Looking down, the bears saw a wall of water stretching out before them.

'How will we cross that?'

They went all the way down to the sea, to the deserted beach. They marvelled at the waves and again asked:

'How will we cross that?'

White birds flew above them. They asked them. And the seagulls answered:

'No! You won't cross that water. Your journey is over.'

Then the bears of Lebanon returned to the ravines of Kaz-Dak and made their second homeland there. They spent a short time in peace. Then man appeared before them again. They were Tzerkezi and Yuruks who killed the big bears so they could take their children, put chains in their noses and teach them to dance.

Again there was great lamentation among their race. Some bears said:

'Let's leave! Let's go away from here! Let's take to the road as refugees again.'

'No! A thousand times no!' said others. 'How can we leave again, how can we leave this new homeland we've made? We can't do it anymore. Let come what may!'

And so many bears stayed in the mountains of Kaz-Dak and were lost at the hands of man. A smaller group, especially those who had children in their bellies, travelled towards the west. On their way, they found the Kimindenia mountains, and they stayed.

ON THAT MOONLIT NIGHT, high in the Kimindenia, the mother bear told these things, the story of their race, to her cub. The little bear listened with frightened eyes and tried to understand the meaning of the world.

'What happened to the other bears of our race that came to the Kimindenia?' he asked.

Very sadly his mother shook her head.

'Man found us here too. They were all lost at his hands.'

'And my father? What happened to my father?'

The mother bear did not want to cause her child sorrow at such a young age. But there was no avoiding it. From now on he had to start learning about the world and to know his fate:

'The snows were just beginning to melt, and the wild bees were leaving their hives and searching among the trees for food,' she said. 'He went to bring us a honeycomb because I had just given birth to you and was weak. He never came back.'

'Why?'

'Man!' said the mother. 'He must have met up with man.'

What a terrible monster this 'man' must be, thought the small bear. And to think that he is everywhere, that he's overrun the world: from Lebanon to Kaz-Dak and the Kimindenia mountains!

'What does man have against us? What does he have against our race?'

'We resemble him,' said the mother bear. 'We can stand on two legs the way he stands. We can dance upright like him. Just like him, we can bear the weight of chains. We resemble him.'

'And why does that matter?'

'Man loves to strike anyone who looks like him,' the big bear replied. 'He loves to kill whatever is like him.'

'Ach,' sighed the little bear, and it was the first sigh that ever came from his mouth into the world. 'How good it would be if man did not exist!'

'How good it would be,' said the big bear.

➢ Chapter Nine ➢

THE HUNTER WITH THE YELLOW STARS
AND THE BLACK BEAR

Dawn begins to break. A silvery light lies upon the mountains and trees and bids them farewell. The dawn star shines alone; the others have disappeared. It stands apart, wrapped in its memories of the night that has passed, and contemplates with indifference what is to come to the Kimindenia on this day that is dawning.

The hunter with the yellow stars, alone astride his horse, crossed the land of the wild oaks and took the path to the great ravine. He had oiled his rifle the previous evening and inspected his bullets. Now he is happy and whistles. He has no presentiment, no unease. He was a youth who had never felt fear. And yet he felt in solitary moments, whenever he was setting out on a difficult hunt, that his heart was beating a little differently, a little more quickly. To conquer this demon from the start, he would ride his *mintili* without a saddle and throw himself into a mindless gallop over ditches and rocks. The wind lashed his face, and the strange beating in his heart would stop. But in time, once he'd become the first shot in his country, once he'd learned to pluck roses with a bullet by shooting their stems at a hundred metres, he didn't need to gallop crazily anymore and make the wind beat his face. The fear had disappeared with the confidence of the hand that never made a mistake.

The hunter goes up the path on his stallion to the top of the great ravine. He whistles an old tune sung by the youths of Aivali, a tune that is sad, like all the songs of Anatolia:

Everyone tells me to fly,
but I don't have wings . . .

His whistling blends with the sound of the birds that have woken up and fly hurriedly above him: wild pigeons, turtledoves and hoopoes. The hunter looks at them tenderly as they pass and is happy. He is whistling a sad song and yet he's happy. The tunes of Anatolia only bring sorrow to foreigners. For the people of this country, they convey peace because they emerged from its very nature and are one with it, just as light is one with flame.

The hunter whistles his sad tune and is happy. He takes a bullet from his cartridge belt. He looks at it, and his eyes shine.

'I'm doing this to please you,' he says, as though he is speaking to someone who is close by, someone who can't be anywhere but close by since he thinks about them so much.

Then he bites the bullet with his strong teeth. He takes his rifle down from his shoulder and loads it with the bitten bullet. He looks up. The dawn star is quivering; it's about to disappear. Sounds are now coming from the distance, from the great road that joins the interior of Anatolia to the coast. The camel caravans have woken up and begun their slow march.

'I have to hurry,' says the hunter, and he prods his horse. 'I have to get to the big bear before she comes out of her den. I have to reach her before the wind wakes up.'

He knows very well where her den is and what her habits are. He knows that she must not get wind of him with that frightfully keen sense of smell she has. But there is no wind at all, not a leaf is moving on the trees. The hunter stops his horse, takes out his tobacco pouch, rolls a cigarette and lights it. He watches the smoke as it moves towards the north.

'Good. I should climb up the steep rock from the north side.'

He keeps on going up. The rising sun is bringing its message of golden light to the distant mountains in the east. As he gets higher, the area becomes more desolate and wild; hoopoes fly back and forth, playing games with the light. A slow-moving hare jumps out of the thicket, rests his startled eyes on the man coming up the path and hurries out of sight. Behind him, way down low, the sea was resting, waiting for the waves to wake it up. The hunter looked at the sea. He saw the tall poplars at their estate. They seemed to him like the masts of a ship. Yes, it was a ship: a white ship, a *pena*. The *pena* is the most beautiful of all the boats that ply our sea. It has only one large sail, and the other sails, the jibs, exist only to serve this one, their king. The sea down there doesn't move, the *pena* doesn't move. Because in her prow sleeps the little mistress who came from foreign lands. She will ask when she wakes up:

'Where is the hunter, for us to go hunting turtledoves? Yesterday we shot the male. The female got away from us, and today she'll be flying around alone. Where is the hunter, so we can go and find the female turtledove, who will be waiting for us to kill her, since only then will she find her companion and be at peace?'

'Oh, he left before daybreak,' they'll say to Doris.

Then she'll get angry.

'Really? He left before daybreak? Why didn't he tell me? Why didn't he ask me?'

No one will be able to answer her, since the hunter told no one his secret. A true hunter never talks to anyone, especially when he is going on a mission like this. What will Doris do when he puts the little bear in her arms?

'But didn't I tell you,' she'll say to him, 'that I don't like bears, that I don't like wild animals in chains?'

'Look at it!' he'll answer. 'It's the most beautiful wild animal that exists today in the Kimindenia. I wanted to give you the most beautiful thing that our mountains possess. I went and brought it to you.'

Then Doris will caress the little bear, she'll caress its black fur. She will look at its little eyes and she'll be crazy with joy.

'But we won't chain him!' she'll tell him.

'No. We won't put chains on him. We'll teach him to follow behind you like a dog. He'll know only you. As for the baby eagle you wanted, what would you do with it? In our parts we don't like eagles. In our mountains we consider the bear king. I went and brought you its cub.'

The hunter keeps going up the path. Now he will have to go through the place where the beeches grow.

Silence. The sounds of the world, the camels' bells, nothing reaches up here. And the sea is no longer visible. The hunter knows he is entering a place of wilderness. Men don't wander here. From here on, he'll be alone. He looks at the trees and listens to the sound that the horse's hooves make on the earth. Here you can speak with the Kimindenia, and no one will ever know what you said. Here . . .

Suddenly the hunter hears a commotion beside him. It's coming from a thick clump of bushes to his right. His thoughts go immediately to the big bear, then to a wild boar, even though his horse doesn't whinny. He is taking his rifle down from his shoulder when three men jump out of the bushes. Their cartridge belts are crossed; they hold weapons in their hands and have daggers in their belts. They are Turkish *zeybeks*. What kind of people are they? The *zeybeks* of this country are gentle creatures, camel drivers, who always go unarmed. Who are these ones, and what do they want?

The hunter stops his horse and instinctively puts his finger on the trigger of his gun.

One of the three greets him in an indifferent tone.

'*Merhaba!*'

'*Merhaba!*'

'Where are you going?'

'I'm going hunting. I'm from around here. Where are you going?'

'We've lost our way,' says the Turk. 'Which is the path that comes out at the sea?'

The hunter shows them. Then he asks:

'What do you want at the sea?'

'Nothing.'

'All right.'

'*Allaha ısmarladık!*'

'*Uğur ola!*'

The three Turks take the way he showed them. Before they're out of sight, one of them turns back again and shouts:

'Are other hunters coming behind you?'

The hunter knows that no one is coming. He knows that he will be there alone. However, out of the need he feels not to be alone, he says:

'Yes, others are coming behind me!'

And he disappears into the trees. For a while he keeps turning it over and over in his mind: 'Who can they be? And what are they looking for? What do they want, armed like that, in our mountains?' But in a short while he has reached the outer limit of the beeches. He dismounts, ties his horse to a tree, takes his rifle and continues. 'Farewell,' the beeches say to him. 'The great ravine starts here. At the brow of the great ravine is the bear's den. From here on you will forget the woman for whose sake you came today to our parts. You will forget the armed *zeybeks*. Now it is just you here, you and the bear.' The hunter understands that that's how it is: only him and the bear. Everything else is erased, disappears. Now, at this moment of truth, only the hunter remains.

With his practised eye, he surveys the landscape. Again he looks at a leaf to see the direction of the wind. It's still from the south. The hunter visualises the path he must take to have the wind in front of him. He begins to very slowly climb and crawl towards the den. The big bear will come out soon to eat acorns and honey from the nests of wild bees. The hunter knows her routine. He holds his rifle tight in his hands.

In the rifle is a piece of lead. A black slave extracted it from the bowels of the earth of Africa. Fire made with coal that came from the depths of the earth in Wales worked it and transformed it into pure metal. Later the lead travelled to the land of Aeolia and fell into the hands of a hunter wearing a scarf with yellow stars on his head. One summer's morning, the hunter's teeth bite on the lead while his heart smiles. And the lead flies to complete the story of a bear from Lebanon and a girl born in Scotland who has the brown eyes of the girls of the Aegean and who lived for one hour in the cave of the wild boars.

⇒ Chapter Ten ⇐

A PISTOL SHOT IN THE LAND OF THE BEECH TREES
IN THE SUMMER OF 1914

The same morning that the hunter is up at the great ravine, I am going around with my little shotgun in the forest of wild oaks so as to become a hunter myself. It is the third day they've let me go out since my illness. I am wandering around in case I manage to shoot a hoopoe.

The first time my mother saw me going out with my gun, she said:

'Don't go far. Don't leave our property. You aren't completely well yet. What are you doing with that gun?'

'Mother, let me be. I'll be careful. Let me have the gun.'

'Let the child have it,' said grandfather. 'I also started shooting at his age.'

'All right. But don't go further than the vineyard.'

I went behind a large grapevine. I sat and waited for the blackbirds that came to eat the grapes. There were so many I managed to shoot one. After a while my mother came and found me. She frowned when she saw the bird I'd shot; she didn't approve of this game at all.

'It wasn't the right time for you yet,' she murmured, as though she were talking to herself. 'They shouldn't have sent you that gift.'

She understood that from now on it was too late, the impulse was inside me. Now that I had succeeded in killing one bird, how could she ever stop me? Especially when even grandfather wanted to see me hunt?

She thought for a minute and then said to me:

'Grown-up hunters never shoot sitting birds. Have you ever seen a hunter from our country do that? It's not manly! You should shoot them on the wing.'

That's what she said to me, thinking it would be impossible for me to hit a bird in flight with a flobert. And then maybe it would lose its charm and attraction for me.

'And now what are we going to do with the blackbird you killed?' asked mother. 'We'll roast it for you to eat this evening.'

I said:

'I can't take it down to her yet; I still can't walk that far. Let me have it sent it to her . . .'

'To whom?' she asked, not understanding.

'To the foreign lady, Mother. The one who gave me the gun . . .'

She came close to me, put her hands on my shoulders and looked at me with her sweet smile.

'You're a good boy to have thought of that.'

I couldn't stand her looking at me that way, and I lowered my eyes. That made her begin to suspect. Why should I lower my eyes as though I had done something bad, or as though I had something to hide? I felt her fingers rest on my shoulders and tap them lightly as though they wanted to dig into my small body and extract its secrets.

'Why aren't you looking at me?'

Shyly, I gathered the courage to lift my eyes again and look at her. She wasn't smiling anymore. She had another expression on her face: as though now she understood, but as though she didn't dare believe it was possible that inside this little boy, who only yesterday she was playing with and rocking to sleep, the stirrings had already begun.

'Do you want very much to please the foreign girl?' she asked me. 'Of course you do! You want to very much?'

I thought she agreed with me, so I was encouraged and answered enthusiastically:

'Oh yes, Mother! I want very much to please her. It's her gun. I should send her the first bird I shoot. Since I couldn't give her the baby eagle . . .'

Surprise was written all over her face.

'Did you say baby eagle? Did you want to give her a baby eagle?'

I had forgotten that I hadn't told her anything about the story of the storm. But now it was too late. When mother looks searchingly like that I can't lie to her. Because I know she'll be able to tell.

'But it's nothing . . . ,' I murmured and turned red, as though I were very much to blame. 'That day that I fell and hurt myself . . .'

'Oh? What were you doing that day?'

'I went to get her a baby eagle from the eagle's nest.'

'Christ and the Panagia!' She let out a terrified cry and hugged me hard. 'Weren't you afraid to do something so dangerous? Did you really do that?'

I couldn't see her face, but now I sensed her anger.

'Ah! How could she let you do such a thing?'

'But she didn't know anything, Mother! She didn't know anything! I went by myself.'

'It's not your fault. It's not your fault,' she murmured, as though talking to herself. 'Why did we let you wander around outside our boundaries at such a young age? God! What a tragedy would have befallen me! Never again . . .'

And then:

'Come now, let's go! You've hunted enough today.'

'Will we send it to her?' I dared to ask, picking up my blackbird.

'What are you saying?' she cried, still in the grips of her fear.

'The bird that I shot, can we send it to her?' I pleaded.

'No!'

And then, as though she sensed the harm she was doing:

'It won't do for us to send her a bird that you shot sitting in the vines. When you grow up and hunt birds on the wing, then you will send her one.'

The next day they very reluctantly let me go back to the vineyard to hunt. Blackbirds came and ate grapes, and as they flew off I shot at them. But I didn't hit any. Then I suddenly saw the wondrous bird with orange and black feathers, the hoopoe, fly over me. My heart pounded. If I could kill the hoopoe! If the first bird that I shot in flight could be a hoopoe for me to send to her . . .

The hoopoe passed above me very low, and I saw its colours so clearly that they dazzled me. That must have been why my hands trembled and I did not even lift my gun in time.

Later, when I told my mother that a hoopoe had passed but I hadn't shot at it, she seemed to take it as a good sign that the desire to hunt had passed. She gave me fritters with honey for not killing the bird. And the fritters tasted particularly sweet to me, sweeter than ever before.

But as time passed, and midday came, and then the afternoon, the hoopoe that had escaped began to torment me. How good it would have been! How good it would have been to have sent her a hoopoe!

I took my gun and went out secretly. I crossed our boundaries and plunged into the domain of the oak trees. I found a lot of birds, but I wanted a hoopoe. I wandered under the great trees and their silence. Then I got tired. I lay down on the dry earth — this way I heard the voice of the trees better. As the sun began to set, their murmuring became more secretive and more distinct. The evening shadows began to come down from the dense trees in waves. I lost myself watching them since I was sure I could clearly distinguish the order the waves of shadows came in, like veils, one after the other. And then suddenly I realized that the shadows had surrounded me and were drowning me. I sprang up terrified and ran furiously to get out of the realm of the oaks. I came out into the open and found the day still poised above it, still blue. At that very moment, a hoopoe passed. But I was still so frightened by the shadows that I didn't even think of lifting my gun.

If anyone asks me, I will say that the hoopoes have left our parts and travelled away from the Kimindenia.

AND YET VERY EARLY THE NEXT MORNING I am wandering around again, on the chance of finding a hoopoe. Then suddenly Doris, on horseback, leaps in front of me from the footpath.

When she had woken up that morning, even though she had not requested the hunter the night before to go hunting today, she sent someone to call him from his hut and tell him to ready the horses.

'He's not there,' they told her. 'His hut is closed.'

Doris is not used to servants doing whatever they feel like without asking her. And the hunter is now exclusively at her service. It cannot be otherwise now; he *must* answer only to her.

What has happened to the hunter?

Doris mounts her horse and rides alone to the country of the wild oaks. She makes a tour of the familiar places, but the hunter is nowhere. Her face has a strange expression. Her upper lip trembles slightly, and her spurs torment the horse. Suddenly, she comes upon me.

I hadn't crossed paths with her in the three days I'd been hunting. I hadn't seen her since the day of the summer storm with the eagles.

I run to her full of joy. I expect her to give me a hug. But her clouded face freezes me and stops me in my tracks.

'Is it you?' she says coldly, as though her mind is elsewhere. 'Tell me, have you seen my hunter around here today?'

'No, I haven't seen him. He hasn't come by here.'

And then, finding a little courage I say:

'Did you know I've been hunting three days now with my gun? I want to kill a hoopoe.'

But Doris doesn't hear; she isn't paying attention. What's wrong?

'And that little sister of yours,' she asks me. 'What's her name?'

'I have lots of sisters.'

'No, I'm talking about the one who's friends with my hunter.'

'Oh, Artemis!'

'Yes! Her! Where is she now?'

'I last saw her at the big walnut tree, down on our property. She was playing with a cicada.'

'Ah, good!'

Without saying anything else, and without saying goodbye, Doris spurs her horse and leaves, taking the path to the sea.

What has become of the hunter?

DORIS RETURNS TO THEIR ESTATE and asks the first person she finds there, a ploughman from Lemnos:

'Has my hunter showed up?'

'No! We haven't seen him.'

She lifts her crop and whips the air hard.

'The minute he shows up, let me know! Do you hear me?'

She goes and shuts herself in her room, but after a short while she hears a big uproar in the courtyard of poplar trees. Men are shouting and women are shrieking.

Her door opens, and the Lemnian runs in terrified, waving his hands in the air.

'Hurry, Mistress! The hunter's horse came back alone. It came back...'

Doris rushes out. She runs towards the crowd that has gathered in a circle around something and is shouting. She pushes the crowd aside roughly.

All the voices fall silent. Doris is amazed at what she sees. Standing in the middle of the circle is the hunter's horse, completely out of breath. Sweat drips from its shining, trembling coat. It is without a saddle, but a wide saddlebag hangs way down below its belly. From one of the sacks on the bag, a small black animal is sticking out its terrified face. Is it a dog?

No, it is not a dog. It is a little bear. It is a bear cub!

The women start to scream again:

'Something bad has happened to him! Something has happened! He went and took the bear from its den.'

Old Vilaras has been notified and arrives at that moment with a worried expression.

'Something bad has definitely happened to him,' he says.

'The mother bear must have mauled him! She must have mauled him!' wails a woman.

'No,' reasons old Vilaras. 'It can't have happened that way. If the mother bear had mauled him, she would have freed her little one. No. The hunter definitely killed the big bear.'

'Maybe he fell off his horse into some ravine,' shouts a ploughman.

'What are you saying,' protests a third. 'Him? A rider like him to fall off his horse? Impossible!'

'Then what?'

'Then what?'

'What happened to the hunter?'

'What if someone killed him?'

The suspicion runs through their faces and fills them with fear.

'Who would kill him? And why?'

Doris listens and looks in a daze at the bear, at the muzzle that's sticking out of the saddlebag. She goes over and takes him out with care. His feet are bound together, two and two, with thin rope. She is very pale. 'Do you want me to bring you the black bear's cub? Do you want me to?' His words fly around her, close in on her. It was then, up there, on the day of the storm at the eagles' cliffs. 'Do you want me to bring you the cub of the black bear that lives in the Kimindenia?'

Doris moves through the small crowd with sudden resolve:

'Who of you know where the bear's den is?'

No one knows. No one answers. Doris becomes desperate.

'Worthless people! How can you live in these mountains and not know them? How is it possible?'

'Calm down, my child,' says old Vilaras. 'Don't speak to them like that. These are ploughmen who work the land all day long. They are not hunters.'

'Now what's going to happen? Where will we go to look for him?' cries Doris, and she makes no effort to hide her distress.

'Didn't he tell any of you where he was going?' old Vilaras asks his men.

No one answers.

'Then we'll send men out in different directions to search the mountain paths. There's no other way,' says Vilaras.

Then an idea strikes Doris like lightning:

'Hurry! Hurry!' she shouts. 'Bring me my horse! Bring me my carbine!'

'In the name of God! What are you thinking?' says old Vilaras. He runs towards her and takes her hands.

'Let go, Father! I know! I know how we'll find him!'

'But don't *you* go! Let's send men.'

'No! No! That won't do, Father! Let your men come with me.'

And looking at the crowd around her:

'You!' she says to one. 'And you! And you! Quickly, get horses! Take your guns!'

Doris mounts her horse and rushes off towards the mountains. Behind her, the three armed men from the estate try to catch up. Speechless, powerless to oppose anything, old Vilaras is enveloped in the dust kicked up by the horses and surrounded by the amazed silence of his people.

Doris enters the outer door of our farmstead at a gallop and stops in the courtyard.

'Artemis! Artemis!' she shouts, looking up towards the wooden stairs and the windows. 'Artemis! Artemis!'

Two or three startled faces peek out from the windows and withdraw at once.

'Artemis! Artemis!'

She calls her more and more urgently in a voice full of anguish.

The voice reaches Artemis. It finds her and fills her with confusion. Could *that* voice possibly call for her with so much warmth?

'Artemis! Artemis!'

Artemis runs down the stairs. As soon as she sees her, Doris jumps off her horse and rushes towards her. She takes hold of her shoulders and looks at her. Her hands are trembling on the girl's shoulders.

'Did he ever tell you about the bear's den? Do you know where the bear's den is? In the name of God! Tell me, Artemis!'

The girl's eyes start to take on a fierce expression. But Doris stops her. 'It's to save his life! To save his life!' she shouts. 'Tell me! Do you know?'

Is it to save his life? Is it to save his life?!

'Yes, I'm telling you, Artemis. He's in danger! Do you know?'

Suddenly, overwhelmed by the anguish of the voice pleading with her, overwhelmed by the fear of death, the girl murmurs:

'I know. . . I know about the big bear's den. Before you came he used to tell me that he'd kill her. He told me he would take her cub and bring it to me.'

'Do you really know where the den is? Did he tell you where the den is?'

'I know where it is. He showed me. It's in the great ravine, beyond the beeches.'

'Come quickly on my horse. Quick! Quick! Get up on my horse!'

At that moment, hearing the commotion, grandfather and mother come down the wooden stairs. They come running towards the riders, looking with amazement at Artemis astride Doris' horse.

'What is it, my lady?' asks grandfather. 'What's going on?'

'Nothing! Nothing!' shouts Doris hurriedly. 'Forgive me, I'm taking your girl for a little run.'

And before they have time to say anything more to her, she spurs her horse and disappears, with the other riders following behind.

'What is this? What is this?' says grandfather angrily. 'What's wrong with old Vilaras? Doesn't he see? This is the last time our children will go off with her!'

THE HUNTER IS LYING WITH A BULLET in his heart where the land of the beech trees ends, on the path that leads to the great ravine. The horse ridden by Doris and Artemis leads the way, with the others following behind. And so their horse is the first to stand before the body lying in the middle of the path.

'Ahhhh!' a loud cry bursts out from Artemis, and she presses into Doris as though she wants to shelter herself from death.

Doris jumps down and runs to the hunter. She takes his hands and shakes them violently. She unbuttons his shirt with violent movements.

The small fountain opened by the bullet has poured forth blood and drenched his breast. Doris puts her ear down to listen to the heart. Above her, the three men and Artemis stand silent, waiting in agony. Doris stands up. Her face is yellow and her lips are white.

'It's over,' she says. 'He's dead.'

Then it's Artemis' turn to fall on the hunter. Shyly at first, and then desperately, she buries her fingers in his hair, caresses his face and calls to him, wailing:

'Why did you do this? Why did you do this? Why did you die?'

The scarf with the yellow stars doesn't wreath his hair. Rumpled and fallen from his head, it is wrapped around his neck.

'He was killed!' says one ploughman. 'Do you see his rifle anywhere?'

'No,' says the other, looking around. 'Nowhere.'

'He was killed!' says the third ploughman. 'Who would have done it? And why?'

Artemis hears the frightful words circling over her, she feels the mystery of their sound envelop her. 'He was killed!' Now death takes on for her a more terrifying gravity. Around the dead body, darkness is starting to fall in waves. Frightened by the darkness, Artemis lets go of the hunter's hair. She withdraws her fingers so they no longer touch him.

Very slowly, she stands up.

'He was killed? You said he was killed? Why would someone kill him?'

Her eyes move away from the men. Now they are riveted there where she senses she must get the answer, where she must look for the answer.

'Who killed him?' she asks Doris. 'Who killed him?'

And right away this question brings with it the other question:

'How did you know that we'd find him on the path to the bear's den? How did you know he had gone to the bear's den?'

During their wild, galloping ride to get here, it hadn't occurred to her to ask; she hadn't thought about it.

'How did you know?' she repeats more fiercely to Doris, while Doris, pallid, says nothing.

'Is there any question?' says one ploughman. 'Since his horse came back with the little bear cub in its saddlebag. It's as clear as day that he went to the bear's den!'

'What?' says the girl, stricken with amazement and distress. 'The horse came back with the little bear cub? He had taken the bear cub?'

And suddenly she starts to wail and weep again.

'You killed him! You killed him!' she shouts at Doris between her sobs. 'He went to get the bear cub for you! You sent him!'

Doris is unable to defend herself, she is not used to this. She gathers all her strength, all her self-control. She bites her hand.

'Be quiet!' she says sharply to Artemis. 'Be quiet!'

And then, turning to her men:

'Tie him onto a horse! We'll take him down.'

They tied him to a horse, lying on his back. They covered his face and hair with the scarf with yellow stars. What could his eyes see now of the beech trees and the Kimindenia? What could they see of Doris' gold hair and Artemis' eyes?

They headed home. They went slowly, so as not to disturb the dead body, for his hair not to blow in the wind. The two riders went in front. Behind, on foot, came the man who was holding the bridle of the horse with the hunter. And Doris' horse followed behind with the two young women joined tightly together, one to the other.

Evening was falling. The beeches took the news, whispered it through their leaves and passed it along throughout their country.

'Did you hear? The hunter was killed! The hunter won't pass under our shade any more.'

Lower down, the wild oaks heard and whispered it to the passing hoopoes and the wild pigeons.

'Did you hear? The hunter was killed.'

'Which hunter was killed?'

'The one who didn't hunt hoopoes and wild pigeons. The one who hunted wild boars in the great ravine.'

'Do you think he killed an old animal that was going to die in the wild boars' cave?'

'Oh, no! He never shot a wild animal that was going to die! He never shot a bird while it was drinking water. He was a true hunter!'

'Then why did he die?' asked the hoopoes and the wild pigeons.

'From love,' said the oak trees.

The birds took the strange word *love* in their mouths and carried it to the Jackal River. The river took it and carried it down to where it joins the sea and sent it into the waters of the Aegean, for it to become waves.

THE PROCESSION LEFT ARTEMIS at our farmstead and continued down towards the estate by the sea.

From Artemis, pale and in tears, we learned what had happened.

'You say they found him killed?' grandfather asked in alarm. 'Did you see him?'

'I saw him, Grandfather, since we brought him down from there tied to a horse.'

'Christ and the Panagia! Christ and the Panagia!' cry out my grandmother and my mother, crossing themselves all the while. 'What did you have to do with this, my little child? What did you have to do with it?'

But now is one of those times when grandfather removes the gentle smile from his face. In its place is the severe expression of the man whom everyone obeys.

'Be quiet!'

Instantly, there is a deathlike silence around him.

'Saddle my horse!' he orders a servant boy.

Grandfather leaves for the estate by the sea to talk to old Vilaras.

He returns when the sun is close to setting. His face is even darker and more clouded. He shuts himself in his room and sends for his foreman. What he had learned about down there was a mystery without an explanation. It wasn't only the hunter who was found killed. On the same day, in another part of the Kimindenia, they shot another Christian, one of Vilaras' men. But this one they only wounded. He survived and brought the news. What kind of men were they who attacked him? They were armed men, Yuruks. Why are the Yuruks armed, and why are they attacking Christians? Do they mean to harm Vilaras in this way? Why? Could they have been robbers? No, they couldn't have been. What would they have had to gain from attacking poor men: a hunter and a ploughman?

And so?

Grandfather gives orders to his foreman.

'Tonight the outer door will close early. Everyone on the estate has to be inside early. If it happens that strangers come to spend the night here, we won't keep them out. But I'll see them myself, one at a time. If they have weapons, you will take the weapons away from them and give them back in the morning when they leave. You will choose three of our

men to keep guard tonight behind the outer door. You will take guns
and bullets from the Yellow Room.'

Then he called grandmother and our mother. We children all came
running too.

'It's nothing,' grandfather says, trying to create an expression of calm
on his face. 'But from now on, none of you,' he says, looking at us children,
'will go far from the big door. Do you hear that? None of you!'

'What is it, Grandfather? What is it, Grandfather?'

'Nothing! Don't be afraid.'

Only later, when grandmother asked him, 'What will happen?' he
said: 'We have taken our measures. Vilaras is going to call for Pagidas.
Pagidas will come with his men.'

When we go to bed in our room that night, we are in a state of agitation
and distress. Above our heads circle mystery and fear. But there are many
other things circling around as well.

'Go on!' says our big sister, Anthippe, after she helps us get into our
beds. 'Go to sleep now. Don't worry.'

She says not to worry, but her face is serious. She goes out quickly,
more quickly than usual, so that we don't start asking her dangerous questions.

Outside it is very still. The night rests in the Kimindenia mountains,
which have lived through so much today. The oil lamp faintly lights the
triptych of the Panagia with the Infant that protects us.

'Artemis . . . ,' says Lena from her bed, and her voice trembles. 'Did
you really see him then? Did you see him?'

Artemis doesn't answer. But Lena is an ignorant and good creature
like grandmother, and she wants to learn.

'What is a killed person like, Artemis? Is it wild looking?'

Artemis starts to cry. I hear her sobs next to me and sense her rending
pain.

'Shh,' I command Lena, since I am the only boy there, the only man.
'You just mind your oven. Go to sleep!'

That's what I say. But I also would have liked so much to know what
a killed person is like.

Then Agapi cuts in, wanting to get her revenge.

'It serves you right,' she says to Artemis, 'for always wanting to roam the mountains like a wild animal! Now you'll always see the killed man in your sleep! It will pursue you! It will pursue you!'

Her terrible words make me shiver with fear. Is it true? Will Artemis see the dead man in her sleep from now on? Poor Artemis! Poor Artemis!

'And did your hands touch his blood by any chance?' continues Agapi with unimaginable malice. 'Then it will never come out! Never!'

Artemis stops sobbing. Now she's flooded with panic.

'Stop! Stop!' she cries to Agapi. 'You are evil! Stop . . .'

'Your hands will always have blood on them! Your hands will always have his blood!' continues the unrelenting voice of the older girl. 'Why don't you want me to teach you numbers? Your hands will have blood on them while mine write about the stars.'

'Be quiet . . . Be quiet, that's enough,' murmurs Artemis' voice more softly now, imploringly.

'Dear Agapi, be quiet,' begs Lena's sweet voice, touched by the pain that she senses in Artemis. 'Don't you feel sorry for her? Be quiet.'

I want to tell her off too, but at that moment my ear catches a slight sound. Memories of our earliest childhood awake at once; they come in waves, moved by the mystery and fear that encircle us.

'Listen!' I murmur softly. 'Listen!'

'What is it?' asks Agapi, startled.

'Listen! Something is moving next door. In the Yellow Room!'

The faint sounds remain, intensify, and then grow weak. The shudder of our childhood fears is here again and envelops us.

'The swords are waking up,' murmurs Lena softly. 'The swords are waking up.'

'What are you saying there!' protests Agapi, trying to react with the logic of her numbers to the panic that is about to take hold of even her. 'Is it possible for swords to wake up? We're not children anymore.'

That's what she says, but the sounds are there; they don't go away. They are mixed with the footsteps of men. They are like men. And Agapi's voice trembles as she struggles in vain to be convincing.

'I'm telling you, swords don't wake up. Go to sleep.'

A murdered hunter, a bear's den, the desolate Kimindenia, blood, and the swords waking up. I go under the covers so that I can't hear the sounds, to be sure that they don't get me.

Quite some time passed. I gather my courage and cautiously poke my head out from under the sheet.

'Artemis . . . Do you hear anything?'

Artemis doesn't answer, but the sounds have stopped now. Lena and Agapi have fallen asleep.

Then the harsh and wild divinity of the mountain can be heard: the voice of the hungry jackals howling.

'Artemis, are you scared? Come close to me.'

I hear the faint brushing of her body against her mattress, and then I see the figure in a white nightgown coming towards me. She lies down beside me. We go under the covers, and I hold her tightly in my arms. Her small body quivers with fear, and her teeth are chattering.

'Calm down, Artemis. We'll always be together, you and I. Don't be afraid.'

It was as though, in some dark and unconscious way, the days that lay ahead were sending a message into the depths of that place where magic and fear reside. It was as though they were telling us now that the Symphony of the Dawn was ending, both for Artemis and for me, with a pistol shot in the Kimindenia, there in the land of the beech trees, on the path that leads to the great bear's den. The pistol shot took the hunter with it, took him away from Artemis. It also took from me the magic of cascading hair. The Symphony was ending.

No one knew that night what it meant, this pistol shot that resounded in our ravines on that summer morning of 1914. No one could guess how many more, countless as the ears of wheat on the earth, were going to follow it. And that's why everyone was able to sleep. Only two children, Artemis and I, with our arms wrapped tightly around one another while the jackals howled, wept because our Symphony was ending. Dense clouds from high above us, and dark waves from deep within us, brought us news of the end. In that way, we were the first creatures who, without knowing it, cried in the summer of 1914 in mourning for the world.

And that night, when sleep finally came and closed her eyes, Artemis did not dream. Not any more. She does not want to go to distant seas, to the land of the Ocean. Why should she go? She doesn't care any more about the country that makes girls' hair look like cascading waves, girls who make hunters with yellow stars pluck roses with their rifles to offer to them. She does not want to go to the islands of Greece either, to fall into their sea crowned with blossoms of the chaste tree. No. She will go and gather blossoms of the chaste tree on the banks of the Jackal River. She won't wear them in her hair. She will take them to the earth where he is at rest, so that they will tell him that Artemis remembers him and weeps.

THE NEXT MORNING, a man came from the estate by the sea. He was holding the bear cub carefully in his arms and looking for Artemis.

'My mistress who came from foreign lands says for you to have it. Keep it and raise it.'

Grandmother and my mother cried out:

'In the name of God! What is this? Are we going to have a wild animal underfoot now?'

But Artemis rushes to grandfather and beseeches him in tears:

'Grandfather, my dear grandfather. Don't say no! Let us keep it!'

Grandfather is silent, absorbed in his worries. But he sees the desperate appeal of the little girl.

'Tie it up!' he says to one of his men. 'Give it milk to drink!'

Artemis runs and kisses his hands. Then she goes to the little animal. Her fingers timidly touch the black fur. They stay there. They stay.

'We will give it to travelling bear trainers when they come through,' says grandfather later to grandmother.

END OF PART TWO

PART THREE

MAN

⇒ Chapter One ⇐

Night came down to the Devil's Table, the legendary mountain of Aivali. She came quietly, treading lightly. She looked to the south and saw the waves of the Aegean breaking on the rocks. She looked to the north and saw the Kimindenia mountains and Anatolia.

Night said:

'Let me ask the waves for news of the smugglers. Let me ask the mountains of the East to tell me where my boys are going.'

She called the wind from the Archipelago and from the mountains of the Aeolian land. She asked:

'How are the brave men of my country, the ones whom I protect? How are the smugglers?'

'They live and reign,' answered the winds. 'Don't worry.'

'Are their hearts still like steel? Are they still always ready for their great companion, death?'

'Always.'

THEY WERE COMPLETELY INSANE, LOST SOULS. A demon burned inside them: the passion for blood and danger. They gambled with their lives every day, getting into fights and starting them. It was a game with fire and death that had to be as crazy and thoughtless as possible for it to have meaning, for it to give a little peace and cool the burning iron a little. They were the most extravagant of men. No smuggler ever held onto the gold from his huge earnings. They squandered it on legendary carousing that lasted for days; they spent it on women; they distributed it among poor housewives. In this way, since it had no practical purpose, their game of fire was unalloyed. It was a compulsion. The crazier it was, the more unattainable the chimera of peace became. The burning iron never cooled down, it just kept on burning. Only in the grave was there peace.

No sign of this unquenchable passion showed in the smugglers' faces. They were serious and laconic. And when they went around in town among women and children, they had the shy awkwardness of children. They never bothered a defenceless person, never affronted a woman. The most sacred sentiment among them was friendship. For a woman, a child, or the good name of a friend, a smuggler had to fight to the death. There was no other way.

They never stole, and they did not excuse robbery. For that reason, no thief could ever have survived in that town. The smugglers would have done away with him. But they did honour murder. They never questioned the grounds on which a murder was committed, whether it was just or unjust. For you to kill meant that there was no other way: it had to be. It also meant that you yourself were waiting for a bullet, that you were among those who could expect it. It meant more or less that you were one of theirs, and that your fate was their fate. Because of this, the murderer was a suppliant in their temple: they were obliged to protect him. All murderers, Christians or Turks, in the surrounding areas of Anatolia knew that as soon as they set foot in Aivali, they walked in the holy city of murder. They had nothing more to fear. The smugglers would take care of them, they would hide them from the authorities and ferry them in caiques to the islands of the Aegean, to the foreign country: Greece.

The smugglers brought the contraband tobacco down from Aounia and the region of Balikeser; they sold it in the city or transported it in their boats. They were in danger at every moment the whole way. They travelled by night to elude the *koltzides*, the smuggling police, the other young men of the country whose work it was to go after contraband. But this made the game boring, and the demon inside the men of fire shouted:

'Not like that! The brave men of Aivali don't do things that way!'

And so, the smugglers attained the height of daring. As soon as their caravan arrived at the outskirts of the city, they sent word to the authorities:

'Tonight, after midnight, we will come down by way of such and such a road!'

The message travelled from mouth to mouth and spread through the whole town. Up until the designated time, the townspeople were asking:

'Will they attack the smugglers? Will they not attack them?
'Will they attack or won't they attack?'

The girls trembled with agitation and emotion. They didn't admit it, but they sniffed the air incessantly because they were raised in blood, and deep inside they longed for the air to smell of blood. They went to the wives and fiancées of the smugglers who were going to make the move. They found them silent and pale, their misty eyes staring and their nerves on edge.

'Angela . . . tonight?'

Angela looks at the cloud that's passing and answers in an icy voice: 'Tonight.'

She wipes her white lips with her hand as her nostrils quiver. No, Angela is not unhappy. She learned as a child, from her mother and her mother's mother, from all the Angelas; she learned to wait for this great moment. She knows, and she waits. She knows that then the eyes of all the women will be turned on her, on her alone, and that in *that* great moment, she will be the leading figure among all the women in the world. They will look at her. They will watch her intently and envy her since it was fated for her to rise so high, to rise and to suffer.

Finally the designated midnight comes. Hidden behind their shutters, everyone waits: women, children, and old men. From a distance, faintly at first, the hoofbeats of horses are heard. The iron-clad hoofs strike the cobblestones on the road. They strike hard, signalling the critical hour. On horseback, wrapped in furs, with their rifles in their hands, the smugglers surround the caravan of camels, which advances without a sound. The camels in this caravan do not have bells — they are not needed. Loaded with contraband, they go silently through the night like ghosts. The procession advances. The horses' gait becomes heavier and harder. From this, the people behind the shutters know that the time has come. They can imagine the eyes of the riders glinting as they try to see through the darkness, into the corners of the roads, to sniff out the enemy that awaits them.

Then the voice of death rushes violently through the night. The Martin rifles and the Gras rifles pour out fire, the horses run about madly and the camels stop abruptly. They stop and go backwards. According to plan, one group of smugglers takes the camels with the tobacco and disappears down a narrow side street. The others stay to hold off the *koltzides*, to protect the escape of the caravan. Shouts are heard through the darkness; bodies that have been hit fall from horses; camels bellow as they're dragged along by force.

And then everything is silent, everything but the acrid blood spilled on the cobblestones. The blood which cries out.

THE RED CUTTER, Andonis Pagidas' famous smuggling boat, with the help of a strong north wind, is leaving 'Bare Island' — the uninhabited island outside the gulf of Aivali. Its prow is pointed straight for the mainland of Anatolia opposite, where the Vilaras estate is. There is no tobacco in her hold this time. There are weapons. Pagidas' whole company — his brave young men — waited on Bare Island for three days and three nights to receive them. They were being brought to them from Syros. But the weather was adverse, and that prevented the smugglers from Syros arriving at the island on time. While they were waiting, Pagidas' smugglers drank and got drunk and sang songs about Tsakitzis for the first and second nights. Then, towards dawn on the second night, the guard who was keeping watch on the northern outlook of the small island saw a felucca gliding into the sheltering cove below his lookout. The watchman waited for the felucca to draw near and then he shouted:

'Hey there, boat!'

'Hey!'

'Are you fishing?'

'*Karantak*,' shouted the man on the felucca, giving the password. 'I want Andonis Pagidas!'

'Drop anchor!'

What unexpected thing has happened for this fellow smuggler to have come in the night to their secret hideout? Had they been betrayed? Were the *koltzides* coming?

No. The smuggling had not been betrayed. The *koltzides* were still acting as though they didn't know where Andonis Pagidas was. So great was the fear that his very name inspired, it would not cross anyone's mind to attack that famous young blood of Aivali or get in the way of his operations. Furthermore, the leader of the *koltzides* was still Stratigos Garbis, the dearest bosom friend of Andonis Pagidas. Their friendship, tested by blood and murder, was celebrated as a legend among the young men of Aivali. They could tell how many times Pagidas had come to blows for the sake of Garbis, and he for Pagidas. Everyone said: 'If Pagidas and Garbis ever worked together in smuggling, no power in all of Anatolia would be able to take them on.' But that never happened. So that one could never impinge upon the honour of the other, the two bravest young men of the country always stayed in opposite camps. And they always found a way to show that they knew how to respect one another. Only in 1908, after the authorities had decided to dispense with Pagidas once and for all and were preparing the attack with the *koltzides*, Garbis decided to pass over secretly one night to the company of Pagidas. He went and met him on the mountain and told him what was going on: he betrayed the secret, the place where they had set up the ambush to kill him. And since Pagidas refused to retreat and run away, Garbis went with him that night, and he fought the authorities beside the friend of his heart.

'Garbis, I will never forget that,' Pagidas told him on that night in 1908.

And he never forgot.

The comrade who'd come in the felucca stood without a word before his leader, not daring to open his mouth.

'What is it?' asked Pagidas.

The other was silent.

Then Pagidas asked again, more savagely:

'What is it?'

Silence.

'Will you talk, man?'

Andonis Pagidas' eyes began to darken. Everyone around him knew what it meant when his eyes started to darken. Do they think there is anything in this world that Andonis Pagidas cannot handle? Is there something they know and are hiding?

The smuggler from the felucca understood that Pagidas would not stand this any more, and he had to talk.

'They killed your brother!' he said.

All the young men standing around their leader were shaken by this blow. They were about to rush at the companion who brought the news and ask him more. But slowly, solemnly, Andonis Pagidas' harsh gaze transfixed them. No one moved.

'Who?' he asked, in a voice that sounded perfectly calm through the darkness.

'Garbis!'

In the position Pagidas had reached, the highest rung of bravery, there was nothing that could surprise him, nothing that could make him lose his harsh composure. And yet that moment showed that Andonis Pagidas had a heart with blood in it.

'Who did you say?' he screamed in a rending voice.

'Garbis, Captain! Stratigos Garbis!'

The younger brother of Andonis Pagidas had nothing in common with his older brother. He was a man without a sense of honour, without any of the qualities of brave young men. Nevertheless, following in his brother's footsteps, he also worked in smuggling and had his own caique and band. Out of respect for Andonis Pagidas, the patrolmen always turned a blind eye to his brother's operations. Since they always treated him this way, he became more and more shameless over time. He thought that whatever happened was because they feared *him*, not Andonis Pagidas. All the brave young men of Aivali had a lot to say about what he did, and secretly they made fun of him. But the *koltzides* always acted as though they didn't see. They knew that for nothing else in the world did Andonis Pagidas have a greater weakness than he had for his worthless brother. Inside this noble man, the only way all the unspent tenderness that he had covered up with blood and iron was shown to exist was in his love for his younger brother.

'Who did you say killed him?' Andonis Pagidas roared for the third time, violently shaking the shoulders of his companion as though he couldn't believe it.

'Garbis, Captain! Stratigos Garbis!'

And in a stark and breathless manner, he gave the details. Something had happened, but it wasn't completely clear what. It seems that Stratigos Garbis was in his patrol boat and encountered Constantine Pagidas' smuggling boat on the open sea of Sarmousak. He didn't recognize it and attempted to stop it. The two caiques exchanged a few pistol shots. Constantine Pagidas was not on board his boat. But once Garbis had confirmed that the boat with the contraband tobacco was his, he let it pass.

When Constantine Pagidas found out what had happened, he

became incensed. His head, swelled up as it already was, grew even bigger. He spread it around here and there that he was going to demand an explanation from Garbis. And as soon as he learned that Garbis' official boat had come back from its patrol, he took his rifle and went down to the beach. He said to Garbis, 'Did you touch my boat?' He made a show of eying his rifle. 'Go ahead and shoot!' said Garbis calmly from the bow of his boat, unarmed as always. Constantine Pagidas said something else. 'Shoot, man!' said Garbis again. Then Constantine Pagidas blasphemed. He let out a mortal curse of the kind that after they are spoken, there is no salvation: they must be paid for with blood. So as not to give Garbis time to pay for it, Pagidas drew his gun and fired at him. He missed. Garbis jumped from the prow to the shore, took the rifle from his hands and killed him.

Andonis Pagidas listened. Silently, he moved apart from his men. His face had recovered its frigid calm. Dawn was breaking. He rolled a cigarette and lit it. The bluish smoke rose, stirred a little in the morning breeze and disappeared. In silence his men watched him there alone. They knew he was planning something terrible. They knew that at this very moment he was resolving to do a thing that would make every brave heart in Anatolia bleed.

Andonis Pagidas threw down his cigarette. He slowly turned his darkened eyes towards the smuggler from the felucca.

'Go back,' he commanded calmly. 'Tell Garbis that I'll kill him. I will meet him outside the farmstead of Yannako-Bibelas on Tuesday at the waning of the moon.'

THE RED CUTTER, Andonis Pagidas' famous smuggling boat, goes tearing through the sea. The waves pound the wood. The wood battles with the water as though one or the other of them must be brought to its knees. But the wood is proud, it does not tolerate being bridled. It is carrying a lot inside it tonight, not just weapons, not just Andonis Pagidas and his men. It carries the fate that will choose between the two most famous lives in the epic circle of bravery in Aivali: Andonis Pagidas or Stratigos Garbis.

Above the sailboat, the night strains to listen. Pagidas sits apart in the bow of the boat smoking endless cigarettes in silence. He hears the waves hit his boat and hears the distant sounds of the great and extraordinary life he had lived, sounds that must all come to him tonight on this sea that he may be crossing for the last time. The more he weighs this thought — that these might be his last hours — the more he understands that he is alone, completely alone. It is a feeling that has been with him since the days of his childhood. When his mother had him in her womb, she had gutted and skinned a hare on Saint Simeon's day. On the feast day of Saint Simeon, pregnant women should sit with their hands folded and not do anything. If they happen to pick something up, whatever it might be, the marks of what they touch will appear on the face or the body of their unborn child. Andonis Pagidas' mother had forgotten what day it was when a neighbour woman came in and saw her.

'How can you be preparing a hare on this day, good woman!' she cried.

Terrified, Andonis Pagidas' mother threw down the hare and brought her two hands to her shoulders.

'Christ and the Panagia!' she said, and turned as yellow as a gold florin.

All night she prayed to God to have pity on her. And Saint Simeon heard her. He didn't let her child be marked on the face. When he was born, all the women in attendance saw with amazement a wide strip of hare's fur on his back. The matter was greatly discussed, and over time, when they wanted to refer to that child, men and women would say: 'The child with the wild animal back.' His mother was very sad and said:

'What will happen when he grows up and learns about it? It will embitter his whole life.'

But she was a mother, and with her deep instinct, she worked out how to help him. One day — the first time he went to the beach to swim with the neighbourhood children — the child came home in tears.

'What's the matter, my son?'

'Why do they make fun of me?' he cried with anguish. 'Why, of all the children who went swimming, am I the only one who has animal skin on his back?'

Then, assuming the most confident air possible, she said:

'So don't you understand? They're jealous! You're the only child in Anatolia who was touched by the Fates!'

'What are the Fates?' asked the child.

The Fates, she told him, are good women who sit in heaven with the angels. Every so often, after many years, it is ordained for them to come down to earth on some stormy night. Men sleep, unsuspecting. Only mothers who are expecting children stay awake watching. They say: 'Let the Fates come this year. May this be their year.' With wide open eyes, they look into the darkness and keep praying: 'Let them come this year. Let them come for my child who will be born.'

Then the blessing comes at last. It comes to only one mother every so many years. The Fates open her door, and the darkness turns to light. They go silently to the mother, smiling sweetly. They place their hands on her head and hold it for a moment, then they smile again and leave. That's all. The unborn child will be marked by the Fates.

'Did you see the Fates, Mother?' asked the boy, amazed.

'Yes, my son. They came then, when it was time for you to be born. You will be strong! You are blessed by the Fates. You will be the most famous youth in Anatolia! Don't cry.'

With words like this, Andonis Pagidas' simple mother, helped by her instinct, brought about the miracle. Not only did she not let her child be broken before his time by a sense of inferiority; she helped him to find pride and self-confidence in the unique fate that marked his body and set him apart from the other children.

One winter day they went together to the sea, to the pine forest beside the beach. A powerful north wind beat the straits and raised enormous waves. Not a single sailboat was out, no human soul dared to contend with the demon. The mother of small Andonis Pagidas stood him face to face with the waves and told him:

'You will struggle, my son. You will become the most powerful sailor in our land. Your name will resound all the way to the Black Sea. They will sing of the sailor with an animal's back.'

In that small pine forest, there was an old tower that was falling into ruins. From inside the tower, the mother and child suddenly saw a hunched old man emerge, dressed in ragged clothes. He went towards the sea, stood for a while looking at the storm, and then returned to the tower.

'Do you see that old man?' said Andonis Pagidas' mother to the child. 'He was once with Father Oikonomos. Father Oikonomos was the most famous man of our country. Every night, that old man comes out and summons him from the waves, calls for him to see that their house is in ruins and to return. He is crazy.'

And as the waves roared, and the wind coming down from the Devil's Table howled through the trees, Andonis Pagidas' mother told her child all about that famous Father Oikonomos. He was a hermit who lived in the old days. Withdrawn from the world, he spent his life in a hut on a deserted shore, where he did penance and prayed for his soul and for the salvation of his enslaved nation. Then one stormy night, he heard a desperate human voice coming from the sea, calling for help. He went out into the night, got his boat, battled the waves and went toward the voice. He pulled a half-drowned body from the sea, brought it to his hut, warmed it and revived it.

The shipwrecked man was trembling from the cold.

'Who are you?' the monk asked him.

'I'm a Turk,' he answered. 'Have pity on me.'

'Are you a sailor? Did your boat sink?'

'No, I'm not a sailor. I am an officer in the sultan's navy. We were defeated by Moscow at Çeşme. For three days and three nights I was battered by the waves in a felucca. As I neared your shore, my felucca capsized.* Pity me and don't harm me in the state you find me, sick and vulnerable. Your God says that He doesn't strike the weak and the defenceless.'

'Don't worry,' the hermit answered him. 'I will do what God tells me to do for the weak and vulnerable, even though you are Turkish.'

The monk took care of the shipwrecked sailor. He attended to him night and day while his fever raged; he gave him herbs from the land and made him well. Then he showed him the road to take to reach an inhabited place.

'Go in peace,' he said to him. 'Don't do harm to my race. Pity my race, just as I pitied you.'

'My name is Hasan,' said the Turk. 'Remember my name and come to me if I can ever help you.'

The monk remembered the sailor's name for many years. Then one day he learned from passing sailors who were travelling to the Black Sea that the Turk of that winter night had become the Grand Vizier. The monk took his staff and went to the town, Aivali, where a race of poor fishermen and toilers of the land groaned under Turkish subjugation. From there he got on a caique and went to the City. He arrived at the throne of the Grand Vizier.

'Do you remember me?' he asked.

Then all the pashas who were gathered there watched in amazement as their vizier stood up and hugged and kissed the infidel monk.

'Good man, how could I forget you?' he said. 'Tell me what I need to do to lighten my soul and resemble you in the things you taught me. Tell me, now that I'm powerful, what I should do to repay you?'

'I don't want anything for myself,' answered the monk. 'I want something for my people and my homeland. Help end their suffering.'

Then the Grand Vizier ordered an edict in the name of the sultan. In it he wrote that not a single Turk would be permitted to stay anymore in the province where the monk lived. All the Ottoman families that lived there would have to settle elsewhere. Christian elders would govern the province with one Turkish governor, whom the people would appoint and dismiss whenever they wanted. A military governor would not only be forbidden to live in the town, he would be forbidden to even pass along its roads. If, in some unusual circumstance, he was obliged to do so, he would have to remove his horse's shoes. The province would pay fifty thousand piastres each year to the Turkish state and would collect all the taxes itself. The area would not have to provide conscripts of young men for the Ottoman army or of children for service in Turkish families. It would be a free place, the only one in the whole Ottoman Empire.

The monk took the edict and returned to his homeland. Then all the tyrannized people, learning the particulars, fell and kissed his feet. They made him the head man of the town, and he governed the province with the elders until the hour of his death.*

First, he built a large church with a tall bell tower, the church of Our Lady of the Orphans. Its walls were decorated with stories from the Old Testament. He adorned it with a pulpit and a bishop's throne made entirely out of ebony, ivory and mother-of-pearl from the Red Sea. He built fine schools and gave asylum to all the Greeks who fled the islands of the Aegean and the old Greece to escape the torments of Turkish subjugation and come to this free province. In this way, the small fishing village in the land of Aeolia grew larger and became a great town. The monk was always the leading town elder. He was fair to good people but unspeakably harsh to the unjust. He became the terror of the Turkish *beys* who governed the neighbouring provinces of Ayiasmat, Adramyti and Pergamum. He armed his men and took them with him to combat injustices done to Christians outside his province. With the same vigour, he shielded his province from raids made by the neighbouring *beys*.

His name was on everyone's lips. They all said:

'Who blessed this man for him to do so much good to our homeland?'

Only when he died and they washed his body and changed his clothes, only then did his secret come to light and was passed with wonder from mouth to mouth among the people:

'The monk was marked by the Fates! On his chest, he had the mark of an eel!'

His most fearsome enemy, the *bey* of Pergamum, didn't believe it when he learned of his death. He came all the way to Aivali, ordered them to dig him up, and when he saw the corpse with his own eyes, he shed tears in the memory of his enemy.

Little Andonis Pagidas listened enthralled.

'Yes, my son,' his mother said to him. 'He was marked, too, just like you! You will also be a great man! You will become powerful!'

In this way, she raised her child in the steady exaltation of his exceptional fate. This helped him not to fall. But he took it to the other extreme. It made him a closed, solitary child who didn't want to associate with other children his age and did not condescend to do so. The unbridled imagination of the people of the Aegean, inherited from their ancestors, helped him in his solitude. All around him, in the air and the songs of the region, in the daily incidents, the supreme moment in the cycle of heroism was lived out — the epic of the smugglers. In his seventeenth year, Andonis Pagidas became a smuggler. In the same year, he committed his first murder, fighting some men who were pursuing him. After that came other murders, and others, an endless succession, all marked by incredible ferocity, incredible fearlessness: he always killed face to face, never through trickery, a libation to the unquenchable passion that ordered him to risk his life and kill like a man.

THE RED CUTTER DROPPED ANCHOR in front of the estate by the sea just as day was about to break. They unloaded the weapons and secured them in Vilaras' mansion. Pagidas asked them to leave him alone in the boat to rest. He would see old Vilaras as soon as he woke up. He slept deeply until evening. On awaking, he dunked his head in the sea and went to see Vilaras.

Doris was there too. She begged them to let her stay while the men talked. The old nobleman recounted the events from the beginning, how the hunter was found killed. He told about the other villager who had been shot.

Pagidas listened silently, smoking endless cigarettes.

'Has anything else happened since then?'

'That's what's awful,' said Vilaras. 'The evil hasn't stopped. Since then, they have shot at three more Christians who were returning from the Kimindenia. They killed one of them. I'm afraid . . .'

'Of what?' Pagidas interrupted him.

'I'm afraid that behind all this there is a plan. I'm afraid to look further ahead . . .'

'We'll see!' said Pagidas.

He thought for a moment, then said:

'Some of the weapons will stay here for your men. The rest need to go to the Christians on the other side of the Kimindenia. Can they pay me for them?'

'I'll pay the whole amount,' said Vilaras. 'But I want you and your men to deliver them.'

'I'll take them. Then I can see things for myself. A trusted man of yours will need to come with us so that the Christians in the villages are not alarmed.'

Then Doris, who was sitting silently, said:

'I will go, Father. Let me go.'

Old Vilaras jumped up, off guard.

'What are you saying, my child? In the name of God! That's impossible! How could you go?'

'This is not women's work,' said Pagidas, calmly. 'You can't come.'

Doris lifts her eyes and fixes them right on him. It's the second time that he, Andonis Pagidas, realizes that he cannot withstand the razor-sharp blade that leaps from her almost childlike face.

He lowers his eyes.

'I'll come with you!' says Doris decisively, in a way that forestalls any response.

'Ah, not this! I can't stand this any longer!' cries the old nobleman, trembling with distress. 'I will have to write to my son . . .'

'Don't worry, Father,' Doris says calmly. 'Don't be afraid for me. My husband will not be sorry to learn that his wife is not afraid of anything.'

'We'll leave tonight!' says Pagidas. 'We'll be gone for two days and two nights.'

'Stay tonight and leave tomorrow night,' says Vilaras, having no other way to buy time and, if possible, change his daughter-in-law's mind.

'No!' says Pagidas. 'I must leave tonight! I don't have time. I have to be back Tuesday night at the waning of the moon.'

'What do you have to do then?' asks Vilaras.

'Nothing!' says Pagidas sharply.

⇒ Chapter Two ⇐

1914

The Kimindenia mountains have grown weary this year, very weary. They wait impatiently for night to come. The beech trees are the first to see it coming, then the oaks.

They say to the night:

Hurry! Come, since the Kimindenia, our mother, are tired. Come and give her rest.'

'What can I do?' the night asks them. 'It's still summer. The days are long, the sun sets late.'

Then the beech trees appeal to the clouds. They say to them:

'The sun won't set until late. Let one of your companions go to cover it. Help our mother, the Kimindenia, go to bed early.'

A black cloud rises in the deep blue sky. It makes its way from the east, moves westward and hides the sun. It is an enormous black cloud; the land of Aeolia darkens abruptly. The hoopoes and wild pigeons playing in the blue light find themselves suddenly enveloped in the shadow that comes from the sky. Guided by instinct, they hurry in fear to hide in their nests. As they fly, they call out:

'The storm! The storm is coming! The storm is coming!'

The green lizards hear them; the jackals in the thicket hear them. Fear passes through their eyes, and they all cry in distress:

'The storm is coming! The storm is coming!'

A small tortoise, turned upside down and waiting for death in the wild boars' cave, hears the cry of the birds and the wild animals. She draws into her shell in fear. Even though she is waiting for death, even though she is waiting only for death, she still shudders, like all the creatures on earth.

'The storm is coming! The storm is coming!'

The beech trees try in vain to combat the panic. In vain they say:

'Don't carry on like that! No storm is coming. It's us who asked the cloud to cover the sun!'

Say what they will, no one hears them. Because instinct reigns in the Kimindenia, deep and indestructible. This instinct gave the creatures the wisdom to know that beyond what they begin by their own volition, beyond their own desires and actions, there exists a dark force that takes desires and actions into its own hands and sets them in motion in its own way, in the direction it chooses.

'No! No! It is the storm! The storm is coming!'

Then the Kimindenia slowly stir. They shake off the sleep that was coming to give them rest. They stand up and look to the left and to the right. They see the black cloud in the west. They turn their eyes to the sky. They know that the stars will come out soon. Maybe the black cloud that the beech trees summoned will disperse and go away once the sun sets. Surely it will go away. And yet now the Kimindenia know for sure. They know because they have lived through many things and have learned much more than the beech trees, the hoopoes, the wild boars and the jackals.

The Kimindenia know for once and for all that the storm is coming. And yet, since this is how it always works, that until the very last minute we keep on hoping for a thing that we already know is beyond hope, the Kimindenia turn to the mountains in the west and the mountains in the east. They ask the Kaz-Dak and the mountains beyond the Aegean, beyond the Hellespont, and beyond the Danube, the king of rivers.

They ask, to make sure:

'Is it true, my brothers? Is it coming?'

And all the mountains, from distant Bosnia and from beyond the Danube, answer sadly:

'It is true, brother. It is coming. The storm is coming.'

Of all the creatures that live in the Kimindenia, man is the last to receive the news, because man is the most far removed creature of all. It comes as a roaring wave, thrashing and beating as it goes, surging and raging:

'It's coming! The storm is coming! War is coming!'

And while the stars above the Aeolian earth watch serenely, the cowering hearts of men, the hearts of wretched humans, open to let in Fear.

IN THAT DEEP NIGHT, away in our room, we children wait for sleep to take us. The nights in the Kimindenia have become more mysterious now and wilder. It isn't only the jackals and the solitude; ever since they killed the hunter, something hovers in the air. The faces of the adults are clouded; they don't let us venture out of the farmstead at all. Our men, armed, stand guard in shifts. We hear their footsteps outside the big door. Sometimes we hear a cough or a voice disturbing the spirit of solitude.

The worst thing is that the beeches will forget us now; the wild oaks and the hoopoes will forget us.

'And what has become of our tortoise up there, and our bat, and the green lizard?'

'What did you say?'

'I mean in the wild boars' cave. What has happened there?'

Artemis shudders. I hear the rustling that her fingers make as they tighten their grip on the sheets.

'I don't want to know,' she murmurs.

'Don't you want to go to the wild boars' cave? Don't you wish they'd let us?'

'I won't go there ever again,' says Artemis, and her voice trembles.

'Our bat must have died by now. We'll hang its tiny bones around our necks. We'll divide them up. After that everyone will love us.'

'I don't want to,' murmurs Artemis. 'I don't want to anymore.'

And she starts to cry.

'Hush, Artemis. Hush. Why are you crying?'

Silence.

'Hush, Artemis. It's all right, don't wear the bat's bones. I'll love you anyway.'

'I'm going out tomorrow,' says Lena. 'I'll ask grandfather, and he'll let me. I'll go with Uncle Joseph.'

'What are you going to do?' asks Agapi.

'We'll go to the place with the red soil. It's the most beautiful part of our land. It's the place that grandfather will give me when I get married. There is a wild pear tree. Uncle Joseph will graft it in my name.'

A few days before, Lena had gone and found Uncle Joseph. She said to him: 'Do you know what? When Artemis grows up she's going to leave us. She'll marry a hunter and they will go to far away places.' 'Why, my girl?' 'Just like that, Uncle Joseph. She's made up her mind. Everyone is going to leave.' Uncle Joseph remembered his own fate, the island he set out from once and to which never returned. 'It sometimes happens that way,' he said. 'It happens that men leave once and never go back. It isn't in their power to return.' 'But I'll stay on our land,' says little Lena. 'I love our land.' 'Come then,' says the old man. 'I'll graft another tree in your name. That way you'll remember me when you eat its fruit.'

Lena says:

'Is it true, Artemis? Are you still planning to leave us?'

There is no answer.

'Artemis! Are you still planning on going to faraway places?'

'I'll leave . . . ,' whispers Artemis in a voice that seems to come from deep inside.

'And will your husband be a hunter?'

There is no answer.

'And will your husband be a hunter?'

Lena is about to ask for a third time, when she first hears the sound.

'Listen! Listen!'

'What is it?'

Bright and metallic, the sound of a bell plays against the night.

'It's a horse, isn't it? Listen. It has a bell! Who is coming?'

We all become quiet and listen. Suddenly, there is a knot in our hearts, and they flood with fear. It is a fear that comes from the secret powers of darkness, from the depths of our existence and from the desolate night.

What can this clatter of a horse's hooves be? What if it's brigands?

Our ears now make out another, weaker sound behind the hoofbeats. It sounds like wheels rolling on the deep earth.

'It's a carriage!' says Lena.

Then right away she adds:

'It must be Vilaras' carriage! That has a horse with a bell.'

The Vilaras' carriage! Thank God it isn't brigands! Of course: the carriage from the estate by the sea.

We are relieved to let go of our fear of brigands. But then Artemis plants the first seed.

'Has the old lord ever before come at this hour, in the middle of the night?' she murmurs. 'Something must have happened. Some very bad thing!'

Her words, delivered in a trembling voice, pour fear again into our veins, our blood, and our hearts.

Our big sister, Anthippe, wakes up.

'What is it?' she says. 'Why are you all awake?'

'Listen Anthippe! The old lord in his carriage is outside the gate.'

Anthippe rubs her eyes.

'Did you say it was the carriage and the old lord? What time is it?'

'Oh! It's the middle of the night.'

'And how do you know that it's the old lord?'

'We heard the bell he has on his horse. We heard the wheels.'

'Shh!' whispers Lena.

From outside, at the big door, a quiet conversation reaches us. We can't make out what they're saying. Old Vilaras must be asking our armed guards to let him pass.

That must be it. After a short while we hear the heavy grinding of the door.

'He's coming! He's coming!'

Artemis throws a shawl over her nightgown. We other children also put something on. Even Anthippe, carried away by the unforeseen night-time adventure and her own curiosity and desire to resolve the mystery, doesn't think to prevent us. She just advises us:

'Get dressed! Get dressed so you don't catch cold.'

We open the door of our room. Anthippe goes first. Behind her Artemis, Agapi, Lena and I follow. Careful not to make any noise, we advance on tiptoe. Shadows are visible in the courtyard: the people who live in the farmstead have woken up and are coming out, frightened, to find out what's happening.

Our hearts are close to bursting.

'What has happened? What has happened?'

A lamp had been lit in the large room with the wide divans where grandfather receives his guests. We guess he's there now, and we keep going. The door is half open. Anthippe, and then all us other children slip in on tiptoe. We stand close to one another.

And with wide-open eyes, we watch.

Grandfather stands straight and motionless like a tall old tree covered in clouds. Beside him stands grandmother, her white hair dishevelled. Her face is stricken with a wave of fear and panic. Beside her is our mother, also silent. And collapsed on a divan is the nobleman from the estate by the sea, old Vilaras. He is pale with distress and runs his hands nervously through his hair.

They turned their eyes slowly towards us when they saw us come in. Then they took them away again. It was as though it didn't surprise them at all, as though they were in a trance.

'It's appalling,' says old Vilaras in an undertone. 'Now the spark will light a fire throughout the world. And what will become of us?'

'What did you call it, neighbour?' asks grandfather softly. 'What did you call that place?'

'Sarajevo,' says Vilaras. 'It's north, in the vicinity of Bosnia.'

Grandfather is naïve, illiterate, and he can't grasp it easily.

'Why?' he says. 'Since the trouble is happening so far north, why should it reach all the way here to us in Anatolia?'

But old Vilaras is not naïve. He reads learned books and newspapers that come to him from Europe; he knows everything.

'But it has come, neighbour! It has already come, I'm telling you! These persecutions of Christians . . . I've heard they began in Kozakia and further inland. Any time now, our turn will come. Yes, now I understand why they killed my hunter and why they shot at my men.'

In a nervous gesture of despair, he digs his fingers into his white hair.

'Any time now our turn will come. We will have to leave the country. And for my child to be in the mountains with the smugglers at a time like this!'

Grandfather doesn't want to make this moment worse than it already is, but he feels choked by a sudden indignation.

'What is with your daughter-in-law, neighbour?' he says. 'Why does a sensible man like you let these things happen? Why?'

'In the name of God, Yannako-Bibelas, be quiet!' pleads old Vilaras in visible distress. 'This isn't the time for that! You're right, but how can I explain it all to you? But what will happen now? What now?'

Grandfather is silent and thinks.

'We have to send our men to the smugglers tonight!' he says at last, and his voice has the decisive tone of a man who has found himself in difficult circumstances many times in his life. 'The woman has to come back! Do you know what road they took?'

Old Vilaras tells which villages Pagidas intended to go to on the other side of the Kimindenia and which paths they would have taken through the ravine.

'How many of your men are truly brave?' asks grandfather.

'I don't have any other than the three who are there. The rest have run in fear.'

'All right! I'll send my men, too. Come with me!'

They went out, grandfather first and old Vilaras behind him.

Silently, all us children, Anthippe, Agapi, Lena, Artemis and I, stand there in the small shadow cast by the lamp. What is this veil that has suddenly been ripped apart, revealing dark chaos to our amazed eyes? What are these mixed-up things that make the tall oak tree of our house, our old grandfather who always used to smile, have such a dark face? Sarajevo, they said, a flame that's coming. They spoke of persecutions, of the hunter who was killed, and of Doris, who is in danger. Dear God, what is all this?

We run like a flock of sheep chased by a wolf and fall at the feet of grandmother and our mother to ask them for protection.

'Grandmother! Grandmother! What is it?'

'Mother! Mother! What is it?'

'My little children … My little children …,' whispers first one, then the other, and it's clear they are trying to keep their voices from trembling, their tears from falling.

'How did you get here, children? In the name of God!' they say, as though they'd only just noticed us.

'What is it, Grandmother? What is it, Mother?'

How can grandmother explain to us, how can our mother explain, when they are now like us children? It is all mixed up and unexplained inside them, just as it is in us. What more can our grandmother and our mother know than us about Sarajevo, about the spark that has caught fire and is approaching? Like us, they are overwhelmed by the dark force that says the storm is coming.

'My little children … My little children …'

Grandmother spreads her arms over us like the wings of a bird that wants to protect her young.

'Come to bed,' she whispers.

We go out into the dark hall. Like a small flock of sheep, we go on ahead, with grandmother and our mother coming behind us. In our room the faint light of the oil lamp that hangs in front of the triptych of the Panagia and Child illuminates our frightened faces. Grandmother goes over to the icon.

'Come, you come too,' she says softly. 'Say your prayers, my children. Pray to the Panagia to help us ...'

And as all of us children silently cross ourselves, grandmother, the chorus leader of the nocturnal supplication, starts to whisper her humble entreaty, for us, for all people, and for the little children of the world.

> *Mighty storms of misfortunes pass over me;*
> *and the swelling waves of afflictions plunge me into the depths.*
> *Accept my appeal and my poor prayer,*
> *and disdain not my weeping and sighs.* *

⇒ Chapter Three ⇐

THE PERSECUTIONS

Night. In the Kimindenia mountains, on the path that goes along the top of the great ravine, the company of Andonis Pagidas proceeds silently, his men on horseback, the mules loaded with the contraband weapons. Four smugglers go ahead to open the road, followed by the mules and then the other men. Pagidas comes last. And beside him is Doris.

Not a sound is heard: not a whisper, not a word. It is always like this during the dangerous hours of their work, when the smugglers are bringing down tobacco or other smuggled goods. Death, which is waiting to jump out in front of them at any moment, gives a severe expression to their faces and stills their tongues. But tonight all the young men understand that above the light murmur of the wind, above the rustling of the leaves, another force is journeying with them and is following them like a cloud. Tonight it isn't the knowledge of danger that tears at their hearts. They know that tonight is the last night of either Andonis Pagidas or Stratigos Garbis. They know that they are walking in company with the highest ideal of manly friendship, that they are present at a moment that will some day be myth and legend.

And their hearts are sad to the point of breaking.

None of the young men dare to approach Andonis Pagidas to tell him what they think or to try to change his mind. They all know that Andonis Pagidas has given his word, that blood is involved, and that this blood will be paid for.

The night is full of stars. Now and then the howling of jackals is heard in the distance. It comes from lower down, from the fields where they've rushed hungrily to eat.

'Let's stop!' commands Pagidas. 'Let the horses rest.'

The young men dismount, tie their horses to trees and gather around their leader. They sit on the damp earth and roll cigarettes.

'Aren't you going to sit down?' Pagidas asks Doris.

'I want to stretch my legs,' she answers, and walks around.

This is her second night of going through the Kimindenia mountains with the smugglers. She feels the strange manner of these dark men she's found herself among at this difficult time weigh on her more and more heavily.

At the beginning, when they'd just set out, she began asking Andonis Pagidas about this and that, trying to get him to tell stories, to tell about his adventures.

He cut her off.

'I don't know!'

Doris fell silent. But after a while, the unquenchable desire for adventure that burned inside her turned into temptation. She tried again to start a conversation with Pagidas. She knew nothing of the customs of these men of fire, nor of the storm that was lashing the heart of their leader.

'Did you ever get into a fight to protect a woman, Captain, or to protect a friend?'

No answer.

Doris tried again during the night:

'I had a hunter. The one who was killed. He told me once that friendship is very highly valued among you. A friend is valued more than a wife or a child. Is that true?'

Pagidas bit his cigarette and spat it out on the ground. He was unable to look Doris in the eyes because it was dark. He began to choke with rage.

'I was a fool to let you come with us, woman, and I regret it. Do you hear anyone else talking? Shut up!'

Doris, who was not used to being spoken to in this way, got angry too.

'What is this? Is it a funeral?'

Pagidas' lip trembled. But he recovered his self-control. He said calmly and decisively:

'I'll send you back! What I command is what happens here. I said: Shut up!'

Then, for the first time, Doris was scared.

That is how the first night passed. When day broke, the smugglers hid in a thicket; they hid their horses and their goods. They set up watches, lay down and slept. Doris slept off to the side until evening came.

The second night came, and they took the road again. They estimated that by daybreak they'd be at the villages where they were to distribute the weapons.

'Let's stop for the horses to rest!' ordered Pagidas.

THE HORSES GRAZE ON THE GRASS. The smugglers roll endless cigarettes and smoke silently. The stars in the clear sky contemplate the men. Everything is harsh and still.

Suddenly through the silence, Pagidas' voice and unexpected words are heard.

'Hey, why isn't anyone talking,' he asks his men. 'Why did you all go mute?'

Is it Pagidas who is saying this? Has a smuggler, has Pagidas, ever been known to ask why his companions are serious and silent, especially in a time of danger?

'What should we say?' asks one, surprised.

'Anything. Say something.'

Anything. Let them say something, let a word be heard, so that this weight might go away. Let it scatter the forces crowding in from the darkness to torment this man who has never cared about anything. It isn't the fear that he will die. It's something else: the fear that he will kill. For the first time, after all the blood that his hands have spilled, Andonis Pagidas feels his heart beating, feels a dark mist enveloping it, because he is going to kill. Because he is going to commit *this* murder.

'Speak, my companions. Say something.'

Then the Anatolian night shook her wings. She struck the wind hard, and the wind stopped. All the whispers, the trees that rustled, the worms that licked the earth, the faraway jackals that howled, all became silent. The companions sat around a brave man from Anatolia who was going to fight and to die, come what may. In a circle around him, they all understood what tonight was: it was their 'Love Feast'* — they were saying goodbye. The blood in their veins was still, only their hearts kept beating. And the woman called Doris who came from a faraway country and had the eyes of Aegean girls, the girl who found herself among them by a strange turn of fate, listened in wonder.

The chief smuggler, the first after Pagidas, began the libation and spoke. His voice was heavy and calm.

He said:

Selim the Moor ravaged the villages of Pergamum, ravaged the people of Agiasmat. Hunted down, they ran away, Christians and Turks, old men and children, to escape and save their lives.

'Selim the Moor is pursuing us! Selim the robber is in our area!'

His terrible name chilled the blood. Not a living soul could be found to fight him. The news arrives. It reaches *him*. *He* sends a message to Selim:

'If you are a man, let the two of us fight. I will be at the great plane tree where the Jackal River divides and becomes two rivers.'

Selim receives the message and goes to the designated spot. He does not go alone. With him are all his Albanian fighters. They sit and wait. They don't wait for long. They hear a noise. Is it horses? They say: 'He must be coming with his men,' and they draw their weapons.

No. It isn't horses; it isn't men. It is him alone. Completely alone.

'Am I seeing right?' asks Selim the Moor, amazed. 'Is it just one man?'

'It is only one!'

'*Allach!*' cries Selim, unable to believe it.

The Albanians are about to fall upon the one man. Their horses are whinnying and their weapons want to blaze forth fire.

'Back!' roars Selim to his men. 'Stand back!'

He spurs his horse and goes alone towards the lone horseman.

'Are you the one who called for me?' he says, and stops a short distance away from him.

'I am!'

'And you came to *me* by yourself?' cries the Moor.

'I thought you were a man! I came alone! I expected you to be alone!'

'Then you don't know who I am?'

'I do know.'

Then the Albanians, who are standing to the side watching, see the two men dismount. Selim the Moor, the terrible Selim, goes up to the other and puts his hand on his shoulder.

'You have defeated me,' he says. 'What do you want from me?'

'Leave this land! There isn't room for both of us. Either I'll kill you or you'll kill me!'

'Join me,' says Selim. 'You'll be the first of my men.'

'I can't,' says the other. 'I am a smuggler. I'm not a robber.'

Selim pauses for a moment. He looks the other in the eye. Then he lowers his gaze.

'*Allaha ısmarladık!*'

'*Uğur ola, Selim!*'

He mounts his horse, takes his men and disappears from the land.

The two brothers, the rivers, see the one and only man who stood up to Selim.

'What did they say his name was?' asks one river.

'Pagidas,' says the other. 'Andonis Pagidas.'

The second smuggler spoke. He said:

The devil shook the pitch off himself, took the lance of fire out of his mouth, assumed human form and came to the world below. He fooled God, he fooled the Archangel with the spear and our Saint George, the rider. He fooled them and became a priest, then a bishop. He came to the Moschonisia, built a tower, double-bolted it, girded it with iron bars and began to torment the Christians. He seized their possessions, stole their crops, and dishonoured their wives. No Turk ever tyrannized the people as much as he did. The people wept and wailed, but there was nothing they could do because, they said: 'He is our bishop, how could you think of touching him? God will burn you! It must be His will that we suffer at the hands of our bishop.' One day the bishop calls for Tramountanas, the smuggler, who had come back from a voyage with a lot of gold. He gives poison to the smuggler and kills him. He takes his gold, and then he does shameful things to his wife. The wife goes to the pier, jumps in the water and drowns. Her old mother goes and finds *him*. Her face is lacerated by her nails, and she's tearing out her hair. She falls at his knees and says to him: 'Will you let it go by like that, the evil that has befallen your bosom friend, my daughter's husband? We cannot take any more.' That night *he* goes to Saint George of Chios,* he crosses himself and venerates him. 'It can't be otherwise,' he says to him. 'I can't do otherwise. I will take even you to task.' He kisses the rock where the saint was martyred, then takes a boat and crosses to the Moschonisia. At midnight, he goes to the bishop's tower. He climbs up, breaks the iron bars and enters. He sets the tower on fire and wakes the bishop. 'Get up!' he says. 'I won't lay a hand on you. I've set this place on fire. We are surrounded by flames. Try to get out. If you pass, you're saved. If I pass, I'm saved!'

The bishop rushed into the flames, caught fire and burned. But *he* rushed in, leapt like a deer and escaped. The people who saw the fire consume the accursed tower gave a great cry, took their saviour and raised him aloft in their arms.

His name was Pagidas. Andonis Pagidas.

It grew quiet. And then the third smuggler spoke. He told a strange tale. It wasn't a tale of their land. A voice from far away had brought it, the voice of one who had made the circle and returned: Cappadocia, the Black Sea, the open seas — the Aegean, the sea of Crete and the Ionian.

This was the story he told:

He lived deep in Anatolia. He was a gigantic man, too big for a house or even a cave to contain. He stepped over mountains, jumped over their peaks. When he stood at full height, he could catch birds on the wing, hawks flying by. The wild ravines that froze a man's soul, that made hearts tremble with fear even when one hundred and fifty men crossed together, these he traversed alone on foot, armed with a sword that was four hands wide. For as many years as he had lived on earth, he had never feared anything. But one day he met with a stranger who had eyes of lightning. 'Come,' says the stranger, 'let us wrestle on the marble threshing floor. Whoever wins takes the other's soul.'

They went and wrestled on the marble threshing floor: Digenis and Charon.*

And Digenis is defeated and about to die. He calls his men and says goodbye. He calls his wife and strangles her, to take her with him.

The third smuggler said no more. The night was tired. The jackals howled in the distance.

'What was he?' asked one of the men.

'Who?'

'The one in the story.'

'It doesn't say,' answers the third smuggler. 'But what could he be?'
'I say he was one of our own. He must have been a smuggler.'
'That's right. He was one of our own.'

THE FIRST TO BREAK THE SILENCE of the Love Feast was Andonis Pagidas.

'Let's go,' he said wearily, and stood up.
The men went to get their horses. No one spoke.
Then one of them heard it. He strained his ears to hear.
'Listen!' he whispered to the others. 'Listen!'
Muffled and indistinct sounds were coming from beyond the ravine.
'What is it?'
'People's voices, isn't it? Do you hear the footsteps?'
'Could it be a flock of sheep?'
They were all silent and strained to hear.
'It's not livestock!' says Pagidas at last, with certainty.
And then:
'Quick! Tether the horses! Take your positions! You, to the left. You, behind the rock! You . . .'
The instinct of danger awoke the captain and drove the torpor from him. With sharp commands, he divided his men into the necessary posts and gave orders.
'No one will shoot until he hears my voice.'
He was about to move forward, to go alone towards the direction from which the voices were coming, when he remembered.
'Where's the woman?'
'I'm here!' Doris says.
Her voice was trying not to tremble, not to show the turmoil inside her. It wasn't fear. It was like the sudden storms that arise on the seas where before there was perfect calm. How had she found herself, a daughter of nobles, born and raised in Scotland, among these wild men with darkened eyes and bloodied hands? She knew nothing of the murderous confrontation that was in store for Pagidas and Garbis. No one had told her. And yet, secretly, she sensed that something was going on, that something terrible was going to happen. First that Love Feast with the men around their leader in a deserted ravine in the Kimindenia at

midnight beside the contraband weapons . . . And now this sudden change: the smugglers getting ready to fight. What was she doing alone among these dark men in these wild ravines? She suddenly understood that she was deserted and foreign, completely foreign. And no one was giving her a thought. That was the worst of it. She wasn't used to being treated in this way — as though she didn't exist. Her humbled pride boiled.

'Where are you?' asked Pagidas again.

'I'm here.'

'I knew it!' murmured Pagidas with irritation, as though he were talking to himself. 'Why did you have to come with us?'

He thought for a moment.

'Hide near some tree behind the horses. Well off the path!'

'No!' says Doris, and her voice shakes with indignation. 'I'm going to stay with you!'

Pagidas says unperturbed:

'All right. I can't waste time. Stay where you are.'

'I'm coming with you!' says Doris. 'I'm not afraid!'

Pagidas goes down the path, and Doris follows behind. He stands about fifty metres from his other companions. He takes cover behind a rock. Doris kneels beside him, her carbine in her hand.

They listen.

The distant sounds gradually become clearer, they are getting closer. There are lots of footsteps and soft voices.

'What is it? Who could it be?'

Doris is the first to make out the unexpected cadence. She's about to say something, but Pagidas cuts her off abruptly.

'Shh!'

She sees his terrible face, just barely lit by the stars. Transfixed on that spot, straining in the darkness, it is as though his face is the only part of his body that is alive.

Doris hears the strange cadence. Again, she hesitates to say it. But she can't stand it any longer.

'I hear women's voices!' she whispers. 'There are women too!'

There are women? On such a night in the ravine in the Kimindenia? What are they doing here?

Pagidas can't believe it. He can't get it into his head. And yet! He can make it out clearly himself now. Soft women's voices and those of children, mixed up with deep masculine voices, are approaching, a flock from the depths of the night.

They keep getting closer and closer until the first shadows are visible moving at the far end of the path. Pagidas holds Doris' arm and squeezes it for her not to move. The flock began to pass in front of the rock where they were keeping watch.

And then they saw it.

They were old people, women, men and children. The women were moaning, and the children were running to keep up with the adults. Heavy with exhaustion and hunger, they moved their bodies pressing onwards like wounded birds. The smallest children were carried on their mothers' backs, and these ones, fast asleep, lived their fate in this way, dreaming of angels and bears. Then another amazing thing appeared. Six men were carrying something on their shoulders that was not a human body and was not an animal. It was a wooden chest, like a coffin. They walked carefully so as not to slip. And the people in front and behind remained at a distance; they didn't crowd the funeral procession for fear of defiling it.

Pagidas looked and looked, trying to understand. Nothing. That coffin disturbed him most of all. He couldn't find an explanation. His mind went to treasure, to smuggled goods.

He could stand it no more. His voice echoed savagely through the night, silencing all the voices of the throng and riveting them where they were.

'Stop! Stop, I said!'

At the sound of his voice, his men jumped out from their hiding places and surrounded the procession with their rifles in their hands. Seeing this, the women began to scream and plead:

'Have pity on us! Have pity on us!'

'Shut up, I said!' roared Pagidas' voice again.

All became silent. Only the wind was heard, playing through the leaves.

Pagidas approaches the funeral procession.

'What are you?' he asks harshly.

'We are Christians! Have pity on us! Pity us if you are Christians!'

'And where are you going at this hour? What do you want?'

'The Bosnians! The Bosnians have come!' wails the throng hysterically.

Hurriedly, breathlessly, they explained. They were Christians from the small villages in the Kimindenia, the ones Pagidas was bringing the weapons to. They said those villages had been destroyed. The Bosnians arrived, Turkish refugees coming from Bosnia, and took their huts and their goods. The Bosnians, together with the armed *zeybeks*, were butchering people and laying waste to everything.

This was it: The persecutions of the Christians of Anatolia had begun in the Kimindenia. The spark that came from far away had arrived.

But Pagidas, unprepared, and uninformed about the spark, could make no sense of it all. What if they were tricking him?

His eyes fall on the chest that looks like a strange coffin. Devious thoughts suddenly disturb his mind. Quick as a deer, he runs towards the coffin with outstretched arms, planning to overturn it.

Then the voice of the throng, full of fear and supplication, echoes through the Kimindenia:

'No! In the name of God, no!'

Whatever women and men were nearby ran to protect their treasure. They made a wall with their bodies between the chest and the smuggler.

Blocked in this way, Pagidas felt his honour offended and he roared:

'Get out of the way! What do you have inside? What do you have, I say!'

He pushed and hit with his hands. The women shrieked.

'What do you have inside? What do you have?'

Unexpected, simple and deep, came the words that explained what they were doing.

'In the name of God! In the name of God!' begged the women. 'Don't harm our Saint. Don't harm him.'

'What did you say? What do you have inside?'

Yes, yes, that was it, they explain. As they fled, driven out, they took nothing else from their country. They took only their household god, the Saint who was martyred in their country. And their youths were carrying him on their shoulders through the dark night and the wild ravine to have him as their helper and their protector in the new land where they were going to find refuge.

'It's our good little Saint ...,' the women murmured more softly now, crying. 'At least don't harm him. Bend down and see ...'

The wall of people parted. A woman opened the coffin. Someone lit a torch. The savage face of Pagidas bent over. And in the light of the flame he saw:

Lying inside, adorned with dry leaves and roses, were the relics of a young lad. It wasn't bones. It was something like a mummy: black skin covered the bones and gave a human shape to the body. It was a skeleton wrapped in black, wrinkled skin.

'Look at his little foot,' murmured an old lady. 'How young he is ... He was martyred many, many years ago ...'

The piety, born of so many years, gave a tone of deep tenderness to the gesture, to the simple act of asking a wild stranger to take pity on the protecting god.

'Look how tender his relics are ... Look at him ...'

The stars saw it. The night saw it. Pagidas saw it. A powerful shiver passed over his whole body. He jumped back, as though pushed by a strong and fearful force.

'What is it?' he whispered, overcome with awe. He took off his cap, and made the sign of the cross.

Then all the people crossed themselves and the women said softly: 'Blessed be his name ... Blessed be his name.'*

PAGIDAS LEARNED THE DETAILS. As the old men of the company had explained to him, all the Christians from the villages in the Kimindenia had been driven out and had fled along different paths to the coast from where they hoped to escape. It was a wild storm that had broken suddenly and unexpectedly, like the storms of spring. How much time was there? for how many more days would peace reign in this country?

Pagidas was thinking. His plan was turned upside down. He no longer had any reason to continue with this plan of distributing weapons to the Christians in the villages, since the Christians had left. Now he saw clearly what he had to do. He had to prevent them from falling into enemy hands.

He made his decision on the spot.

'Divide the rifles and bullets among all the men!' he ordered. 'How many are you?'

They brought the rifles and divided them among the men in the company. Then Pagidas gave them directions.

'Go to the estate of Yannako-Bibelas! You'll be there by tomorrow evening. I'll come on your heels. I'll see that no one attacks you from behind!'

The company was about to start along the road when Pagidas remembered:

'Where's the woman?' he shouted. 'Where is Vilaras' wife?'

'I'm here,' came Doris' soft voice.

In silent distress, she had followed the whole nocturnal story. No one had cared about her during those wild moments in the ravine. She saw the frantic throng writhe. She saw, by the light of the flame, the fearful god they had brought with them. She saw the weapons distributed, the orders given — all dimly, confusedly, as though she were living a strange dream.

'I'm here . . .'

'You must leave with them!' shouted Pagidas.

What did he say? For her to leave?

'We will come behind, we could be attacked!' explained Pagidas. 'You need to go with them.'

She started to beg him, truly breaking down, trembling at the idea of going with that wordless flock, with the black god, foreign and desolate.

'Keep me with you . . . Don't leave me . . . Where will I go?'

She was like a child, small and powerless.

'Keep me with you . . . Don't leave me . . .'

Pagidas still hesitated. He was weighing his decision when one of his companions ran up and told him:

'Captain! Listen! Horsemen are coming! They are coming from the direction of the sea!'

'On the ground! All of you!' shouted Pagidas in a stifled voice.

There was terrible confusion. The women screamed. The voice of Pagidas cut them off again, like a blade.

'Shut up! Not a breath out of anyone!'

Quickly he took his men down the path in the direction of the approaching hoofbeats.

The hungry jackals howled. The trees rustled — a light whisper.

The moist stars flickered indifferently. Only the human heart, hounded as it was, pressed against the earth, seeking refuge. And the astonished worms stopped and listened to its beating.

Some time passes. What is happening there where the smugglers have gone? Is the enemy coming? Will they fight? Doris is sitting there, wrapped in shivers of fear and remembering. From the time she was very small, she had heard fairy tales, not about dragons and princesses, but about the bright land of serenity: fairy tales about Greece and the Aegean. There were sea nymphs and gods of the forests there, river gods and gods of light, gods of hunting and of the wind. Bit by bit, the blue land took shape in her mind as a magic world. When she began to understand, she asked her grandmother one day: 'Do people really live there too, grandmother?' 'They do,' she answered, smiling. 'And are they like us?' She didn't want to ruin the atmosphere of pure wonder that the child was experiencing. 'They are a little different, a little different,' she told her. Later, when Doris grew up and learned the history of her country, the harsh history of Scotland, she again asked her grandmother, who came from the magic country. 'Are the people there like the people of our country? Were they ever so cruel?' 'Doris,' the old lady from Mykonos told her gravely, 'in that respect, all human beings are the same. All of them.'

Yes, all human beings, she repeated. They are all the same when the terrible demon that lurks in all of us wakes up.

Now Doris remembers her words. Surrounded by the flock of hunted people who seek refuge by the sea, she guesses *that* must be it — the demon, those instincts, must have woken up. But she knows nothing yet of the spark that woke them. And she tries to understand.

Not a voice is heard from the furthermost part of the path. But suddenly a fierce shout rattles the night. It seems that it orders the approaching horsemen to stop. One moment passes, then another. Now they will fight! Now!

Nothing. After a while, there comes the sound of the smugglers' footsteps returning. The horses. A frightened voice is calling for Doris.

'Mistress! Mistress!'

Andonis Pagidis also shouts:

'Where is the foreign woman? Where is Vilaras' wife?'

Doris recognizes in amazement the men from their estate, the ones that old Vilaras sent to find her.

'Come quickly, Mistress! Quickly! Come back! We came to get you.'

'What is it? What is it?' asks Doris.

'It seems that a great evil is coming to our country!'

The chorus, the throng, on hearing this, gives out a desperate, wailing cry.

'Woe to us! Woe to us!'

'Read this letter that my master gave me for you!' says one of the men from the estate, and he gives Doris an envelope. 'You'll see here...'

They light a torch. Pagidas' men, the smugglers, the women of the throng, the children and old men, all gather around the flame that blazes in the still night. Their bitter, clouded eyes open as though they want to take in their fill of light. Hearts cringe, voices are silent in their mouths, while the sleeping body of the Saint lies desolate and powerless in its box.

Doris reads by the shaky flame. Everyone follows her movements, her hands, and her face that is turning pale.

She lifts her eyes. Her words fall one at a time like blows:

'War! The biggest war that's ever happened in the world is coming!'

The group of women and old men, upon hearing the terrible word, falls on the ground and starts to lament:

'Woe to us and our children! Woe to us and our children!'

They stop for a while, as though they want to understand, to think about it, and again they wail:

'Woe to us and our children! Woe to us and our children!'

Andonis Pagidas runs and takes Doris aside.

'Explain to me! What is it? What did you say?'

With agitated words, the girl from Scotland tries to explain to the brave man who rules the Kimindenia and to pass on the message that crossed the mountains beyond Kaz-Dak, those beyond the Hellespont, those beyond the Danube and came to the Aeolian land from faraway Bosnia.

'Quickly! Quickly! Let's escape to the sea!'

'Quickly! Quickly! To the sea!'

Trembling and wailing, the people took the Saint on their shoulders and started to hurry towards the plain.

And the night recovered its serenity in the Kimindenia; the stars recovered their calm.

≫ Chapter Four ≪

ON THE AEGEAN AS THE SYMPHONY ENDS

The sun was getting low. We spent our day at the farmstead in terrible anguish. We didn't set foot outside the big door. The plough-men move around the courtyard in small groups, speaking in hushed voices. A dark cloud covers grandfather's face. None of us dare to go near him. His men keep coming and going on horseback. Sometimes they bring news from the estate near the sea, sometimes from the patrols he sends out to the surrounding area to see whether they're coming to attack us.

I stand at a distance and watch silently, trying to read his face. Later I run to bring Artemis the news of Doris and the smugglers.

'Are they coming?' she asks, before I've even opened my mouth.

'Not yet! Not yet!'

'Have you heard anything?'

'No, nothing. Again they sent men on horseback along the path to the Kimindenia. He says they should be here tonight.'

She doesn't want to talk any more. But I guess why: Artemis' heart is beating as much as mine for Doris. Let nothing bad happen to her!

'Artemis, why did she go into the mountains?'

'I don't know, Petros.'

And yet she senses it. It must have to do with the hunter. It can't be anything else — she went for him. She went to find out what happened, so that his blood would not be crying out alone. She went to find out who took the hunter's life and to make sure they put him behind bars. Now that the hunter has died, Artemis can't hate anyone. She wants to love everyone who remembers him.

'When will they come back?'

From the conversations of the grown-ups that we manage to overhear, we know what they're planning. They believe that the road to our town is still open. They're waiting for the smugglers and saying that we should set out tomorrow for the town, under the protection of those brave men of our country.

'Why aren't they here yet?'

Grandfather gave the order: everyone should prepare their bundle, only what each can carry. Men and women run back and forth getting things ready and shouting. Only one person is calm and doesn't move. It's the old man who came to us once upon a time as a young man from Lemnos, who was going to stay for a short while with us to earn some money and then go back to a girl who studied the stars and was waiting for him. But he grew old among us and never went back: Uncle Joseph.

Little Lena goes to find him.

'What a pity,' she says to him. 'You were going to graft a wild pear in my name, Uncle Joseph, in the place where the earth is red. What a pity that we're leaving!'

'Don't be sad, my little girl. I won't forget you.'

'But we're leaving, Uncle Joseph! That's what grandfather said. We're all going to go away from our land.'

'Don't be sad, my little girl,' said the old man again tenderly. 'I won't forget your tree.'

Lena doesn't understand what this answer means, but she doesn't persist. Many confused thoughts are going around in her mind. She jumps from one to another. She keeps coming back to the word that's been on everyone's lips for the last few hours: 'War'.

'What is war, Uncle Joseph?'

Lena imagines it like a dragon bigger than the forty dragons that imprisoned the little princess in the fairy tale. It must be something like that. But this terrible dragon doesn't hunt only princesses. It hunts all people. And they are running to escape and to save themselves.

'What is war, Uncle Joseph?'

'My girl, why should you learn?' answers the old man. 'Wait until you grow up.'

Lena comes to find Artemis and me. She wants to find out. Since the grown-ups won't tell her anything, maybe we can.

'Do you know what war is?'

Then it came back, from the depths of our childhood years.

'Do you remember?' asks Artemis. 'That first time, with the jackals?'

Yes. It was then we had heard the terrible word for the first time. For the first time, we saw the men rush out at night with shouts and drums to chase away the jackals whose hunger had brought them to our borders. 'War.' That's what they had told us. And yet we had learned to remember the hungry jackals of the world in our prayers, along with people. We had run to grandfather, searching desperately to find an explanation. But he, wise as he was, did not understand, and laughed. 'We have to beat them back,' he had said.

'We have to.'

Now we have to leave our land, Lena. We have to leave and follow Artemis, we who never planned on leaving the way she did. You, who were going to ask grandfather to give you the land with red earth when you grew up. You would have raised rabbits there and made round loaves of bread. And I, who said I would become a hunter and roam in the ravines in the Kimindenia, in the land of the beeches and the land of the wild oaks.

'We have to.'

That must be what war is.

THE SUN WAS SETTING when the news came:

'They're coming! The smugglers are coming! And there are people with them! Lots of people!'

There was terrible commotion. All the farmhands, grandfather, grandmother, and all of us ran to the big door.

'What is this?' said grandfather, amazed, seeing the throng that was approaching. 'Where do they come from?'

Now you could clearly hear the wailing of women and children, and the groans of old men, exhausted from the long march. All the smugglers were on foot leading their horses, which carried the sick, the pregnant women, the old and disabled. Doris was also walking. Her face was completely white, her clothes were torn, and her head was no longer crowned with cascading locks. The dust of the road had covered their golden sheen.

Way in the back, on the shoulders of men staggering with exhaustion, came the Saint with his young, desiccated body.

Speechless, we made room, moving away from the great door. The crowd poured into the courtyard and fell onto the ground with heart-rending groans.

'Water! Water!'

Grandfather ordered that the refugees be attended to and given frumenty and milk.

He took Andonis Pagidas aside and found out what was happening. 'We must send Vilaras' daughter-in-law home immediately.'

She was sitting alone on a rock with her head bowed. She was like a child who had misbehaved and was being punished. I stood at her side and watched her. Artemis stood on her other side.

'What do you want?' asked my sister compassionately. 'What do you want me to bring you?'

She didn't answer.

Artemis went and brought some warm milk.

'Drink it. It will do you good.'

Doris lifts her eyes. Then she sees it. In the courtyard, tied to a nearby tree with a thin rope, the bear with black fur sits on the ground, watching the world around it in amazement. Doris looks at it for a long time. Then she looks at Artemis. Something trembles on both their eyelashes before turning into a teardrop.

'Drink,' whispers Artemis again, giving her the cup with milk. 'Drink it,' she says, and does not look her in the eyes, so as not to give herself away.

Doris takes my little sister by the hand, pulls her close and kisses her on the cheek. The abandoned cup tips, and the milk spills out slowly until the cup is empty.

'Come, daughter,' says grandfather to Doris, coming near to us. 'You must go home.'

She mounts her horse. Four smugglers go with her. I see her disappear into the brilliant colours of the summer sunset. No, her hair is not dusty anymore, and her clothes are not ragged. The distance erases the details and the sorrow that stamps her face. She leaves, wrapped again in the golden light of the Aeolian land, just like then, when she first came into my life.

Farewell, Doris.

NIGHT FELL. In all the rooms and in the courtyard, the throng lay and moaned. They had placed their Saint in the middle of the courtyard. Every so often the women stood up, went to their household god, bowed before him and kissed the wood that protected his body. An oil lamp placed on top of the box lit the tortured faces as they prayed.

Artemis and I wander around among the prone bodies, upset and overwhelmed by the terror of the catastrophe. No one in our family seems to take any notice of us. Only very late does Anthippe come looking for us.

'What are you doing here? Hurry up! Go to bed!'

We go up to our bedroom and lie down, but cannot fall asleep. Time passes. The many noises outside grow silent. There is only the howling of jackals.

'I can't sleep,' I say quietly to Artemis. 'I'm going back down.'

'I'm coming too,' she whispers.

We tiptoe out and down to the courtyard. In the middle of the crowd, the lamp still lights the body of the Saint. All the people have now gone to sleep. But in one corner of the courtyard, beneath the big, locked door, black shadows are keeping watch and smoking cigarettes.

We move closer, going along the wall so as not to be noticed. We hide behind a stone seat and wait. The little bear, tied up nearby, smells us and growls. But nobody notices. Then he quiets down.

Pagidas' men are awake, their leader in the middle. None of them is speaking. No one breathes a word.

'What are they doing?' I whisper softly to Artemis.

She takes my hand and squeezes it for me to be quiet. A short time passes. Andonis Pagidas has stood up. We can't make out his face but understand from his height that it's him.

He looks up at the night to calculate the time. The stars tell him.

'I'm going,' he says.

There is no answer.

'Goodbye!' he says again, in a voice that is frigid and unwavering.

He takes two confident steps toward the big door.

Then one of his men stands up.

'Captain!'

'What?'

'Don't go, Captain!' he pleads. 'Look at the evil that's come to our land. Can you leave at such a time?'

For one uncertain moment, the departing footsteps stop. It's as though they want to think about it. But the hesitation lasts for less than the time it takes for a bird to fly by and disappear.

'It's not possible' says the voice of Pagidas calmly. 'Goodbye!'

He draws the bolt, opens the big door and disappears into the desolate night.

IT IS A CLEAR, a very clear night.

Pagidas walks alone, heading to the place where Stratigos Garbis should be waiting for him. A thought crosses his mind. Was he able to get through, or were the roads cut off and he couldn't? Deep inside, his whole rough being is praying: let him not have been able to get through! Let there have been opposing forces, forces outside of their own wills that came between them to prevent what otherwise has to happen!

He keeps going. With his eyes wide open, straining to see, he looks around. Nothing. Not a soul is heard, only the rustling of the trees. It is very cold.

Pagidas reaches the appointed spot. He looks around. There is nothing to be seen. His heart, which has beaten so much in its life, is now on the verge of breaking.

Could it be?

No. A shadow detaches itself from the earth and moves. It gradually grows larger. It comes with assurance, silent, like a tree that is walking.

'Is it you?' asks Pagidas.

The familiar voice of his friend answers sharply:

'It's me!'

They stand a few feet apart from one another.

What is it that struggles inside them, that troubles their blood, trying to rise to their lips and then flees, driven away?

A moment passes. Two moments.

Pagidas asks again:

'Is the road open?'

Garbis:

'No!'

It isn't open, but Garbis got through. *He had to.*

The wind blows, pure and sprinkled with stars. It is so pure that it enters the hearts of two men who don't want to fight and yet who cannot not fight. The wind blows. For one moment, one moment only, it manages to enter more deeply.

'Stratigos,' says Pagidas.

And in the way he pronounces that first name, his love trembles, as hard as steel and the rocks of Sarmousak.

'What?' says the other voice.

'Leave, man,' says Pagidas, and his voice betrays his pleading.

'You called me here,' says Garbis, 'and I came. You leave.'

Several critical moments pass. Who will give way?

Then, at the crowning hour, the blood awakens. It is dreadful and merciless; it will not be silent.

'Why did you kill him, man?' says Pagidas. At the memory of his brother, his teeth gnash.

Then Garbis, pouring out all his rage at the murdered man who was about to come between them, between him and his bosom friend, and destroy them, he cursed Pagidas' brother hideously.

That was it.

'All I have is a knife!' cries Pagidas.

Garbis unslings his rifle from his shoulder and throws it on the ground. He takes his knife from his belt. He is calm now, ready for the inescapable libation of their friendship.

'Come!'

Now he, too, says his friend's first name. It's as though he's saying goodbye.

'Come, Andonis.'

There was something heart-rending in that invitation — tenderness mixed with fate.

The knives flashed in the night and the two bodies rushed at one another. They moaned and raged. The rustling trees around them fell silent, and the stars leaned over to watch what was happening. They watched for a long time.

HIDDEN BEHIND THE STONE SEAT, Artemis and I don't move. We are waiting. We sense that something is going to happen, that our eyes are going to see something awful. Where did the leader of the smugglers go? Why did his men try to keep him?

We think we'll catch something of what they're saying. But none of them speak. They only smoke.

'Should we leave?' I whisper to Artemis, shivering from the cold.

She squeezes my hand. She is shaking too.

'No! Let's stay. Let's see . . .'

Let us stay. Let us watch until the bitter end. Let our dreams, gold and blue until this moment, fill with the new wave, the message of the times: let them fill with red.

One smuggler stood outside the big door and strained to hear something from the direction where their leader had gone. Every so often he came inside.

'Could you hear anything?' his companions would ask him.

'Nothing.'

'Not even a voice?'

'Not even a voice.'

Then the lookout announced:

'I hear footsteps! Someone is coming!'

The smugglers jumped up and ran to the door with their rifles in their hands.

We wait and wait.

'Who is it?' came the lookout's fierce voice.

Softer, calm and tired came the response.

'It's me!'

We saw the dark mass of men part. Through the black river that opened came Pagidas. The lamp burning above the body of the Saint cast a faint light on the leader of the smugglers. His face was wild. His fur cap was missing from his head, and his hair was in disarray.

'Go get him,' was all he said, and he collapsed against a door.

They went and brought him back on their shoulders. They placed him reverently beside the body of the Saint.

'Bring me water,' said Pagidas and stood up.

He himself took the water, wet his hands and washed the bloodied face of his murdered friend. He arranged his hair. He alone. No one else. Then he moved away.

'Bring me rum,' he said.

He drank, and surrounded by his men, by the silence, and by the storm of the approaching war, Andonis Pagidas kept the friend he had killed company for the last time.

We saw those things on our last night in the Kimindenia.

EARLY IN THE MORNING, the smugglers attended first to their dead. They buried Stratigos Garbis under the great oak at the entrance to the farmstead. They fashioned a cross out of thick olive branches and placed it on his grave.

Grandfather, grandmother, and the whole throng of people sheltering in the farmstead learned the news with amazement when they woke up. They asked for details. But no one gave them.

They all kept a distance from the grave.

When the burial was over, Pagidas took grandfather aside. His face had recovered all its harsh decisiveness.

'We'll see if we can get to the town,' he said.

He sent horsemen to see if the road was open.

They came back around noon.

'No, Captain! The road is closed! The Turks will attack any time now! We have to leave by sea! They're burning and killing, and they're coming!'

'Woe to us! Woe to us!' wails the throng on hearing this. 'Woe to us who must leave our country.'

Up until the very last moment, they had harboured the hope that they would be able to stay at the coast until the storm passed and then return to their villages. It was clear now that they would not be able to.

'Woe to us! Woe to us!'

The refugees from the villages were the first to set out. It was agreed they would go down to the shore at Dikeli, where they would find caiques to board. They took their Saint on their shoulders. They took to the road, guarded by their men and armed with the weapons Pagidas had distributed.

We watched them from the big door until they disappeared in the distance.

'It's our turn,' said grandfather.

These events had come about with such force that they shook the old oak tree of our house to the very roots. He struggled to hold himself together and not fall at this critical time.

The first to leave were the people who worked at the estate, both men and women. Loaded up with their bundles, they passed one by one in front of grandfather, who stood at the big door. They leaned over crying and kissed his hand as he said goodbye and blessed them.

'Farewell. Farewell.'

They all left.

'All right, Despina, it's time for us to leave too,' he says to grandmother as he takes her hand and squeezes it.

We were going to embark from the beach below the Vilaras' estate. We would go there in the *dalika*.

Grandmother is the first to get into the carriage. She is crying inconsolably. The white hair that crowns her sweet face is no longer cared for; it blows in the light wind. Her knees are shaking. Grandfather and our mother support her as she climbs in.

Next, our mother gets in, then Anthippe, Lena and Agapi. Agapi holds her bundle of clothes in one hand and in the other hand her Cosmography — the book of numbered stars.

Then Artemis' turn comes. She hadn't slept the night before, neither of us had. Her face is as white as a sheet.

'Come on, Artemis.'

She pulls her bear by the rope by which it's tied, and it comes quietly. She turns to one side and looks. It is there, nearby. It is a little tree now, the walnut she planted once with her own hands, driven by the deep desire and need to learn whether she would pay with death for planting a walnut tree. She looks at the little tree and says goodbye.

'Little walnut tree, Artemis is leaving. Will she pay, I wonder, in the place where she's going? Will she not pay?'

Artemis unties the rope holding the bear cub. The small black animal looks first to one side, then to the other. Then, drawn by unfailing instinct, he takes off running up the path to the Kimindenia as though he were drunk.

We waited until last, grandfather and I. Pagidas and his men are waiting to escort us. Grandfather turns and looks behind him to say goodbye to the trees and the Kimindenia mountains. Then he sees him:

He is coming from inside the farmstead. He walks slowly on legs that tremble with age and stands there next to the big door.

Uncle Joseph!

'Haven't you left, old Joseph?' says grandfather in surprise, going towards him.

Composed, quiet and serene comes the voice of the old man from Lemnos:

'No, Master. I am going to stay.'

'You're going to stay?!'

Grandfather is not prepared for this on top of everything else. 'Where will you stay?' he says. 'The Turks are coming. They leave no one alive!'

Uncle Joseph listens. But he has made his decision. He didn't leave the Kimindenia when it was time to. He didn't leave when another voice, more powerful than death, cried for him to return, when the voice of his heart called, the girl who studied the stars on Lemnos, their barren island. He couldn't then. Now it is too late. Why should he go now? His days, his hours are numbered now. It is too late.

'I'll stay, Master. What will they do to me at this point?'

'Old man, they'll destroy you!' shouts Andonis Pagidas. 'Leave!'

But the resolution in the sad eyes of the old man is as strong as his love of the land.

'I'll stay.'

Everyone understands there is no way to make him change his mind. Pagidas sees the sun getting lower.

'We don't have time!' he says to grandfather. 'We have to hurry!'

Grandfather goes to Uncle Joseph with shaky steps. The old man from Lemnos starts to bend down to kiss the hand of the other old man. Grandfather takes him in his arms, looks into his tear-filled eyes and then kisses him on the forehead.

'Farewell!'

Grandfather stands fixed again. He stands for one moment in front of the big door to the farmstead with his eyes turned to it. Upright, our regal oak, crowned with hair that time has made white, wrapped in the golden colours of the setting sun, stands there as though he is praying.

Then he takes off his cap, kneels humbly and leans over and kisses the earth that he blessed with his life.

'Farewell.'

WE GET INTO THE CAIQUE that is waiting for us. The estate by the sea is deserted. The Vilaras family has already embarked. We see their caique under sail moving further away from the mainland. I try to make out Doris, but cannot. For a moment only, something in the bow of the boat moves, a golden light that mingles with the azure sea and disappears again behind the jib as it comes about. It must be her hair.

The smugglers board their red cutter one by one. Pagidas watches them, astride his horse. The last has embarked. Not a soul is on the shore. All the men look at their leader.

'Captain! Come on!'

Pagidas turns his head slowly from left to right. His face is red, illuminated by the setting sun. He sits tall in the seat of his saddle, pulling hard on the horse's bridle.

'Goodbye!' he shouts to his companions.

Was their captain not going with them?

No, he was not going. The men in the cutter know now that their leader is leaving them. He is leaving them to do battle alone with the multitude that is coming. And to die. He cannot do otherwise. He is going to meet the friend that he killed.

I see him disappear on his horse, galloping in the red light. The smugglers in the boat shoot farewell shots into the air with their rifles. Their metallic sound falls into the sea and dies out in the waves.

THE STARS HAVE ALL COME OUT. Our childhood dreams are travelling on the Aegean. The waves striking the bow of our caique put them to sleep. Go to sleep, dreams. What is waiting for us in the foreign country we are going to as refugees? What days will dawn for us?

Lena has fallen asleep. She wanted the land with red earth very much. She would have lived there with the man she married and would have had lots of children. She would have kept rabbits and doves and much more. No, Lena did not plan on journeys by sea, she did not want them to separate her from the Kimindenia. It's not what she wanted.

Agapi has fixed her eyes absentmindedly on the stars. How much she has studied them recently, how much she has measured their distances with numbers! But looking at them now, as she leaves the land of her birth for a difficult journey, only now does she see how that was her mistake, her irreparable mistake. The stars ran away from her. While we were living our chimeras in the ravines of the Aeolian land, while we were creating eternal companions who were going to follow us through all the bitter days in the future, she, small as she was, wanted to bring the sky down to earth.

Poor Agapi . . . Poor Agapi . . .

There is somewhere, in a farmstead in Anatolia, below the mountains they call the Kimindenia, a Yellow Room. The swords that are hung there wake up at night. A man once passed by there. He was travelling the roads of Anatolia looking for a camel with a white head, the only camel with a white head, which passed once through his life and disappeared. People made fun of him, but he didn't hear them. Because he couldn't believe, because he didn't want to believe, that the camel with the white head was lost, that it would not be in his life again.

Another man passed by that same place. He was headed for far-off Jerusalem, trying to catch sounds, to make the sounds inside a clock with gold satyrs never cease. 'Do you know where the Holy Land is? Do you know where Jerusalem is?' sympathetic people would ask him. 'You'll have to cross all of Anatolia . . .' 'I will cross all of Anatolia,' answered the deep voice of passion, stubborn and serene.

There, under the mountains they call the Kimindenia, is a cave where the wild boars go to die when they've grown old. A salamander, a small tortoise and a hanging bat are waiting for death. Artemis, we didn't have time to hang the bat's thin bone around our neck, next to our gold cross. That way everyone would have loved us. But we didn't have time.

Further on, however, beyond the Jackal River, is the eagle's nest. It was there one summer day that the storm came. May it be blessed. Now all storms to come will recall that one. May it be blessed.

And even higher up, beyond the land of the beeches, beyond the land of the wild oaks, on the brow of the great ravine, a gunshot rings out and finds the big bear from Lebanon. She has a child, a baby bear with black fur. The big bear will die. And a hunter who has a scarf with yellow stars on it will die too. 'Why?' ask the hoopoes and the wild doves. 'For love,' answer the oaks.

Artemis, you and I will never be alone in the foreign land. From now on, in all the days to come, to the end of the end, we will not be alone.

OUR DREAMS travel on the Aegean.

Grandmother is tired. She wants to lean her head on grandfather's chest. His eyes are riveted on where we came from, in the hope of making out something of the mainland, something of the Kimindenia. But now nothing is visible. The night has drawn the shapes and forms into herself.

Grandmother bends down her head to rest it on the chest that has protected her all the days of her life. Something is in the way, and her head can't get settled. There is a lump under the old man's shirt.

'What is that there?' she asks, almost indifferently.

Grandfather lifts his hand. He puts it under his shirt and finds the small foreign body that is lying on his body and that hears the beating of his heart.

'What is it?'

'It's nothing,' answers grandfather timidly, like a child who has done something wrong. 'It's nothing. It's a little soil.'

'Soil!'

Yes, a little soil from their land. So that they can plant a basil plant, he tells her, in the foreign country where they're going. To remember.

Slowly, the old man's fingers open the kerchief containing the soil. They sift through it. Grandmother's fingers sift through it, too, as though they are caressing it. Their eyes, full of tears, rest on it.

'It's nothing, I tell you. Just a little soil.'

Earth, Aeolian Earth, Earth of my country.

THE END

ENDNOTES

Page

3   The island of Lesbos lies opposite the town of Aivali (see note to p. 9 below) in the northeast Aegean sea, just five and a half kilometres distant from the Turkish mainland. It is a mountainous, forested and verdant island with millions of olive trees. Its main town is called Mytilene, by which name the island is also known. It was under Ottoman rule until 1912 when, during the first Balkan War, it became a part of Greece. It was famous in antiquity as the home of the great lyric poet Sappho. Because of its proximity to Turkey, Lesbos was one of the main destinations for Asia Minor Greek refugees fleeing Ottoman persecutions from 1914 to 1922. A hundred years later, it became once more a major stopping place for refugees from Syria, Afghanistan, Iraq and other countries.

3   Aeolia is the ancient Greek name for the region along the northern coast of Asia Minor. It was named after the Aeolians, a Greek tribe who migrated there from Thessaly in northern Greece before 1000 BC. The founder of this tribe was Aeolus, son of Hellen, the mythical progenitor of all the Hellenes. The Aeolus mentioned in Homer's *Odyssey* as a guardian of the winds is identified with the grandson of this original Aeolus by his illegitimate daughter, Arne, and the god Poseidon.

5   The Sarmousak (*Sarımsak* in Turkish) quarries, near the entrance to the bay of Aivali, provided stone for many of the buildings in Aivali and the nearby town of Mytilene on Lesbos, including the famous church of Saint Symeon. Samousak stone is much esteemed and has a reddish colour.

7   Rose Slipper is the heroine of a very old Greek fairy tale that resembles, and prefigures, the Cinderella story. The story is based on that of Rodopis, which was recorded by the Greek historian Strabo in the late first century BC or early first century AD, a beautiful Greek girl who was captured by pirates and sold into slavery in Egypt. While she was washing clothes in the Nile river, the god Horus, in the guise of a falcon, flew away with one of her red slippers. He dropped it into the lap of the young king of Egypt who then searched the whole country to find the girl on whose foot the slipper would fit. In this way, he found and married Rodopis.

pirates and sold into slavery in Egypt. She was lonely and had only animals for friends. While she was washing clothes in the Nile river, the god Horus, in the guise of a falcon, flew away with one of her red slippers. He dropped it into the lap of the young king of Egypt who then searched the whole country to find the girl on whose foot the slipper would fit. In this way, he found and married Rodopis.

9   Aivali, Ayvalik in Turkish, is a town on the coast of Asia Minor, opposite the island of Lesbos. During the Ottoman era, it was inhabited almost exclusively by Greeks and had virtual autonomy from Ottoman rule in the nineteenth and early twentieth centuries (see note to p. 203 below). It was an important cultural centre for Asia Minor Greeks, second only to Smyrna, with many Christian churches and Greek schools. It is located on the site of the ancient Aeolian port town of Kydonies, meaning 'land of quinces', of which the Turkish name Ayvalik is a translation. Both Herodotus and Pliny identify the city as the capital of the Aeolia region of Asia Minor. Greeks continued to call the town by its ancient name of Kydonies into the twentieth century.

29   Nestor is a figure from Greek mythology who appears in both the *Iliad* and *Odyssey* of Homer. He was the King of Pylos in the southern Peloponnese and the commander of the warriors from Pylos in the Trojan War. Nestor is older than the other Greek captains at Troy and known for his wisdom and kindness — and for his long-windedness. When Agamemnon and Achilles quarrel, Nestor intervenes to reconcile them. In the *Odyssey*, Nestor shows kindness and hospitality to Odysseus' young son Telemachus, who sails from Ithaka to Pylos to seek news of his father.

29   Lemnos is an island in the northeastern Aegean sea, north of Lesbos, some twenty kilometres from the Turkish coast. Like Lesbos, it was under Ottoman rule until 1912 when it became part of Greece. The ancient Greeks considered the island to be sacred to the god Hephaestus. According to Homer, Lemnos was the island where the Greek warrior Philoctetes was abandoned by his army on the way to the Trojan war. He remained alone there for ten years, suffering from a festering snake bite on his foot.

47   Tsakitzis was a kind of Turkish Robin Hood, a robber who stole from the rich but protected the poor. He was legendary in Anatolia in the beginning of the twentieth century. Although Turkish, some Greeks thought he must be a crypto-Christian.

67   The names that the street urchins hurl at Stephanos refer to two

well-known carnival characters from the festivities that took place in Aivali every year before the beginning of Lent. In his earlier work, *Number 31328*, Venezis names Kambesa-the-bear and Eros-with-wings-on-his-back as two beloved carnival characters. The children here confuse Eros with Erotokritos, the hero of a famous seventeenth-century romance from Crete. In any case, to be seen as a carnival character when it's not carnival marks you as crazy. The folk painter Theophilos, whom Venezis would encounter later in Lesbos, was mocked for regularly dressing as Alexander the Great or a hero of the Greek Revolution. There was also an ancient belief that dimwits sprouted wings on their backs.

76 The City with an upper case C (*Poli* in Greek) refers to Constantinople, the City of Constantine, known today as Istanbul. The Roman emperor Constantine the Great founded the city in 324 on the site of an older Greek city called Byzantium. Constantinople was the capital of the Roman Empire until the end of the fourth century and then capital of the Eastern Roman (Byzantine) Empire for one thousand years after that, until it fell to the Ottomans in May 1453. The city was the capital of the Ottoman empire from 1453 until 1923 but never stopped existing in the hearts of Greeks as their mother city and an important seat of Orthodoxy. Even today, Greeks refer to Turkish Istanbul as simply *i Poli*, the City.

78 The Salutations, *Chairetismoi* in Greek, is a famous and much beloved sixth-century hymn to the Theotokos, the Mother of God, which is attributed to the noted hymnographer Saint Romanos the Melodist. It has twenty-four verses, twelve long and twelve short, each beginning with one of the twenty-four letters of the Greek alphabet. The word *chaire*, meaning 'hail!' or 'rejoice!', is used frequently throughout the hymn, hence the Greek name *Chairetismoi*. This hymn is chanted in the Greek Orthodox Church on successive Fridays in Lent. Many Greeks know the words of the hymn by heart and it is often recited at home before the icon of the Theotokos, or in times of trouble.

86 The words grandmother says in this prayer are from a beautiful supplicatory hymn to the Theotokos, or Panagia as she is most frequently addressed. This hymn is not part of the official liturgical canon and is sometimes chanted during the distribution of blessed bread following the liturgy. In some monasteries on Mount Athos, it is chanted after the procession back to church after the meal following a vigil on the feast days of the Panagia. In Greek, the hymn uses the epithet *Despina*, Lady, in addressing the Panagia. Despina is also grandmother's first name. (Special thanks to Irene Bullock for finding the English translation of this hymn.)

85   The method of divination involving a lamb's shoulder, or scapula, is known as scapulimancy. The cleaned bone is held to the light and the future is revealed in the patterns on the transparent part of the bone. A clear scapula indicates a positive outcome. The practice is still known to some Greeks today and is mentioned in the memoirs of warriors from the Greek War of Independence. Part of my research for this translation involved holding a lamb scapula to the light: it was clear!

113   The Moschonisia, meaning literally the Fragrant Islands, is a group of twenty-two islands situated around the sea coast of the town of Aivali. The largest island, Moschonisi — Cunda in Turkish — had a large, almost exclusively Greek population during the late Ottoman Empire. There were fifty Greek churches scattered throughout these islands. In 1922, at the end of the Greco-Turkish war, hundreds of Greeks were massacred on Moschonisi, and the bishop of the Greek metropolis of the island was tortured and buried alive there.

118   The Greek War of Independence, or the Revolution of 1821, was the Greek uprising against the Ottoman empire that led to the establishment of Greece as an independent sovereign state in 1830 after four centuries of Ottoman rule. A secret organization called the Filiki Eteria or Society of Friends was founded in Odessa in 1814 with the goal of establishing a Greek state. The revolution was declared in the Peloponnese on 25 March 1821. As the conflict expanded, Egypt sent a navy to support the Ottomans while Russia, Britain and France sent navies to support the Greeks.

  The Greek revolution captured the imagination of young European and American intellectuals who felt that the heritage of ancient Greece made the modern Greeks worthy of their support. In addition to raising money and sympathy for the Greek cause, hundreds of young philhellenes from Germany, France, Britain and America travelled to Greece and fell fighting beside the revolutionaries.

  For Greeks, being descended from the fighters of the War of Independence bestows a particular prestige.

118   The Phanariots were a class of wealthy Greek merchants who lived in the Phanar district of Constantinople, near the court of the Patriarch, and held important political and administrative positions in the Ottoman empire. Phanariots were the best educated members of Greek society during the Ottoman period and were influential in the Greek National Assembly during the War of Independence.

132   The chaste tree, *Vitex agnus-castus*, *aligariá* in Greek, is a shrub or small tree native to the Mediterranean and common in Greece. It has soft

fragrant foliage and spikes of lavender-coloured flowers. In antiquity, the tree was considered sacred to the virgin goddess Hestia/Vesta, hence its Latin name and also its English name. In evoking this plant, we are reminded of Artemis' connection to the virgin huntress goddess with whom she shares her name. There is a folk tradition in Greece that you should not walk past a chaste tree without picking one of the blossoms for your loved one.

155 On Easter Good Friday, in Greek Orthodox churches, an embroidered icon of the dead crucified Christ, called the *Epitaphios*, is laid on a wooden bier representing the tomb of Christ, and then is processed around the church, village, or city, wherever the Easter celebrations are taking place, with the faithful following with lighted candles as at a funeral. It is then placed in the centre of the church where the Easter services are being enacted. The wooden bier and the cloth icon of Christ laid upon it are sprinkled with rose petals, fragrant leaves and herbs before the final hymns of the Good Friday service. The faithful often gather these flowers and perfumed offerings as possessing special spiritual power from having been laid on the body of Christ, and take them home to keep for occasions when special blessings are needed. It was these dried leaves that Lena was burning on the censer.

202 The naval battle of Çeşme in July 1770 during the Russo-Turkish war was a great victory for the Russians and a disaster for the Ottoman fleet. Çeşme bay is between the coast of Anatolia and the island of Chios, making it plausible that survivors of the battle might have been swept along the coast near to Aivali.

203 The story Pagidas' mother recounts to her son was passed on orally by Greeks in Aivali. Apparently, the Ottoman admiral Cezayirli Gazi Hasan Pasha was shipwrecked on the Aeolian coast after the naval battle of Çeşme and a Christian priest with the rank of Oikonomos, a title meaning a manager or treasurer, saved his life. In appreciation of his deed, the priest, Ioannis Dimitrakellis (1735–91), obtained an extraordinary firman from the sultan in 1773 granting Aivali self-government and banishing most Turks from the town.

214 The words that grandmother whispers before the icon are taken from the Great Paraklesis (Supplicatory Canon) to the Most Holy Theotokos (Mother of God), which is chanted in Orthodox churches during the first fourteen days of August prior to the great feast day of the Panagia on 15 August. A much loved hymn, it is also sung, as with the Salutations (see endnote to p. 78 above), in times of great distress.

217 The 'Love Feast' or *Agape* Feast, was a communal meal shared among early Christians. The purpose of the Love Feast was to strengthen bonds of goodwill among its participants and affirm their love for one another.

220 Digenes Akritas was a medieval Greek hero of superhuman strength who was celebrated in folk ballads and a famous epic poem from around the ninth century that bears his name. He was a brave warrior who defended the frontier of the Byzantine Empire from the Muslim states to the east. He is eventually defeated only by Death, here named Charon, after a single combat on a threshing floor.

220 Saint George of Chios was martyred in Aivali at the beginning of the nineteenth century. He was born into a Christian family on the island of Chios, but converted to Islam while still a child and when working as an apprentice in the northern mainland town of Kavala. He later returned to Chios, repented of his conversion and became Christian again. In danger from the Turks for renouncing Islam, he hid in Aivali until young adulthood. When the story of his past was revealed, he refused to renounce his Christian faith and was imprisoned for eighteen days, then shot in the back and beheaded. He was initially buried on the deserted island of Nisopoula of the Moschonisia, but his relics were later translated to a church built in Aivali on the site of his martyrdom.

225 The physical description of the saint carried by these refugees suggests an identification with the major Orthodox saint from Asia Minor, Saint John the Russian, whose relics now lie in the church that bears his name in the village of Prokopi on the Greek island of Evia (Euboea). Prokopi has subsequently become one of the most popular pilgrimages centres in Greece.

Saint John was born in Ukraine into a Christian family in, approximately, the year 1690. As a soldier in the army of Peter I during the Russo-Turkish war, he was captured and enslaved by a Turkish cavalry commander in the town of Prokopio (Turkish Ürgüp) in central Anatolia. Despite bad treatment and degradation, he refused to renounce his Christian faith. He lived in the stable with the horses he cared for and went secretly each week to the cave church of Saint George.

Over time, John's humility and hard work won the affection of his Turkish aga. The saint's first miracle was on his master's behalf: at the request of the aga's wife, John prayed that a plate of pilaf from his home be transported to his master who was on a pilgrimage in Mecca. When his master returned home bearing the very plate on which the pilaf had miraculously been sent, both Christians and Muslims began to view John as a saint. When he died on 27 May 1730, he was buried in the church of Saint George in Cappadocia which later became a place of pilgrimage. In 1832 the church was ransacked and twice his relics, which had remained uncorrupted, were thrown into a fire and although blackened did not burn.

When, in 1924, the Christian inhabitants of Turkey were expelled in the exchange of populations mandated by the treaty of Lausanne, the refugees from Prokopio carried, together with their few possessions and icons, the wooden casket containing the saint's relics over land and sea to the island of Evia. The refugee settlement provided for them was named New Prokopi, after their home town in Anatolia. In 1930, the refugees began building a grand church there dedicated to their saint which was completed twenty-one years later and in which his relics are kept.

I made my own pilgrimage to Evia last summer and went to the church of Saint John the Russian in Prokopi to ask for the saint's blessing for this book project. I saw the silver reliquary bearing his remains. The visible parts of his small body, which was dressed in fine vestments, were covered in blackened skin. A little unclothed foot protruded at the bottom, just like the one the old woman in this story describes with such tenderness.

GLOSSARY

Allaha ısmarladık: Turkish, goodbye, used by the person departing and meaning something like, 'I leave you in the care of God.'

bey: Turkish title for a chieftain, also used for the governor of a province in the Ottoman Empire.

dalika: Greek, from the Turkish *talika*, in the story, an enclosed, four-wheeled carriage; in Greece today, a heavy transport lorry.

deves: from the Turkish *deve*, camel.

ghiolia: etymology unknown, infertile swampland.

kafir: Arabic, an unbeliever, non-Muslim, infidel.

karantak: Turkish *karadağ*, meaning black mountain, the Turkish name for Montenegro.

koltzides: Greek plural of *koltzis*, from the Turkish *kolcu*, a guard or sentry.

kontrabatzides: Greek plural of *kontrabatzis*, smuggler, from the French *contrabande*, smuggled goods.

meltemi: Greek, from the Turkish *meltem*, a strong northerly wind that blows in the summer in the northeast Mediterranean.

merhaba: Turkish, 'hello', also used in Arabic.

mintili: from the Turkish *Midilli*, the name for the island of Mytilene (Lesbos), and by which a type of shaggy pony that comes from that island is also known.

nargileh: Turkish, a water pipe or hookah that originated in the Near East. The word is derived from the Persian *nargila*, meaning coconut, from which the bowl of the pipe was made.

nyfitsa: Greek, weasel.

pastra: Greek, also called *xerí* in Greece, a simple card game resembling 'Go Fish'.

pena: a type of sailboat, from the Italian *penna*, meaning feather, which describes the shape of the boat's lateen sail.

Tzerkezi: Turkish *Çerkez*, meaning a Circassian.

tegki: Turkish, a type of saddle.

Uğur Ola: an old-fashioned way of saying of goodbye in Turkish; it means something like 'let there be luck!'

ulan: a Turkish interjection used to get someone's attention in a rude manner, or as an expression of reprimand, frustration or anger.

yemitzides: Greek plural of *yemitzis*, from the Turkish *gemici*, meaning sailor.

Yarabis: God, from the Turkish *ya Rabbi*, meaning O my God, as addressed in prayer.

PROLOGUE TO THE SECOND GREEK EDITION OF
LAND OF AEOLIA
by Angelos Sikelianos

[*Angelos Sikelianos (1884–1951) was born on the Ionian island of Lefkada. He first begΑΝΑ publishing his poems in literary journals, and in 1907 he married the American heiress Eva Palmer who became his greatest supporter, enabling him to publish his poetry in book form. Together they went on to organize two Delphic festivals, those of 1927 and 1930, as part of Sikelianos' vision of the 'Delphic Idea', the establishment of a world spiritual centre and university, a vision and attempt which ultimately failed. During the German occupation of Greece he was a source of inspiration to the Greek people and engaged in public acts of symbolic resistance.*

There are two main aspects to his poetry: the lyrical affirmation of the natural world and the vision of the seer who knows that the natural world is doomed to tragic suffering, and within both these aspects he celebrates all life's forms and sensual energies with an almost mystical intensity. It would seem that similar aspects and qualities expressed in Land of Aeolia *inspired Sikelianos to write the prologue to the book's second edition in January of 1944, when Greece was still occupied by the Axis powers.*]

FATE HAS ENCOMPASSED THE PERSON WRITING THIS PROLOGUE in a spiritual perspective that we should probably by and large call Doric, were we for a moment to see it as distinct from another, the Ionic spiritual perspective, whose fusion with the former produced, from time immemorial, the fullness of our entire historically expressed Greek civilization. This person has known since his childhood, in his blood, and later in full consciousness, that an essential spiritual note, an unambiguously masculine register, had one day to wed the purest Soul of the ancient world: the Doric had to fuse with the Ionian, so that could be born that miracle of life, of thought and of art — that miracle which, whether we recognize it or not, in its deep essence continues to embrace us, to follow us, and to light our way. But, for that very reason, he also knows the value of each of these two individual elements and the contribution of each to the world, before their union and the creation of the great fusion I mentioned earlier: of on the one hand the radiant, all-encompassing, intellectualistic and edifying tenets of the Doric element, which had the vigour and mission of the strong sperm in the creation of what is commonly known in its wholeness as historical Greek civilization. And on the other hand, of the pre-existing civilization, which we might call pre-Hellenic, a flowering of the same Ionian Soul before it was wed to the great 'Male Logos', where simplicity was combined with contemplativeness in the gentlest hue of spontaneous idealism, in which was reflected with boundless sweetness the entire morphology of the Earth, the sea, the valleys, the mountains, animals, human beings, all enfolded in the same, intrinsically virginal and maternal embrace. And this pre-existing civilization once constituted for me (why should I hide it?) the locus of an Edenic nostalgia, something like a revelation by my cosmic subconscious memory itself of a life full of the nurturing warmth of some sweet prehistoric great-grandmother, some watchful age-old Mother, some tender Virgin sister. Not that you might suppose that the purely male element was absent from this civilization. But because it was more intensely imbued with the breath of an all-encompassing matriarchal womanliness, which also enclosed the purely male element within the warmth and depth of some intrinsically pantheistic and cosmic womb. So that, as I said before, my soul drove me often, nostalgically, to re-live that atmosphere, although I did not truly know whether I would some day be able to feel it, reborn, around me, like the flesh of my flesh and the spirit of my spirit, by some conjuncture, by some chance, by an unforeseen revived surge, vividly, essentially, truly.

And then, the other day, I happened upon Venezis' *Land of Aeolia.*
A sweet, serene warmth flows all at once from its pages, no longer the leaves of a book but leaves of a tree, a tree both very young and ancient, which stirs around me, rustles very gently in my ears, connects to my blood, my mind, my heart, and in its turn helps me to commune once again through some vast new bond with the entire world: with the sea, the mountains, the fields, with animals, with souls. A deep, serene, impulsive movement propels my reading — as effortlessly as lymph moves within a plant, or a sympathetic response is created between the roots of a tree and some faraway spring, between a butterfly and a flowering field — unexpectedly offering me a means and a way to a sweeter and calmer breath both of body and of soul. It is the gentle Ionic atmosphere, it is the mystical, lost warmth of the secret flesh of the world that unexpectedly enters once again into a matriarchal contact with me, it is the pure Ionic breath of the forgotten civilization that I yearned for, as I explained earlier. Here no single note dominates, neither male nor female, here sound together all the voices of the world, like the string of bells of the camel-driver, the Tsitmis, of the Land of Aeolia.
'Nothing,' writes Venezis, 'can disturb the strict discipline of these sounds. They affirm nature's harmony, the symphony of the world. The Tsitmis hears them going along behind him and knows that all is well on earth. It can happen for one second — a single second — that one sound is missing. The harmony is

affected at once and the Tsitmis understands that something has broken the world's order. Only then does his face take on a worried expression, and he turns his head back to see. He stops, gets down from his donkey, goes and refastens to the caravan the camel that had broken its rope. Then the symphony begins again.'

And Venezis, like the good Tsitmis, acts in the same way within this book. He does not tarry on any particular note, he does not require that it dominate, he does not underline that part of his work that has its roots in history — History per se, and so recent — rather than that which springs only from his own sensitiveness. Like the Tsitmis, this writer does something very wise. He seeks to attribute to everything, whether individuals or things or events, which populate his book — and therefore also the soul of the reader himself — their lost ancient forces, their secret sympathetic properties, bringing them close to Nature, integrating them within the harmony of life in its wholeness, rebuilding the ancient sacred and necessary bond between the 'creature/created' — animal, plant or human — and the entire Creation.

In order to realize this miracle Venezis simply descends — not violently, nor hurriedly, but rhythmically, smoothly, serenely — into his first, his fundamental and sensuous self.

Shall we give pre-eminence to his youthful self as that fundamental self? Certainly not, if by this we only refer to chronology. Certainly yes, if we give the term an essential, spiritual meaning, which assures to the creative hypostasis of Man truth, authenticity, a living and sensitive spiritual space free of the influence of rationality. The space from which rise, with the same vigour and purity, thought, dreams, feelings, a deep biological persuasiveness, a discrete intuition, the secret rhythm of synthesis, all of this together with some sort of responsive correlation and some comprehensive organic co-vibration, such as that which in ancient times gave us Ionic philosophy and — do not be surprised by a comparison with something as distant in time as this — in these latter days, Venezis' book. Because, without a doubt, as with those influential all-embracing spiritual forefathers of Ionia who, communicating with Nature, immersed in it and proceeding from it, discovered in a gigantic cosmic diapason of Matter, Soul, and Ethics pulsating in unison as though they constituted the strings of the same eternal Lyre; so too, in this new book, led by the same essentially youthful sensitiveness, Soul, Nature, Ethos once again find, under the Poet's hand, their vital fundamental union and at the same time the vitality to advance rapidly towards a kind of mystical dialectical wholeness, where the visible and the invisible, the palpable and the imaginative, affect and contemplation, weave and vibrate in consonance to produce a general and indivisible reality: a purely Poetical reality, which is also the only one that is essentially authentic and true.

Would we want better confirmation of what I am saying than the wondrous story of the eels of the Aeolian Land? It comes to us from the great mind of a man such as Thales, from the soul of the writer, from the heart of Nature, from our own heart. In order that all may draw their own conclusions, I transcribe here, just the wonderful end of this charming story:

'That is how it came to be that the two eels travelled very close to each other, together with their swarm, and reached the bottom of the distant Ocean. They lost many companions on the way in battles they had with other fish. But nothing happened to the two companions, because they helped one another. When they reached the place in the depths where they would mate, they chose a spot at the root of the coral to make their nest. Then the other eels in the swarm began to change their skin and be dressed in silver — their wedding clothes. But the two companions of the coral didn't need to wait. They had been ready since the beginning of the journey. They fell in love sweetly, and when they were tired, they waited quietly for the children that would come. Every so often the male eel would bend over the body of his wife, and when he heard heartbeats, he would ask impatiently:

' "Have they come? Is it our children?"

' "No," she would say. "Not yet. That is *that other heartbeat*. It is the voice of our country."

'But when the children formed inside her, the heartbeats got mixed up. And then even she could not tell them apart.'

There are many such confirmations and examples; they are the entire book. The guardian of a supreme tradition, which we thought lost. That of Ionia. Its secret voice:

'In this way, this secret voice becomes the most imperceptible and reliable bond between the generations of our ancestors and of those who are to come: a resonance that will remain when the memory of the people themselves is lost.'

And there is the supreme example, the ultimate one, that concludes the whole book. It is that of the little kerchief containing within it a clump of soil from the homeland. Here there is no longer a voice. Here there is the flesh and soul itself of Ionia. We hold it, touch it, seek it in this fistful of Ionian earth. A sweet, elemental faith flows from its touch into our veins and our hearts. Ionia is not gone. Ionia lives on. Her lost, age-old civilization exists. The terrible drama of History has brought it to us. The refugees have brought it to us. You, Ilias Venezis, have brought it to us.

I bend down and kiss that soil first. Then, on behalf of all our brothers and older in years, I bend down and, through this prologue, I deposit a kiss on your brow too, brother Venezis.

9 January 1944

(Translated by Daphne Kapsambelis)

257

PREFACE TO THE FIRST ENGLISH EDITION OF
LAND OF AEOLIA
by Lawrence Durrell

[*Lawrence Durrell (1912–1990) needs little introduction to English readers. Born in India he was sent at the age of eleven to school in England, which he disliked intensely, and after failing to get into Cambridge and various casual jobs he decamped with his family to Corfu in 1935 since when he was much connected with the world of the Mediterranean and its cultural milieu. For many years Durrell supported his writing by working in the British Foreign Service, including for the British Council in which capacity he would have met the translator of the first English edition of* Land of Aeolia, *Elizabeth Scott-Kilvert, and her husband, Ian, who worked for the British Council in Athens. By 1949, when* Land of Aeolia, *under the title* Aeolia, *was first published in England, Durrell's reputation as a writer and poet of import was beginning to be established.* Aeolia *was reprinted in the United States, under the title* Beyond the Aegean, *in 1956, the year before the publication of* Justine, *the first volume of Durrell's renowned* Alexandrian Quartet.]

THE TRAGEDY OF HIS EXPULSION FROM ANATOLIA still weighs heavily upon the heart of the modern Greek, whether he is a metropolitan or an exile from the bountiful plains and wooded mountains of Asia Minor. He cannot forget it. If he is an exile he returns again and again to Anatolia in his dreams; he broods upon it as Adam and Eve must have brooded upon the Garden of Eden after the Fall. The blazing fires of Smyrna lit up the skies of the whole Levant; they say that even across the straits the walls of the cells in Mount Athos caught some of the fugitive glare of the burning cities. The waters of Smyrna were choked with dead bodies.

But it is more than the injustice, the cruelty, the madness of the whole episode that sticks in the mind of the modern Greek. It is also a sense of a lost richness, a lost peace of mind. Walking today among the towns of metropolitan Greece, he inevitably comes at last upon the refugee quarter, with its earth streets and its rows of minute houses constructed out of petrol tins and shattered sugar-boxes. He hears snatches of an old-fashioned Greek — fragments of Doric that were once carried up to the shores of the Black Sea, and that have now been washed down here to this barren littoral by the waters of history. A song split suddenly into quarter-tones like so many prisms speaks of Smyrna, the streets with their huddled cafés, the glass birdcages swinging in the honeyed summer air, the bubble of the *nargilehs*, the red *fezzes* dotting the plaster walls, where once every client owned his own peg... Stumbling through the refuse and filth of these mean little streets (and what town in Greece is without its refugee settlement?) he thinks of Anatolia. It has become a memory that he touches from time to time, like a man fingering a cicatrice.

The author of this novel is such a man, and, in order to understand the appeal his work has for the modern Greek, one must first turn one's face away from Europe to gaze out across the blue straits to where, once, in the rich fastnesses of Anatolia, life was simple and rich, and a man owned his own peace of mind. The golden ambience of *Beyond the Aegean* springs out of an imaginative reconstruction of a way of life that has vanished, the re-evaluation of an inheritance that has been forfeited.

Venezis' novel is a poetic commentary upon life as it once was in the Kimindenia, before the expulsion from the Garden, so to speak; yet it never becomes sentimental documentary, and it never degenerates into self-pity. The poignance of its evocations comes perhaps from their very calm. The sadness is never explicit — it wells up out of the beauty of the book and gives a darker, richer colouring to its characters and incidents.

The world it describes is strangely archaic; it is nearer to the pastoral world of Hesiod and Homer than it is to our own. Yet the intellectual charm of Venezis' style interprets it perfectly. *Beyond the Aegean* is not a narrative — how could it be? History only begins with the expulsion from the Garden. In Eden there was no time, but only a blessed continuum of happiness; and this novel, with its skillful arrangement of moods and atmospheres, makes another Eden of the lost Anatolia.

Since 1923 Venezis has been a resident of metropolitan Greece, where he has published two other novels besides this one. He has also written a play that gives an account of his imprisonment, during the recent war, by the Germans. Together with Mirivilis he is considered to be one of the greatest Greek novelists of today — a reputation no reader of this present work can fail to feel justified. *Beyond the Aegean* is a delightful book, and we are lucky to have this clear and melodious translation of it into English.

BIOGRAPHICAL NOTES

ILIAS VENEZIS, the pen name of Ilias Mellos, was born in 1904 into an affluent Greek family in the coastal town of Aivali in Asia Minor. He attended elementary school in Aivali and spent the summers with his several siblings at his maternal grandparents' farming estate in the foothills of the Kimindenia mountains. In 1914, at the outbreak of World War I, the family had to flee to the Greek island of Lesbos to escape the persecution of Christians by the Ottoman State. During these war years, Ilias went to school in Lesbos. His sister Artemis, to whom he was closest, died on the island in 1918, probably of the Spanish flu. The following year, at the beginning of the Greco-Turkish War, when Greece controlled western Anatolia, he returned to Aivali with his family and completed his secondary education there in 1921.

After the overwhelming defeat of the Greek army in September of 1922, Ilias, still a teenager, was taken prisoner by the Turks and force-marched into the interior of Turkey in one of the infamous labour battalions. Of the 3,000 Greek men taken then from Aivali for slave labour, he was one of only twenty-three to survive. He was released after fourteen months in captivity, managed to join his family in Lesbos in 1923 and began working to support them. Encouraged by the Greek writer Stratis Myrivilis (1890–1969), a native of Lesbos whom he met there, he wrote an account of his ordeal as a Turkish prisoner. It was first published in installments in the island's weekly newspaper and later, in 1931, was published as a book with the title *Number 31328*. The book won great acclaim and established Venezis' reputation as a literary figure in Greece and leading member of what became known as the 'generation of the thirties', a group of Greek intellectuals, writers, poets, artists, critics, who made their debut in that decade and are regarded as responsible for introducing modernism into Greek literature and art.

In 1932 Venezis settled in Athens where he worked for the Bank of Greece until his retirement in 1957. In 1938 he married Stavritsa Molyviati, whom he had loved since their youth in Aivali, and the following year their daughter, Anna, was born. The year 1939 also saw the publication of his second major work, the novel *Serenity*, which tells the story of a group of Asia Minor refugees trying to start a new life on a barren piece of land given to them by the Greek government. This book won both the National Literature Prize and that of the Athens Academy.

The German occupation of Greece began in April of 1941 and lasted until October 1944, during which time thousands of Greeks died of starvation and from Nazi reprisals against civilians. It was in these calamitous years that Venezis wrote *Land of Aeolia*. On October 28, 1943, he took part in a clandestine gathering in the Bank of Greece convened to honour the memory of those who had died fighting the Italian fascists in Albania in 1940. The meeting was betrayed to the SS, who arrested a number of the participants, including Venezis, who was subsequently condemned to death. While he awaited execution, he was able to give instructions for the publication of *Land of Aeolia*. At the last minute, protests and petitions from friends and supporters, including Archbishop Damaskinos, somehow reached Berlin and led to his release after eighteen horrific days and nights in German hands. His 1945 play *Block C* portrays this ordeal. *Land of Aeolia* was published almost directly after his release, in December of 1943. The initial print run of 5,000 copies sold out in two weeks. It was reprinted immediately and has remained in print continuously ever since. It is presently in its 69th edition.

After the war, a succession of translations and reviews of his main works appeared in most European languages. Venezis was acclaimed as a major pacifist writer; he had now acquired fame beyond the confines of Greek literary circles. But as his daughter, Anna Cosmetatos, writes:

'One thing never changed: his loving, generous, warm personality; his irrepressible, joyous approach to humankind. His deep love of nature, developed in childhood and expressed powerfully in his writing, continued to sustain him throughout his life. He went on weekly excursions and climbing expeditions and was deeply touched by the beauty of mountains.'

Venezis continued to write prolifically throughout his life: newspaper articles, short stories, novels, histories, and travelogues. He was involved in the creation of various modern Greek institutions, such as the National Theatre, for which he became the advisory director after his retirement from the bank. In 1957 he was elected to the Athens Academy, the first Greek writer from Asia Minor to attain this honour. In the mid 1960s, he built a house in Lesbos with a view to his beloved Kimindenia mountains, to which he would never return, and was able to spend some six months of every year there until he died of cancer in Athens in 1973.

I am very grateful to Anna Cosmetatos for sharing a number of personal details about her father's life. She helped me appreciate Venezis as a man in whom there was no dichotomy between his life and his writings.

T. S.

THERESE SELLERS is a writer, translator and Hellenist who lives in New England. In 1987 she came to Greece to follow the traces of the American philhellene Eva Palmer Sikelianos. In 1988 Therese purchased land in a traditional village in the Peloponnese and built a house that has kept her connected to Greece ever since. While her children were young, she worked as a teacher of Latin and Greek and wrote *Alpha is for Anthropos*, an illustrated collection of nursery rhymes for teaching Ancient Greek to children. In addition to translating Venezis, Therese has translated stories by Alexandros Papadiamandis that are included in Volume II of *The Boundless Garden*, also published by Denise Harvey. She is currently at work on her first novel.

BRUCE CLARK is a writer on history, culture and ideas, especially that of the Greeks, for *The Economist*. His posts as a journalist have included those of diplomatic correspondent for the *Financial Times*, Moscow correspondent for *The Times*, and editor of the *Economist*'s international news pages. Earlier he worked for Reuters in Paris and Athens. He is the author of *Twice A Stranger*, a prize-winning study of the Greek-Turkish population exchange, and of *An Empire's New Clothes*, a personal view of post-soviet Russia. In 2018 he was named Archon-Interpreter of the Ecumenical Patriarchate.